M000310759

"*Directing the Power of Conscious Feelings* can help us peel off decades of pain and numbness to unearth our powerful, authentic selves. Genuine, here-and-now feelings are messages to help us behave appropriately and courageously, and to make the changes we need in our lives. Callahan's book is full of potent, accessible tools for clear, effective communication and responsible action. This—our ability to be real and true—is what activists, ecovillage pioneers, and all of us (in my opinion) need to make the world a better place."
>　　—**Diana Leafe Christian**, author of *Creating a Life Together*
>　　<www.ecovillagenews.org>

"I am so glad to have this book. Its enlightened distinctions changed my life: they changed the way I think and feel about myself and the world. This book maps higher consciousness and is a work of Conscience. I recommend this book wholeheartedly for its honor, insight, wisdom, and integrity. You can spend $10,000 on therapy or you can buy this book and change your life, which changes the world."
>　　—**Red Hawk**, author of *Self Observation—the Awakening of Conscience.*

"To be alive is to feel; not to think we feel based on what society tells us we should feel, not to imitate superficial emotions programmed by TV and the movies, but to be in touch with the richness of our shared humanity and be able to bear it all with grace, dignity and, eventually compassion. Clinton's book teaches just that to all those among us who aspire to get closer to what it might mean to actually be a human being. A song of experience and innocence regained, may it serve those who are ready."
>　　—**Gilles Farcet**, author of *The Anti-Wisdom Manual—a Practical Guide to Spiritual Bankruptcy.*

"Learning to feel is essential to us being able to stay alive as a species. We need to open our hearts and minds to the shift that is happening on the planet, allow it to penetrate deep into the center of our being, allow the pain to be felt and released, feel ourselves re-awaken to who we are as sentient, pulsing human beings, deeply connected to the Earth and the universe at once. Numbness is suicidal."
>　　—**Peter Merry**, author of *Evolutionary Leadership*
>　　<www.humanemergence.nl>

"In the Middle East one experiences numbness not only as hopelessness about achieving any solution to the conflict, but as a tactic for survival itself. In this book Callahan introduces individuals, communities and nations to tools that allow awakening and transformation to occur. Here is an opportunity for all of us to gain a future worth living for."

> —**Sami Awad**, Executive Director of Holy Land Trust
> <www.holylandtrust.org>

"We project the horror of what happened to us as children onto the world. We cannot heal Gaia because we don't believe in ourselves, in our true value. Thus we have turned ourselves dumb. It is in this that Clinton's work is so precious. This great book is a guide to consciousness. Only this level of self-development can bring out the attitudes that we and the world need to heal the Great Mother, our Earth."

> —**John James**, author of *The Great Field* <www.cruciblecentre.com>
> <www.planetextinction.com>

"It has been with great appreciation that I have found Clinton Callahan's work and writing. He so clearly and comprehensively details the path of feeling that those who approach it with a sense of open inquiry will likely feel compelled to undertake their own feeling journey. The work to regain such a fundamental ability as feeling is revolutionary, and inevitably transformative, both personally and collectively. And once one has a long drink of the experience of feeling that Clinton writes about, it will be difficult to quench one's thirst with less."

> —**Sally Erickson**, Film producer <www.whatawaytogomovie.com>

"Clinton blends a rare combination of accurate psycho/political state-of-the-world awareness with truly valuable emotional-healing skills. We deeply need them both and this book leads the way."

> —**Bill Kauth**, co-founder of New Warrior Training Adventure, and
> author of *A Circle of Men*. <www.sacredlifeboats.com>

"This book puts a simple key in your hand: Allow yourself to feel. The key releases you from paralysis, opens true insights, and gathers energy. It awakens the inner adult to step forward and make the changes we long for. Thank you for this guide to a new culture. May this book spread in the world."

> —**Sabine Lichtenfels**, peace activist, author, co-founder of Tamera
> <www.sabine-lichtenfels.de>

Directing The Power
of Conscious Feelings

Living Your Own Truth

Clinton Callahan

HOHM PRESS
Prescott, Arizona

Cover design: Adi Zuccarello, <www.adizuccarello.com>
Layout and design: Kubera Book Design, Prescott, Arizona
Photo of author: Laurent Belmonte <www.LaurentBelmontePhotographe.com>
Cover photo: Shinichi Maruyama, <www.ShinichiMaruyama.com>
Photo team: Sonia and Tassilo Willaredt, Roswitha and Peter Kuder, Marion and Clinton Callahan, Regina and Jürgen Birlinger, Britta Vrettos, Layla Scheffler, Christian Thoma, Simon A. Westermann, Joachim Antweiler, Nicola Nagel, Stefanie Heidtmann, and Moritz Krause. Thanks to Joachim for sticking his head in the sand, and Simon for photo editing.

Library of Congress Cataloging-in-Publication Data

Callahan, Clinton.
 Directing the power of conscious feelings : living your own truth / Clinton Callahan.
    p. cm.
 Includes index.
 ISBN 978-1-935387-11-4 (pbk. : alk. paper)
 1. Emotions. I. Title.
 BF511.C25 2010
 152.4--dc22
                                    2010006781

DISCLAIMER: This publication is designed to provide accurate and authoritative information regarding the subject matter covered. It is sold with the understanding that the publisher is not engaged in rendering relationship, emotional, or psychological counseling, medical treatment, or other professional services. If professional advice or expert assistance is required, readers are advised to seek the services of a competent professional.

HOHM PRESS
P.O. Box 2501
Prescott, AZ 86302
1-800-381-2700
<www.hohmpress.com>

This book was printed in the USA on recycled, acid-free paper using soy ink.

THANKS

Finding one's way along the path of personal development seems to depend on three things: your teamwork with fellow explorers, the quality of your maps, and the accuracy of your compass.

My compadres on this journey are the most trustworthy of friends; for you I am truly appreciative.

My maps come from raw research at the intersection of worlds; for these experiments I am extremely grateful.

Until I was thirty-seven years old I specialized in being in discovery groups and collecting treasure maps.

Then I found a compass. His name is Lee Lozowick. He exactly pinpoints my little X on the map that says, "You are here," without which all treasure maps are useless. Now I specialize in expressing gratitude for my compass.

Any value in this book derives from the heartful kibitzing of Lee Lozowick.

CONTENTS

Midsummer 2008, I was standing alone on a luscious green mountainside behind a hut in the Austrian Alps. It was beautiful. I noticed a momma horse trying to get my attention. Horses are not normally my thing, but I climbed through the fence and started rubbing her nose, scratching her back and shoulders. After a while she looked over to her baby who was observing us from a safe ten meters away. She told him I was okay. He came over and presented himself for the same treatment. Since he was smaller, I could give him a complete back massage digging my fingers deep into his thick soft fur. For fifteen minutes we were both in ecstasy. In my heart I planned to tell my horse-loving daughters about this interaction. They would love hearing about it.

Then the farmer came out. He had seen me with the baby horse. He said, *Too bad it's a boy.* I said, *Why is that?* He said, *In a few months we have to kill it. Can't have boy horses around here. The sausages will be very tasty, though.*

I couldn't say anything. I started walking up the mountain. The trail is steep and narrow. I didn't seem to notice. At the ridge I sat on a bench. Tears streamed down my cheeks. I had just heard the human prescription for planet Earth, and the cause of the end of civilization.

I connected into the mountain, trying to share my pain. The mountain said, *Idealizing the strong numb hero has possibly exterminated the human race. Write a book about conscious feelings. Make it safe for people to become no longer numb.*

FOREWORD

Here's the thought that kept springing to mind as I read *Directing the Power of Conscious Feelings*: something picked Clinton Callahan up, sat him down, and used him to write this book. And that something—that muse, that force, that helper, that spirit, that consciousness—was exactly right to do so. For the task of showing the path out of our collective cultural insanity, through our true and authentic feelings, and back to our birthright of sanity and connectedness, you'll find few voices as clear and conscious as Clinton Callahan's. Good choice, Cosmos. Thanks!

It's all here: straight talk and a courageous willingness to look unflinchingly at our individual and collective situations; gentle acceptance and encouragement; clear teaching and practical insight; personal revelation and cultural analysis. The tone is sober and open and friendly and real. The maps take you right where you want to go. As George Gershwin wrote and Gene Kelly sang, "Who could ask for anything more?"

Directing the Power of Conscious Feelings organizes and makes plain my own messy journey through feeling from numbness and distraction to conscious feeling, something approaching sweet, sweet sanity. And it gives me useful language and images and metaphors, which, by sharing the book, I can then share with others, expanding the conversation and spreading the healing that is available to all who choose to take this path. I've already started a list in my head, of the people with whom I can share this book. And sharing this book is essential. We cannot do this work alone.

I guess I'm just trying to help you understand what it is you have in your hands right now. This book is not just "a good read." It's full of *exercises*. It's a *training*. A *movement*. The maps take you places. You *have* to go somewhere new. A species of living creatures may have gone extinct in the time it has taken you to read these four paragraphs. Maybe two. Climate is destabilizing. Oil is slowing. Oceans are dying. Forests are falling. You know the drill. This book is a way to navigate your way through this mess in a manner that might actually help the situation. Clinton Callahan says, and I agree, and so, apparently, did the forces who spoke through him, that learning to consciously feel is a fundamental and necessary step to take if we wish to make some sane response to our present predicament.

Imagine what might happen if scientists and politicians and industrialists and economists and you and I and the man-on-the-street and the girl-next-door were able to sit with our feelings of anger and grief and fear and joy and fully feel them. Imagine us facing head-on into our helplessness. Imagine us fully feeling the impacts in the world of our actions to-date. Maybe we'd stop inventing plans to launch millions of old shoes and used ABBA CDs into the upper stratosphere in order to stop those pesky sunbeams from reaching the planet. Maybe we'd sit down for a minute, bow our heads, admit that we are powerless in the matter of controlling the world and that our culture has become unmanageable, and begin the process of sobering up. Maybe, just maybe, we'd begin to open up to a power greater than our collective ego. Maybe we'd start to actually be of service to the planet.

There's an old joke, one I've told many times, one I've heard others tell. When looking at the "missteps" and "wrong turns" and "lost years" of my life, I've said this: *Well, it's not like we come with an owner's manual when we're born.* As if to say, "Hey, I'm doing my best!" As if to say, "It's not my fault!" As if to say, "If only. . . if only. . . if only. . . "

Well, guess what, folks? Whether true or not before, it's *not* true now. We *have* an owner's manual. It's in your hands. You're reading it right now. It's an owner's manual for Sane Human Being. Follow the diagrams. Reconfigure the wires. Adjust the dials. Pretty soon you'll reclaim who you have always been, who you came here to be. Deep and authentic feeling. A conscious life. And a chance to play a part in the healing of our collective nightmare, and the creation of What's Next. Not too shabby, eh? A human life lived in alignment with the Cosmos. Yours if you really want it.

This book can help with that.

May your copy become dog-eared and yellowed with use.

Touching the ground,
Tim Bennett
Filmmaker <www.whatawaytogomovie.com>
Rochester Abbey
August, 2009

INTRODUCTION

Every man, woman and child on Earth lives within the continuously fluctuating sensations of intelligent feelings, but this intelligence remains suppressed and misdirected under the brutal imperatives of a patriarchal empire.

Many of us are lost between two shores, not truly committed to supporting the greedy madness of a globalized consumer society, yet not knowing what else to do. We wait in timid fear, hoping that the ship of state will somehow right itself and sail us into a bright future. But will it? Can it?

The question remains, how much longer will you wait? This book is for people who have waited long enough.

This book is about taking responsibility for the intelligence and power of your own feelings and using them to lead a life closer to your own truth.

SOURCE OF THIS KNOWLEDGE

These ideas do not come from mainstream culture. Neither are they derived from psychology, sociology, Christianity, Eastern traditions, aborigines, or the new age. These ideas come from more than thirty years of unprecedented exploration with private groups of people. For days at a time, in spaces of great safety and mutual trust, we repeatedly ventured beyond traditional understandings into unknown territory. Together we wrestled with our deepest uncertainties, tried numerous approaches, distilled the outcomes, and brought back a collection of distinctions that permit men and women to create extraordinary lives. We have come to call that work *Possibility Management*.

You will find these pages directed toward the practical: filled with thoughtmaps, examples and exercises. The skills are to be practiced with feedback and coaching from peers until their effectiveness becomes experientially undeniable.

In some ways this is an extended version of the feelings information in *Radiant Joy Brilliant Love*, my previous book, yet it is more than that. *Directing the Power of Conscious Feelings* takes you by the hand, builds a foundation of understanding beyond mainstream culture, and then experientially leads you into reclaiming your own feelings as steps across the bridge into next culture.

These skills become vitally urgent in the moment you recognize that global climate disruption combined with peak oil and population growth will collapse civilization as we know it within the span of our lifetimes.

The devastating consequences of humanity's collective actions during the twentieth century remain concealed from view of the majority (as of March 2010), but I predict they cannot remain so much longer. The clarity and power of your own feelings will support you to create a new life for yourself when civilization is no longer there to create a life for you.

As Tim Bennett writes in his blog, *Bambi vs the Collapse of Civilization* (included as Appendix C): "Some of us need to do this work, because most will not. Refusing to feel their fear now, they will be forced to feel it upon impact, when the trauma is greatest, the losses so hard to bear. They will need our help."

WHO SHOULD READ THIS BOOK?
Social entrepreneurs, leaders and managers who read this book equip themselves with new clarity for empowering their team, organization or project.

Educators, social workers, healers, parents, coaches, and especially students can use these ideas and tools to enhance their effectiveness even during times of rapid change. Especially young people need activated feelings for transitioning into their own adult lives. Feelings provide real-time energy and information when students discover that much of what they learned in school is at best irrelevant.

Each person reclaiming the power to consciously feel and to communicate with feelings not only benefits themselves but contributes to the lives of their colleagues, friends and relations. Studying the ideas in this book opens a real chance that your heart could break out of its long-familiar prison. Learning to feel could become the most profound experience of your life.

BOOK CONTENTS

What would it be like to claim your adult masculine or feminine feelings with clarity? How can you distinguish and express your own feelings? How could you effectively listen to and relate to other people's feelings? How can feelings serve you professionally? How can feelings be the gateway to archetypal ways of life? How could reclaiming your feelings empower you to establish truly sustainable culture? These are questions addressed by this book.

The first three chapters establish foundational understanding to support new feelings experiences. One model is the *numbness bar*, an internal intensity regulator which our cultural training has encouraged us to adjust so that we feel nearly nothing. With our numbness bar set so high we equate feeling numb with feeling good. By lowering the setting of your numbness bar you regain physical, intellectual, emotional and energetic sensations. This is the equivalent of slowly opening long-closed Venetian blinds, letting the sun shine in. Things which have been cold, numb or dead start warming up.

By chapter four you start doing conscious feeling experiments yourself, and by then the experiments go almost effortlessly. The first steps may, of course, be sobering, while you become more conscious of your previous level of numbness. Long-repressed feelings may burst out this way and that, like cooking popcorn without a lid. This is to be expected in Phase 1 of feelings work. Before you can apply the energy and intelligence of your feelings you must first learn to feel!

Through integrating conscious feelings with new thoughtmaps about what is happening to you, Phase 2 of feelings work begins. You start applying the impulses and information of conscious feelings through responsible practice. Everything changes. Responsible, clear feelings catalyze the long-awaited transition into adulthood, and the gateway opens to the archetypal masculine and feminine.

Experiential clarity produces the surprising possibility of living in a more conscious and responsible relationship to other people, to the Earth, and to your own purpose. Human precision and vulnerability come together, forming diverse new societies—tiny at first—where men and women, families, friends, neighbors and colleagues collaboratively create technically and spiritually sustainable cultures in which success means developing the potential of each person.

THE MISSING INGREDIENT HAS BEEN YOU

These first years of the twenty-first century are times of sudden and drastic transition. Continuing business as usual brings ominous consequences, yet the shift to sustainability involves immediate and unprecedented personal, organizational and societal challenges. The efforts you apply toward bringing consciousness to your feelings make you a leader in this transition.

We need leaders in the shift to next culture. A "leader" in this sense is simply a person who goes first.

Brave people have the courage to ask embarrassing but obvious questions, and then to follow through on the answers they discover without subjecting themselves to the conceptual limits of their birth culture. You are such a one, a key element in humanity making the leap to a more promising future for our children.

This book is full of strong clarity that becomes the basis of *next culture* through you bringing that clarity to common practice in your daily life and interactions. Some of these ideas may at first seem intimidating, but please keep trying—even through the shadowy unsettling times when things might not make sense. Please be one of the experimenters who never gives up. I thank you for your efforts.

1. THE NUMBNESS BAR

A NEW DECISION

Idealizing the strong numb hero has possibly exterminated the human race. The present conditions of environmental degradation, mass extinction of species, global warming beyond critical tipping points, greedy consumption of nonrenewable resources, economic injustices, overpopulation, weapons of mass destruction, and the general failure of seemingly intelligent human beings to create a sustainable future for ourselves on this garden planet are all consequences of revering numbness.

Personally choosing numbness may have been unconscious for you. Perhaps you patterned yourself on the numbness of modern culture, taking on machine-like qualities of being fast, hard and impersonal. Perhaps you obediently followed in your mother's or father's footsteps by adopting the level of numbness handed down from generation to generation in your family's tradition.

Either way, this book confronts you with making the choice to consciously continue your old behaviors or practice new ones. Either you will tighten your internal restraints and stay numb, or you will break the chain around your heart and simply allow yourself to feel.

At any moment your new decision may prevail.

If deep sobs of grief over lost years of feeling erupt from your heart and convulse your lungs and chest for hours or days while reading this book, do not worry. That is okay. Nothing is wrong with you. You are coming back to life.

Deep grief over missed opportunities and loneliness long endured is the healing path toward a more humane future. Seen in this light, your sadness equates to a celebration. Intimacy is still possible for you.

Your heart is not dead. The remainder of your life can be filled with inner sensations of belongingness that no one can take away from you ever again.

Your feelings are fine. Having your feelings back is so simple. Yet, like a sudden down-pouring of rain after a long drought, the new experiences may change everything. Nothing can prepare you for the awesome abundance when green shoots sprout miraculously out of dry desert sands.

FEELINGS COME KNOCKING

Some of us are forced to learn about feelings by unwanted side effects from years and years of numbness. We may suffer rashes, nail biting, hair plucking, skin picking, depression, overeating, burnout, anxiety, hypertension, drinking, shame, drug taking, adaptive behavior, confusion, insomnia, indigestion, intestinal problems, frustration, hopelessness, headaches, asthma, nervous twitches, fatigue, listlessness, lack of financial success, family stress, failed relationships, sexual dysfunction, infertility, despair, oversleeping, back pain, accidents, self-injury, angina, bulimia, anorexia or attempted suicide. Even such conditions as bipolar, borderline, schizophrenia, multiple sclerosis, Graves' disease, and Parkinson's disease are suspected of being related to unexpressed feelings.

Some of us are driven to investigate feelings after years of hysteria, aggression, shouting, violence, rage, destructive temper tantrums, claustrophobia, paralysis, melancholy, a gambling or shopping addiction, lying, speeding, theft, corruption, engaging in intrigue, mobbing, indiscriminate sex, betraying or being betrayed. Ignoring such expressions does not make them go away. On the contrary, denial only intensifies their destructive impact on our lives. For example, a brilliant and successful professional consultant friend of mine recently found himself arrested and in jail because he was caught walking out of a bookshop with an unpurchased book in his pocket. He was completely flabbergasted by his own behavior! He had no explanation.

Perhaps the question of feelings has come knocking more surreptitiously. Are you alone? Divorced? Has a loved one complained that he or she just can't get through to you? That you don't listen? That you're not open to intimacy or sexuality? Do they say they don't really know who you are?

Perhaps your children are distant, keeping themselves away from you.

Perhaps intimacy disturbs something deep within you rather than being genuinely satisfying. Perhaps you feel disconnected from the human race, isolated in your own separate world.

PASSIONATE PROFESSIONALISM

As a modern professional you may categorically reject the need for feelings. You may barricade your thoughts and speech behind scientific reasons and logic. Yet you may experience a certain twinge in your heart watching people simply fall into each other's arms with tears in their eyes, grieving the death of a loved one, sharing rage and fears over the coming climate crisis, or outrageously laughing together, while you feel nothing, remaining unmoved, still untouched.

Perhaps your true passions are a mystery, although now and then you sense a vague longing to experience the richness of manhood or womanhood before your life passes. Perhaps you ache to fulfill your life's destiny no matter how big or impossible it may seem.

After all, it *has* been done! It *is* possible! There existed a Richard Burton! He lived. There existed (or still lives) a Wangari Muta Maathai, a George Gurdjieff, an Aung San Suu Kyi, a Tatanka-Iyotanka (Sitting Bull), an Arnaud Desjardins, a Nelson Mandela, a Mother Teresa. There are so many examples of human potential fully lived! Why not you too? Why not reclaim your own passionate vision and live your life's adventure with full commitment and enthusiasm? Something noble. Something daring. Why not gain a sense of having *at least once* done something else in your life?

THE POSSIBILITY OF BEING NO LONGER NUMB

Numbness has been artfully woven in as a foundational element of our modern way of life. We have unwittingly grown accustomed to staying well distracted from our feelings: busy, reactive, drunk, drugged, worried, overstressed, overfed, overstimulated, overstretched, and cerebral.

Proposing that a person could actually learn to feel turns out to be rather revolutionary in modern culture. It goes against the entire systems of education, psychology, medicine, religion, politics, science and technology.

Giving numbness a name implies that there is a condition of *not numbness*. Your willingness to recognize the existence of numbness suggests your willingness to recognize the personal costs of staying numb, and the personal opportunities of becoming someone who is *no longer numb*.

CONSPIRACY AGAINST FEELINGS

For a man to enter the patriarchy at birth he must give up his option of being himself. This sacrifice causes the deepest kind of pain. Few women understand the source of this pain, though they may recognize an intense resentment festering at the core of patriarchal men. Unexpressed pain drives us men to cause an equivalent pain in the world around us. Only tortured souls could condone the physical and spiritual starvation of children, aggressions against women, war among elected gangsters, and the rapidly expanding ecological holocaust. Patriarchal men are not allowed to be innocently themselves. Why should anyone else get to?

Since the beginnings of patriarchy some five thousand years ago, authoritarian voices have delivered clear proclamations against feelings. After all, patriarchal empire needs its mercenaries and merchants to siphon the wealth of conquered lands into the empire's sequestered coffers.

How could a worker or soldier endlessly rape and pillage in the name of the empire unless he shut down the dignity and nobility of his own natural feelings?

The Spartans said, *Come home with your shield, or on it!*

The Vikings said, *Victory, or Valhalla!*

The Muslims said, *Allahu Akbar!*

The Christians said, *Deus vult!*

The Japanese said, *Banzai!*

The Germans said, *Seig heil!*

The Russians said, *Ura!*

The Israelis said, *Kadima!*

The Americans said, *It's show time!*

Modern parents say, *Boys don't cry! Indians feel no pain! Shhhh! Nothing happened!*

We have been well instructed to stay numb.

In modern society, the worst names you can be called are *Yellow! Chicken! Scaredy Cat!* We learned at a young age that it is disgraceful to feel.

The man or woman who wins in business, politics, war, or sports is the *last man standing*, the strong numb hero.

Each generation finds a way to bury the pain of sending their own children into war to do the dirty work of the ruling classes. Specialized numbing techniques have become familiar features of today's society. We were sent to school to study numbing topics. We brought home numbing homework, preparing us to work long hours at numbing jobs with a numbing commute and constantly droning numbing news. We work for money to shop for things we don't need, to buy drugs and entertainment that seduce our attention and deaden the horrifying recognition of modern empire's proudest success: globalization.

Corporate-controlled international financial institutions encourage businessmen to invade, subvert and globalize forty thousand years of diverse human cultures around the world using any means available. By reducing cultures to Disneyfied caricatures, local customs and traditions are disempowered and replaced by mass-produced brands sold at franchised shops to make ever-increasing profits. No mechanism exists to monitor or stop the manufacturers of monoculture, not even the United Nations. The globalization steamroller has gone berserk. Being numb, we blindly participate.

Unbridled empire will dig up and burn everything on Earth because there is only one goal of a corporation: profit. The plan is being meticulously executed as you read these words. In many ways you are an accomplice. Me too.

The plan has one suicidal fault. It ignores the fact that we live on a planet. A planet has limited resources and a limited capacity to absorb contaminants. Those limits are being reached.

Like a cancer, the paradigm of empire is killing its host. Having come full circle around the globe, modern empire finds no more societies to enslave, no more resources to plunder. The world's oil production curve goes downhill from here while the ravaged planet suffocates in toxic wastes, rapidly becoming inhospitable to the human species.

Collective numbness permits us to degrade the only spaceship that can support human life in this part of the galaxy. More easily than most people realize, Earth could become frozen and airless like Mars, or more likely, blanketed in superheated poisonous gases through a runaway greenhouse effect like Venus. Numbness toward the consequences of our individual actions may self-exterminate Homo sapiens. Modern civilization arranged its own demise.

HIERARCHICAL PSYCHOPATHS

Arrogantly ignoring the warning signs, we modern citizens continue organizing ourselves using hierarchical organization designs, even though the pyramid is but one of many possible designs for flowing power through people to accomplish our common goals.

In a hierarchy, whoever does what it takes to climb the ladder wins the coveted leadership positions. An utter lack of empathy is a key success factor. The hierarchical design causes our government, military, religious, medical and educational organizations to be top-heavy with people tending toward psychopathic behavior.

It is not that power corrupts; it is that corrupt individuals seek power.

A hierarchy automatically replaces people of integrity with the most ruthless psychopaths, and the closer you get to the top, the more this pattern prevails.

In the last fifty years the transition to organizational psychopathy seems to have reached a tipping point. As proven by the failure of the COP15 Climate Change Conference in Copenhagen 2009, global leadership no longer serves to create a bright future for humanity. Instead, it preys on humanity as a resource of slave labor and dull-witted consumers, and we citizens are complicit. Our parents were busy so they sat us in front of a television to follow the hypnotic instructions for giving our authority away to so-called experts. Now, even when we have the chance, we do not take our personal authority back. We don't even think of it.

Modern society is terrified of cults or sects whose leaders might brainwash their victims to surrender their will to serve evil purposes. Actually, this is a perfect description of what already exists in modern society. Perhaps the greater fear is of a force that might awaken citizens from their walking sleep so they regain natural capacities for living that modern society tries to convince them they never had. Personal feelings could well be this awakening force.

It is discouraging to look around the world and notice how few people choose to live in a culture where respect, human dignity and creativity thrive. For the most part, humanity is dominated and controlled by those most capable of gaining and retaining power and least capable of thoughtful human leadership.

The people we have entrusted with making wise decisions about our health, well-being, education and a sustainable future are committed to no such things. They are instead committed to assuring their own security, wealth and power. We have handed over the reins of society and the keys to our treasury to a loose affiliation of psychopathic millionaires and billionaires maximizing their own holdings without regard for humanity's future.

Psychopathic leaders can only continue serving their own agendas if they remain unrecognized and unobstructed. Could this be why the general population is kept distracted with sporting events, movie star scandals, the so-called threat of terrorist attacks, and a series of never-ending wars with a never-vanquished enemy? Lacking an objective overview and busily occupied with the worries of modern life, we stay disconnected from each other and from the wisdom and power of our moment to moment feelings while psychopaths proceed undisturbed.

Astonishment when you discover the degree to which feelings have been scrubbed from modern society is only surpassed by your embarrassment that nothing has been done to remedy the lack. In the 1960s it became apparent that schooling could expand to include more balanced aspects of human development, but too few people took radical responsibility to change their lives and the lives of their children.

Architects of modern culture already had control of the majority vote. The somnambulant momentum prevailed.

Economic productivity is determined by the effectiveness of the machinery. Captains of industry required only machine operators, so schooling was designed to address only the minimum intellect, as if a human being stops at the neck. Feeling skills and introspective capacities have been systematically eliminated from modern society through corporate curriculum design.

This is why reclaiming your feelings will require extending your experiments beyond the thought limits of mainstream culture, well beyond what is provided in modern education.

Why does your heart ache? Because you never used it before.

PRETENDING TO BE WHAT OTHER PEOPLE WANT YOU TO BE

It may surprise you to hear that you have feelings about nearly everything all the time: where to go and how to get there, what to see, what to wear, what to buy, who to talk to, what to say, what to eat, what to study, and how to relate to what is going on. You have feelings about politics, religion, business, sports, science and the arts, about philosophy, about beliefs, about what you possess and don't possess, about what you think and what others think, about stuckness and change, about experiencing life and experiencing death. We even have feelings about our feelings!

Through accessing your true feelings you can sense what is authentically going on for you, become more present to yourself, find out how you really want to live, discover what is important for you and what you deeply wish to be doing.

Some of your feelings might surprise you completely. If you could consciously feel what your heart is feeling, you might be moved to take actions that are the complete opposite of the actions you have been taking.

Decisions to act in contradiction to your true nature commonly arise because, lacking your own feelings, you are easily distracted from being yourself. Then instead of enacting your own life you animate a life that fulfills other people's expectations. By welcoming back your own feelings, previously unseen features of life resolve into focus and ignite unquenchable inspiration about what you are doing.

I know of what I speak.

IT HAPPENED TO ME

After graduating from the university with a degree in physics in 1975 I took various jobs as a research assistant in technical development and manufacturing companies. Eventually I started my own business, Computer Effects Company, in Northern California, a tiny electronics prototyping and production firm. We developed biomedical equipment for DNA research, such as thermal cyclers for polymerase chain reaction (PCR) and fly-back transformers in power supplies for gel-phase electrophoresis. This is all standard equipment now, but back then it was cutting-edge technology. We were making very cool stuff.

As a hobby I attended seminars and classes here and there that interested me. In 1989, at the encouragement of my wife, I participated in my first *training*.

A training is quite different from a seminar or class where you *learn* something new. In a training you *become* something new. I was not prepared for this. Perhaps one *cannot* be prepared for this.

In any case, the profound safety of this particular training space permitted me, for the first time in my life, to truly experience and express my deep feelings with clarity. People encouraged me to feel and listened to me with respect. They made distinctions for me about things I'd never suspected distinctions could be made. As a result of the training, my door to feelings was opened. I went through that door. Feelings began flowing through my nervous system in a completely different manner.

A short while after the training somebody casually asked me, *Why do you do the work that you do?* I had never considered this question before. It turns out to be a dangerous question to consider.

I liked my work. I had fun fooling around with the latest circuit boards and electronic manufacturing processes. But when I allowed myself to truly *feel* into the question, a completely startling answer arose in me. I opened my mouth to speak and what came out was, *I do this kind of work because my father does this kind of work.*

I was shocked. Feelings raged through my body. Something old and tired in me began to die, and at the same time something new and joyous was being born. One future dropped away while a new future became more probable. Suddenly I did not have to do that kind of work anymore. Plans outlining the next decades of my life dissolved into a horizon that was less predictable, less defined, less oriented toward technology and more oriented toward liberating human potential. Something in me relaxed and levitated itself effortlessly into a new level of excitement. I felt deeply elated. On that day I took possession of my own inspiring life. I was thirty-seven years old.

I am not saying that something so dramatic will happen for you when you begin learning to feel. On the other hand, I am not saying it won't. By finding out what you actually feel you will find out who you are and what your life is about. You will move toward taking your own steps, and will move away from being a known character stamped out by modern society's mold, fulfilling other people's plans.

THE REWARD FOR NUMBNESS

The central distinction in this book is between *un*consciously feeling and consciously feeling. Don't worry! At this point you are not expected to have *any* idea what this means. The rest of this book will explore the world of conscious feelings.

As you read through these pages, practicing skills and engaging processes, you will build onto your internal foundation for experientially understanding feelings. While your understanding grows, the distinction between *un*consciously feeling and consciously feeling becomes tactile. Newly recognized sensations lead to developing internal navigation skills. Whole new forms of experience, perception and behavior will flourish in you. But there is preparatory work to be done.

Since we have a heart, we have feelings. But since modern culture trains us to repress rather than express our feelings, we don't discern our sensations. Just as a person born blind can't imagine the brilliance of a rainbow's spectrum, we who are trained to stay numb can't imagine the visceral sensations of feelings.

How could our lack of feelings continue so long undetected? How could we sacrifice such an intimate aspect of being human?

It turns out that numbness produces an ambiance of stability and security. When we are numb, life seems to be more manageable and consistent, less volatile, more civilized, exactly the way life looks in magazines and TV ads. If we are not in touch with our ever-changing true-heart feelings then we will not be moved in unpredictable directions.

Our life can then be scheduled to fit into a linear plan, regulated to be the same from day to day, week to week, month to month, planned years in advance, another mass-produced item. We feel powerful to have diminished life to be so predictable. We find security in life's repeatability.

This is our reward for staying numb: we become socially acceptable. We become a source person promoting the expectations of civilization.

My guess is that you would not be reading this book unless you have become somewhat uncomfortable with your comforts. Perhaps you are moved to discover who you are and what will happen if you end the reign of numbness in your life.

NUMBNESS VS FEELING

Because the benefits of numbness have been actively marketed to us since childhood, and the benefits of consciously feeling may still remain a complete mystery, it makes sense to approach the subject of feelings with some caution. Let's begin with an analysis that compares numbness with conscious feelings. The Map of Numbness vs Feeling presents two lists:

- What we already get from staying numb, and

- What we *could* get from consciously feeling.

By comparing these two lists you gain a sense of the present balance in your life on the continuum between numbness and feeling. You can assess to what degree you choose numbness compared to making use of your feelings.

Each aspect named in the list is a different facet of life. Each step you take in the direction of abandoning numbness in favor of clear responsible feeling will inaugurate a breakthrough in your life quality and

MAP OF NUMBNESS vs FEELING

Numbness and feeling, two sides of the same heart.

WHAT YOU GET BY BEING NUMB	WHAT YOU GET BY FEELING
Can blindly follow authority.	Self trust. Having own authority.
Gain a false sense of security.	Appreciation of self and others.
Achieve the illusion of stability.	Being present, in touch, in contact.
Self-separation, -incompletion, -betrayal, -deception, -manipulation.	Listening, being listened to.
Distrust of self and others because you cannot detect what is coming.	Acceptance. Being known.
	Making clear boundaries.
Trying to stay safe. Survival.	Making precise distinctions.
Trying to follow the rules.	Asking for what you want.
Fear of what the neighbors think.	Authentic sharing of self.
Righteousness—trying to be right.	Intimacy. Exchange.
Frustration, boredom, rigidity.	Creating clarity and possibility.
Lack of possibilities. Lack of flow.	Making decisions. Relaxation.
Communication breakdowns.	Taking care of what arises.
Belligerence, obstinacy.	Creating, art, innovation.
Aggressive outbursts. Hopelessness.	Enjoyment. Sensuality.
Isolated. Seemingly alone, unheard.	Satisfaction, flow. Sense of erotic.
Defendedness. Positionality.	Experiencing your experience.
Tending toward fantasy worlds.	Intuition, insight. Simple joy.
Out of relationship. Depression.	Self-inquiry. Humbleness.
Preferring power-over and control.	Personal growth. Discovery.
Ongoing annoyance over trivialities.	Pleasure, ecstasy, delight.
Seeing only competitors.	Togetherness. Connectedness.
Desperate for stimulation.	Being with friends. Communion.
Having ongoing resentment.	Delicacy of sensations.
Confusion. Nervousness.	Full communication. Love.
Using or being used by others.	Compassion. Abundance.
	Collaboration with others.
Heaven comes in the afterlife.	Heaven on Earth. Peace. Grace.

relationships. The more facets that vibrate and shine with the information and energy of feelings, the richer your life.

CULT OF COMFORT

Modern society has taught us to be strong numb workers and obedient numb consumers—*sheeple* instead of people—and to seek further numbness through labor-saving and entertainment devices. Modern satisfactions include life being easy, efficient, convenient, and comfortable.

Conveniences have been historically powered by slave labor. Picture yourself sitting on the shaded porch of your southern mansion. It is a sweltering day. You sip a mint julep while a slave wafts a fan over your head to keep you cool. Hordes of other slaves plant and harvest in your fields, wash your clothes, carry your messages, and do the other chores of daily life.

What you are imagining to be true in this exercise is actually how it is today.

It is so natural for us to turn on a stereo, grab a root beer out of the fridge, or send an email. We hop in the car and stop by a fast-food joint or the supermarket if we get hungry, leading a life of extravagance that kings and queens of yesteryear only dreamed of.

At the same time, we are generally oblivious to the fact that many luxuries of modern empire rely on human slave labor in the third world—to sew our latest fashions, dig minerals from the mines, assemble cheap electronic devices, and farm exotic foods like coffee, tea, bananas and chocolate.

As much as modern society depends on children laboring in sweatshops, it depends even more on enslaved fossil fuels. We no longer need to go out in the cold, soil our hands, suffer the ache of sore muscles or the sting of blisters while chopping wood and carrying water. Oil- powered machines do it for us at the flick of a switch. We have found the secret of the sorcerer's apprentice! One barrel of oil provides the equivalent of twenty-five thousand hours of hard physical labor. That equates to one person working eight hours a day, five days a week, fifty weeks a year, for more than twelve years! Even if a barrel of oil costs three hundred dollars, the oil slaves cost you little more than one cent per hour to accomplish the most exhausting hard work.

Think about being paid one cent per hour for pushing a car along the road, hoisting or lowering someone in an elevator, or pedaling a generator to keep the lights on or someone's computer running. Would you do that work for one cent per hour for twelve years? I will answer for you: *No, you would not.*

But currently around the world, eighty million barrels of oil slavery is occurring *each day* without one single complaint! Oil is the motive force of modern culture to an almost unimaginable degree, providing a massive army of nearly free slaves, laboring for every comfort in modern society at the flick of a switch.

Without realizing it you have padded yourself in multiple layers of numbness from the real world: numbness as in *cut off from your feelings*, and numbness as in *cut off from the ordinary labors of daily life*. As a modern citizen in the first world you do not live in the *comfort zone*. You live in the double-protected, sticky-sweet, warm soft *center* of the comfort zone called the *marshmallow zone*, far away from the raw edges of life. The path to authenticity will require that you dig your way out of *that* sticky mess!

Not to worry. Half of that digging work is being done for you. The slaves of modern empire are dying off. By most rational accounts, the world's oil production peaked in the few years around 2005. We are burning far more oil than we are finding. No matter what efforts are made, we will most likely never produce more oil than we are producing right now, and there is nothing available to replace the slave energy of oil. For example, it would take 750 new nuclear power plants to replace the oil that the US imported in 2009. This is more than *double* the total number of nuclear power plants operating in the *whole world* in this year, and more than *seven times* the nuclear power plants already polluting America. A free-energy replacement for oil is not going to magically appear, and aliens are not coming in large spaceships to save us from our own stupidity.

Repressing feelings leads to additional kinds of repression, which is the reason why the following publicly accessible information is not widely known: the widespread fear would be unbearable for a population that has learned that it is not okay to feel fear.

Global oil production is peaking, but the population *and* industrialization of both India *and* China are not. As expanding Asian industry builds cars for an expanding Asian population, the demand for oil continues to rise. At some point in the not too distant future the world's demand will exceed the world's total production. At this point oil prices will take a one-way trip to the sky, forcing oil-dependent businesses into rather sudden and irremediable bankruptcy . . .

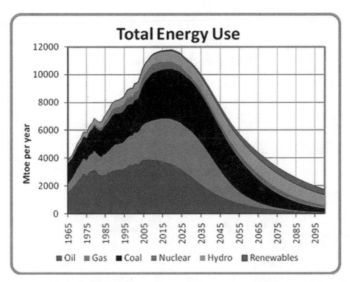

Total Energy Use

Oil ■ Gas ■ Coal ■ Nuclear ■ Hydro ■ Renewables

PEAK OIL This conglomerate graph reveals that oil, gas and coal are by far the most important contributors to the world's present energy mix. Recent data indicates a combined per capita peak of all fossil fuels by 2012 in tandem with Peak Oil, although production is maintained above 10 boe (Barrels of Oil Equivalent) per person per year (the 1979 peak) from 2010 up to 2020. By 2050 that number is below 6 boe per person, and by century's end, oil, gas and coal will have dropped out of the picture almost entirely. USA oil peaked in 1970. Mexican oil peaked in 2006. Russia and Saudi Arabia oil are peaking now, 2010. (This graph and further explanations can be found in World Energy and Population, by Paul Chefurka, an article I encourage you to read, available online here <www.paulchefurka.ca/WEAP/WEAP.html> with additional peak oil information at <www.aspo-usa.com>.)

. . . irremediable bankruptcy for oil-dependent businesses such as agriculture, for example. Modern food production succeeds exclusively due to the cheap slave labor of fossil fuels:

- Diesel-powered pumps to bring up irrigation water from rapidly falling water tables.
- Fossil fuel-based fertilizers and pesticides.
- Diesel-powered tractors to plow, plant, harvest and process the crops.
- Coal-powered electric plants for nighttime greenhouse lighting.
- Oil-derived plastic films, hoses and fittings.

- Petroleum-powered trucks, ships, trains and planes to transport food to your local markets.

And, of course, fuel for the car when you drive to town for groceries.

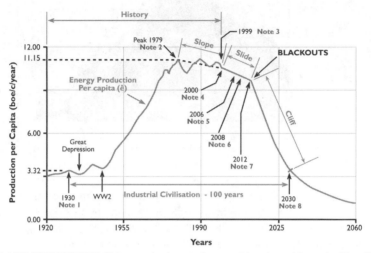

THE LAST CIVILIZATION This graph shows the combined world total of fossil fuel production divided by the number of people on the Earth (boe/c/year is Barrels of Oil Equivalent of all fossil fuels used per capita per year). Present data confirms the Olduvai Theory that Industrial Civilization has a much shorter lifetime than most of us ever imagined, perhaps only 160 years, from 1910 to 2070. Unlike previous civilizations which have risen and fallen to be replaced by others, industrial civilization would be the last civilization because we would have used up all the easily obtainable resources needed for a civilization to form. (This graph and explanations for the notes can be found by going to <www.wolfatthedoor.org.uk> then clicking on the Olduvai Theory button. An updated analysis with latest population and energy data can be found at <www.europe.theoildrum.com/node/3565>.)

When oil becomes scarce compared to the world's demand for it, just how long do you think you will find your local grocery store stocked with food? When shelves are bare, what do you plan to eat? Compounded with climate disruptions, heat waves, drought, and vanishing fresh water, our petroleum-based global farming industry could completely unravel at any time during the next decade. Then you won't be numb anymore. You'll be hungry. This half of your numbness will handle itself.

The other half of digging out of your marshmallow zone you will need to do yourself.

KEEPING THE NUMBNESS BAR HIGH

The level of your numbness bar establishes your threshold of feeling awareness. Any feeling that is less intense than the level of your numbness bar may not be experienced *at all*. The combination of idealizing a pain-free hero cut off from his or her feelings and a pain-free modern life cut off from chores pushes our collective numbness bar to its highest point in the two hundred thousand–year history of Homo sapiens.

For example, you may live in an apartment in a city. All day and all night long the sensations of city life pound on your senses. Sirens wailing, traffic honking and spewing exhaust, trains and trucks shaking the building, factories belching toxic fumes, flashing neon lights, dogs barking, telephones ringing, TVs droning on and on, lawn mowers, construction sounds, loudspeakers, jets, helicopters, all contribute to the nerve-pounding roar of city life.

When a person who normally lives in the countryside first visits a big city the roar can be crushing. To survive the onslaught, the country person may quickly raise their numbness bar to block the assault or they won't even be able to hear themselves think, let alone be able to sleep at night. Without blocking the avalanche of sensations they would go crazy.

In reverse, the city person visiting the countryside is struck by the thunderous silence, the awesome *lack* of sensations. To them, *nothing* is happening. Everything seems slowed down, almost stopped. A trip to the countryside can feel like entering a sensory deprivation tank. So much space and time can bring a city dweller into a fidget verging on panic. They can hardly wait to get back to the swarming city where *something* is happening!

A recent six-year study by a prominent cancer institute in India showed that some 70 percent of the population of Calcutta, both young and old, suffers from respiratory disorders caused by toxic air pollution. For the eighteen million inhabitants of Calcutta, the numbness bar must be desperately high, higher than the detector for personal well-being. In such a circumstance humans act like the proverbial frog, who instantly leaps out if dropped into a pot of hot water but sits placidly until boiled if the water is gradually heated. Children born into Calcutta regard shortened breath and shortened lifespan as normal. As they grow up, most of these children keep their numbness bar high and therefore find no reason to ever leave the contaminated city.

To modern people, so mesmerized by the idea of "progress" and "the good life," the idea of becoming *less* numb may actually seem insane. Why would you want to remove a buffer that makes you more comfortable? Removing numbness could make everything hurt more. That is why we invented doctors, psychologists, and therapists, to make the hurt go away! Lowering your threshold of numbness to pain seems like a form of masochism. Is this smart?

AVOIDING CONSEQUENCES

Maintaining a high numbness bar promotes not having to feel the consequences of your behavior. If you do not feel the consequences of your actions, you can do horrendous things to yourself, to your environment, to other people, and to animals without feeling the pain of it.

For example, if your numbness bar is high, you can join the army and go to war to fight for your country or religion. Even more remarkably, you could enter war as your profession. You could become a police officer, a prison guard, a mercenary, a foreign legionnaire, a member of special operations, a member of the National Guard, SWAT, CIA, DIA, INR, NRO, NGA, NSA, FBI, OICI, OIA, TFI, and so on. (If you do not recognize some of these abbreviations for American organizations employing hundreds of thousands of people in the name of war, I invite you to look them up for your personal enlightenment.) If your numbness bar is high you could work as a double agent, or a triple agent, even as an assassin. You could work as a corporate headhunter, a drug dealer, a gun runner, a weapons manufacturer or transporter, a child-advertising specialist, a pimp for child prostitution, a banker, parochial school teacher, or lawyer.

Without the numbness bar set to a high level, such occupations could well be too painful to tolerate. If you allow yourself to feel your true feelings, you might have reason to change careers rather than continuing with whatever you must do or say to remain in one of these professions.

Numbness, once achieved, sustains itself forever. Or does it?

CONSCIOUSNESS EVOLVING

Things don't seem to stay the same. If you search for an overall pattern in the universe there appears to be a trend for life to become more complex. From simple cells to complex cells to multicellular organisms. From cold-blooded simple hearts to warm-blooded four-chambered hearts. From simple clumps of nerve cells to complex brain structures. Increasing the sophistication of biological design increases its capacity to manifest consciousness.

Typical group photo from the late nineteenth century, courtesy of M. Reusser Collection.

Typical group photo from the early twenty-first century, courtesy of *Expand The Box* training.

You can see this if you study the faces of people in older photos compared to photos that are more recent. The psychoemotional personality of modern people is more multifaceted. The performance put on by ego is more complicated and versatile.

As consciousness develops you become more aware of the consequences of your actions. Increased awareness is both a benefit and a burden. For example, far more American soldiers returning home from the wars in Iraq and Afghanistan have committed suicide than were killed in battle.

As of this writing, eighteen US soldiers are committing suicide each day.

The American Veterans Health Administration confirms that an average of 126 veterans per week—6,552 per year—kill themselves. Actual numbers may be even higher than this because these statistics only include deaths reported as suicides. They do not include deaths reported as accidents or murders.

American A-10 *Warthog* designed specifically to fire Depleted Uranium DU weapons.

One cause of these suicides may be consciousness expansion during battle experiences. Previously numb soldiers get sent into combat conditions. Suddenly they are faced with the shocking and perhaps gruesome consequences of their choice to be a soldier. Irrepressible feelings may arise about what they see, what they have done, or what happened to them, and they may have no idea what to do with these feelings, how to consciously feel them, or how to communicate their feelings to others.

Further reading in alternative news websites online will reveal another harrowing scenario unfolding. There are now *tens of thousands* of soldiers discovering the hard way that, as a consequence of choosing to participate in one of the various wars since 1991, they returned home *contaminated for life* with radioactive dust from Depleted Uranium (DU) weapons. These soldiers (both men and women) were neither warned about the health hazards of DU nor properly protected, even though the dangers have been known since 1945.

By following the orders given to them by military authorities these courageous young men and women have consigned themselves to a shortened lifespan and a drawn-out painful death without care or compensation from either the government they trusted or from the oil, weapons, communications, and construction corporations who financially benefited from the ultimate sacrifice these men and women made.

Exposure to DU dust can cause multiple simultaneous cancers and genetic disorders. Perhaps by now the soldiers have also contaminated their wives with DU, have had malformed miscarriages, or are caring

Jayce Hanson at his father's legs, from a *Life* magazine cover story, *Children of the Gulf War*. Photo © Copyright 2005 by Derek Hudson, all rights reserved <www.derekhudson.com>.

DU plays no favorites in terms of creating horrific genetic disorders.

for a child with horrible birth defects, just like mothers and fathers in Iraq, Afghanistan, Kosovo, Bosnia, Lebanon, and Gaza, where DU weapons have been (are being) heavily used by the US, UK, NATO and Israeli militaries.

If soldiers have pointlessly killed or hideously tortured other human beings in the name of following orders, they may be discovering that memories of having performed such actions can *never* be erased.

Blocking unwanted memories and feelings through the use of drugs, alcohol or adrenalin rushes from risky or violent behavior simultaneously blocks the possibility of intimacy, tenderness, vulnerability, acceptance and love.

After a while one might begin to question the value of a life without intimacy.

If your buddy is killed and you do not feel and express your feelings about his death, your numbness does not bring him back to life, nor does it fill the gaping hole in your heart where your friend used to be.

If you lose your self-respect by seeing the true motivations of the forces with which you have been naively collaborating and your numbness bar is so high that you cannot express your feelings even if you wanted to, the resulting self-hatred may become intolerable. Suicide may creep in as a preferred alternative.

Staying numb to the consequences of your actions does not avoid the consequences.

Ask the ostrich if it protects him to stick his head in the sand.

GOING BEYOND THE LIMITS OF MODERN CULTURE

The level of your numbness bar is not permanently set. It can be adjusted up or down to vary the intensity of sensations it allows you to perceive. However, the controls for adjusting the level of your numbness bar are not located within the comprehension of modern culture.

Gaining control of the numbness bar level involves extending your own personal capacity for responsibility and awareness beyond the reach of modern culture. What does this mean?

Unless you employ serious interventions, the culture you were born into and raised in largely determines how the world works for you. For example, the single strongest influence over a person's choice of religions is the religion of their parents.

If you were born and raised in a modern society, then you hold the viewpoints of patriarchal empire. Patriarchal empire blatantly encourages maximum numbness. If you are numb, you will have no problem agreeing that having a franchise coffee shop and hamburger joint on every street corner in the world is a really good idea, even if it destroys local culture by forcing original neighborhood coffee shops out of business, multiplies methane greenhouse gas concentrations by maintaining colossal herds of hamburger cattle, uses slave labor to grow the sugar cane and coffee beans, generates millions of tons of nonrecycled plastic wastes, and burns the rain forests, killing the lungs of the Earth.

Modern culture declares itself to be the only culture worthy of calling itself a culture. According to modern culture:

- There is nothing beyond the reach of globalization.

- No other culture has ever equaled modern culture's grand achievements.

- No other culture actually exists.

- In its own eyes, modern civilization is the ultimate triumph of humankind.

- Stepping outside of modern culture could only mean devolving toward the monkeys.

- Leaving modern culture equates to insanity, if not death.

This is really funny.

Think about it. If going beyond the limits of modern culture means that you abandon your security, you are thinking about the world in the same way that people five hundred years ago thought about it. You are still using the flat-world map!

On the flat-world map, if you sail away from known territory you will fall off the edge of the flat world and die. It's funny to realize that you might still be thinking this way, and yet, *most modern people still do think this way.*

What other ways could you think?

Here is an experiment. Permit yourself to view the lifestyle of the culture you were raised in as merely one of many possible perceptions about the world, as if you were gazing upon only one kind of flower in a beautiful flower garden. When you look upon your culture as a flowering plant, you are suddenly outside of its grip. Stay out there and study it for a while. Take the time to examine the many strange and unique qualities of this cultural organism. Start with the most common things. Credit card shopping? Very strange. A supermarket? Supermarkets are one of the most unreal things in the world.

Plastic litter on the streets? Kids divided up into different age groups and forced to sit in rows in classrooms? A three thousand-mile supply chain for your Caesar salad? Pet dogs? Graffiti? A TV in every house? Advertisements for alcohol, cigarettes, casinos, new cars, penis enlarging pills, sex on computers? Large pharmaceutical corporations lobbying for favorable government regulations rather than for health? People working at jobs they don't love just to earn money? Retirement homes?

See the whole thing as a package deal while you observe it from the outside. How long can you keep this perspective? How are you doing, standing outside looking in at your culture? Are you okay?

Seen from outside of a culture, the mythology that is believed within the culture to be unquestionably true (e.g., profit is good, free market capitalism serves humanity, America is a peace-loving democracy) is suddenly recognized as mere myth.

MYTH BUSTING

Myth busting is equivalent to naming a superstition as a superstition. For example, if I asked you to tell me a superstition about black cats, broken mirrors, or spilled salt, you would smile and relate what you would consider to be an old wives' tale. The smile comes from being slightly embarrassed to think this way. We recognize these ideas to be superstitions. But before something is known to be a superstition it is known to be the truth. A superstition is not a superstition until it becomes a superstition. Before that, it is fact. The same is true of the myths that are inherent in every culture, including modern civilization.

As soon as you look at modern culture from the outside, as merely another set of superstitions, it loses its mafia-like grip on your perceptions. Your broadened vantage point permits you to inquire about modern culture in ways that modern culture itself would ordinarily forbid. You might, for example, start asking what may previously have been regarded as dangerous questions.

LEVEL OF RESPONSIBILITY

One such dangerous question might be about responsibility.

If a child makes a mess, who cleans it up?

If you ever lived with children the answer is obvious. Children do not have the capacity to be responsible for cleaning up their own messes. When a child makes a mess, even a teenage child, the adults are responsible for seeing that it gets cleaned up. Certainly, some children are trained to clean up some messes some of the time. Parenting is about creating environments where children can develop their muscles of responsibility. But until around the age of fifteen, children cannot be held responsible for their level of responsibility.

This distinction about levels of responsibility permits you to classify cultures according to the responsibility they take for cleaning up their messes—in other words, their sustainability.

Applying the level-of-responsibility test to modern society reveals that modern society makes huge messes with no intention of ever cleaning them up.

Think of the expanding dead zones in the world's oceans. Think of the tons of permanently lethal nuclear wastes. Think of the US national debt. Think of children being given brain drugs that make them unfit even to join the army. Think of the gigatons of methane frozen forty thousand years ago under Siberian tundra now bubbling out as heat-capturing greenhouse gases.

When you position modern society on a graph showing the number of people and their average level of responsibility, you find modern culture centered directly on child level responsibility. *Modern culture is a child level responsibility culture*, far below adult level.

Modern society does not require that a person grow up prior to being given (or allowed to take) positions of responsibility. In general, even the most powerful leaders of modern culture—leaders of international corporations as well as in politics, the military, entertainment, religion, media, medicine and education—make their decisions and take actions with a child's level of responsibility.

Our society makes messes without having consciousness of, or taking responsibility for, the consequences of those messes. For example, today's business and government leaders specialize in *externalizing costs*. To externalize a cost means to create a devilishly clever excuse for passing the cost on to someone else. That "someone else" could be the

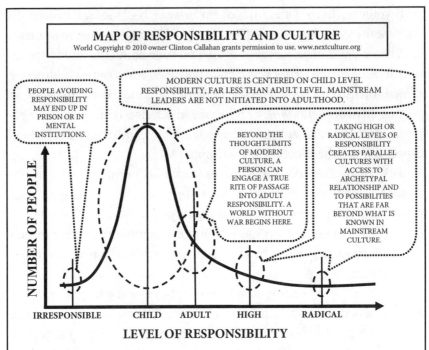

MAP OF RESPONSIBILITY AND CULTURE

World Copyright © 2010 owner Clinton Callahan grants permission to use. www.nextculture.org

MODERN CULTURE IS CENTERED ON CHILD LEVEL RESPONSIBILITY, FAR LESS THAN ADULT LEVEL. MAINSTREAM LEADERS ARE NOT INITIATED INTO ADULTHOOD.

PEOPLE AVOIDING RESPONSIBILITY MAY END UP IN PRISON OR IN MENTAL INSTITUTIONS.

BEYOND THE THOUGHT-LIMITS OF MODERN CULTURE, A PERSON CAN ENGAGE A TRUE RITE OF PASSAGE INTO ADULT RESPONSIBILITY. A WORLD WITHOUT WAR BEGINS HERE.

TAKING HIGH OR RADICAL LEVELS OF RESPONSIBILITY CREATES PARALLEL CULTURES WITH ACCESS TO ARCHETYPAL RELATIONSHIP AND TO POSSIBILITIES THAT ARE FAR BEYOND WHAT IS KNOWN IN MAINSTREAM CULTURE.

NUMBER OF PEOPLE

IRRESPONSIBLE CHILD ADULT HIGH RADICAL

LEVEL OF RESPONSIBILITY

When a child makes a mess, who cleans it up? The adults clean it up. Modern culture is classified at child level responsibility because modern culture makes horrific messes with no intention of ever cleaning them up (e.g., nuclear wastes, children on brain drugs, deforestation, greenhouse gases, peak oil, over fishing, unsustainable lifestyles, etc.). Experiments with creating new sustainable cultures are becoming more plentiful and more powerful. For example, the number of known international NGOs has grown from 6,000 in 1990 to 26,000 in 2000, to over 40,000 in 2008. (Sources: *High Noon: Twenty Global Problems, Twenty Years to Solve Them*, by J. F. Rischard, p.48, <www.rischard.net>, and <www.wikipedia.org>). You can connect with others of similar interest and exchange with them in a committed community of practice. Then if you establish critical connections to other communities of practice, you build a system of influence that facilitates the emergence of next culture. If you do your part by handling the jobs that land on your bench, the emergence of next culture is self-organizing (For more on this, s the M. Wheatley and D. Frieze article <www.berkana.org/pdf/emergence_web.pdf>).

consumer, the general public, the people living under corrupt governments, or even future generations.

Business and government collude to externalize costs, for example, the costs of cleaning up toxic wastes from coal- and oil-burning electric power plants. Power stations produce 70 percent of the sulfur dioxide in the acid rain that destroys wildlife, crops, forests and lakes, and strips minerals from topsoil. They also produce 40 percent of the carbon dioxide in ocean acidification, killing off coral reefs, shrimp, clams, crabs, lobsters, abalone, and krill, which is the main food source of some of the most magnificent creatures ever to have existed on Earth, the great whales. The financial consequence of so much unconscionable destruction is inestimably huge. Do power station directors and government officials think they can escape paying?

Externalizing costs creates the illusion of profit. If the manufacturer of an item, say a plastic bag used at a fast-food restaurant, was responsible for paying the full costs of their product, including collection after use, transportation, and recycling of the product (instead of merely burying it in a landfill and thinking this is responsible), there would be no profit. It costs seventeen times more to recycle a plastic bag than it does to make it in the first place. In a closed system, there *can* be no profit. Earth is a closed system. Modern society assumes it can ignore that the Earth is a closed system. That assumption is suicidal.

PARALLEL CULTURES

Since we are exploring beyond the understanding limits of modern culture in order to find ways to adjust the level of our numbness bar, we can imagine the existence of cultures with higher levels of responsibility than modern culture.

Perhaps there could be cultures with, on average, *adult level* responsibility.

Perhaps there could be cultures with a *high level* of responsibility.

Perhaps there could be cultures with *radical level* responsibility.

Since these cultures would coexist in the same environment, they would be *parallel cultures*, not necessarily visible to each other. In particular, the parallel cultures of higher levels of responsibility would not be so visible to the parallel cultures of lower levels of responsibility. It is doubtful that the people who were burning cars and spraying graffiti in Paris had much comprehension of the level of responsibility it takes to own cars and maintain buildings.

You respond according to what you perceive. Certainly the world must look different if you take adult and radical levels of responsibility than it does if you perceive your circumstances from child level responsibility. The difference in perception comes from your *thoughtmaps*.

MAP OF EVOLVING THOUGHTMAPS

What is a *thoughtmap*? A *thoughtmap* is the set of distinctions that formats the way you interact with the world. Your set of thoughtmaps constitutes your personal *identity*, your *mindset*, your *worldview*, your *comfort zone*, your *belief system*.

Your thoughtmaps present you with the options you have to choose from: to make the decisions you make, to take the actions you take, to produce the results you want to create. If you want to change your results, you would most effectively start by changing your thoughtmaps.

MAP OF CHANGED RESULTS
World Copyright © 2010 owner Clinton Callahan grants permission to use. www.nextculture.org

If you are interested in change it pays to study where new results come fro m. Did you ever try to get new results without changing your actions? (We all do. It doesn't work. This shows how disconnected the mind can be from reality.) New results come from new *behaviors*. So where do new behaviors come from? They come from conscious or unconscious *decisions* to act differently. Where do new decisions come from? They come from new *options* to choose from. But where do we get the new options? From new *thoughtmaps*. Without changing your thoughtmaps it is unlikely that you will create changed results.

NEW THOUGHTMAPS

⇩

NEW OPTIONS TO CHOOSE FROM

⇩

NEW DECISIONS
(decisions can be conscious or unconscious)

⇩

NEW ACTIONS OR BEHAVIORS

⇩

NEW RESULTS

Imagine two people looking out over the horizon, each holding a different map of the world. One person holds a map where the world is shown as a flat disc. The other person holds a map where the world is shown as a round ball. The world they look at is the same, but what they see is completely different because they are using different maps.

If the flat-world map-user exchanged his flat-world map for the round-world map, would this person gain new options, powers, and possibilities? Yes, he would.

When this person exchanges his map, does the world itself change? No, it does not. The world remains the same world it has always been.

This person's new map gives him new possibilities because human beings do not interact with the world as it is. We interact with the world through our *thoughtmaps* of the world. If you change your thoughtmap, you get a new world.

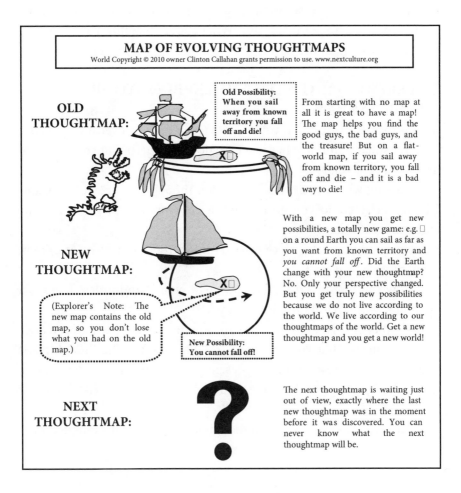

MAP OF EVOLVING THOUGHTMAPS
World Copyright © 2010 owner Clinton Callahan grants permission to use. www.nextculture.org

OLD THOUGHTMAP:

Old Possibility: When you sail away from known territory you fall off and die!

From starting with no map at all it is great to have a map! The map helps you find the good guys, the bad guys, and the treasure! But on a flat-world map, if you sail away from known territory, you fall off and die – and it is a bad way to die!

NEW THOUGHTMAP:

(Explorer's Note: The new map contains the old map, so you don't lose what you had on the old map.)

New Possibility: You cannot fall off!

With a new map you get new possibilities, a totally new game: e.g. ☐ on a round Earth you can sail as far as you want from known territory and *you cannot fall off*. Did the Earth change with your new thoughtmap? No. Only your perspective changed. But you get truly new possibilities because we do not live according to the world. We live according to our thoughtmaps of the world. Get a new thoughtmap and you get a new world!

NEXT THOUGHTMAP:

?

The next thoughtmap is waiting just out of view, exactly where the last new thoughtmap was in the moment before it was discovered. You can never know what the next thoughtmap will be.

So it turns out that thoughtmaps are quite influential in a human being's quality of life.

Of course, changing thoughtmaps may be the most frightening thing to consider doing. After all, we may well have regarded our thoughtmaps as *the one true way that things are,* rather than as merely a personal set of thoughtmaps. Seriously considering changing your thoughtmaps may seem like vaporizing the solid ground you have stood on for your whole life. What remains of the real world if thoughtmaps are recognized as merely thoughtmaps?

Still, you have probably changed your thoughtmaps before, and you will probably change them again. What about changing your thoughtmaps *now* to obtain the new results of being no longer numb?

EXPERIMENTING WITH THE LEVEL OF YOUR NUMBNESS BAR

In this case, the result that you want to change is the level at which your own personal numbness bar is set. To do this experiment you will need to start where you are.

Starting where you are is a powerful thoughtmap itself. For example, how else could you go through a doorway unless you are at the doorway? You can't.

How can you eat a piece of cake unless there is a piece of cake in front of you? You can't.

How can you pick up a hammer with your hand unless there is a hammer within hand's reach? You can't.

In other words, to cause a change you need to start where you are.

This means that you will need to take a look at the thoughtmaps that produce the results you are presently getting before you can replace those thoughtmaps with different thoughtmaps that produce different results.

Specifically, what is your old thoughtmap about your numbness bar?

FLAT-WORLD THOUGHTMAPS

If you have been raised within modern society then your flat-world thoughtmap about the numbness bar is that *it is better to be numb*. The higher the numbness bar is, the less pain you feel. The less pain you feel, the more comfortable you will be.

Modern culture's Standard Human Institutional Thoughtmaps include:

- The goal is to be rich, happy, and famous, no matter what.

- Pain is bad.

- Feelings are mostly negative.

- Buy low. Sell high.

- Do whatever it takes to achieve success.

- Maximize profit through externalizing costs to society or to the next generation. Ignore the social and environmental consequences.

- Follow society's plan: Get born, go to school, get a job, get married, buy a house, get a different job, start your own business, sell your business, retire, go to an old people's home, die.

- Pay no attention to the man behind the curtain operating the illusion-making levers.

- Chase the carrot.

- Run the rat race.

- Whoever dies with the most toys wins.

- Only the good die young.

Standard Human Institutional Thoughtmaps are not bad or stupid. They are simply the set of thoughtmaps that produce standard human intelligence results. If you want to produce other results, then use other thoughtmaps.

A thoughtmap to begin experimenting with is the Old Map of the Numbness Bar.

MAP OF THE NUMBNESS BAR (OLD)

Modern culture teaches you to move your *numbness bar* ever higher to obtain the sensation of comfort. The mainstream motto is: *avoid pain*. But numbness blocks us from appropriately responding to present conditions. That is why idealizing the strong numb hero has possibly exterminated the human race.

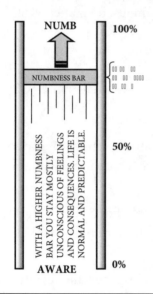

NUMB

100%

NUMBNESS BAR

50%

WITH A HIGHER NUMBNESS BAR YOU STAY MOSTLY UNCONSCIOUS OF FEELINGS AND CONSEQUENCES. LIFE IS NORMAL AND PREDICTABLE.

AWARE

0%

Keeping your numbness bar high assures that pain with an intensity level below the bar does not consciously register. You don't feel it. With a high numbness bar you can pointlessly stay in school, watch infantile TV, fight in wars, be in a gang, work a job you don't love, lead without integrity, accept corrupt leadership without objecting, consume endlessly, watch mainstream news, go into debt, believe government officials, live in waking sleep, and stay oblivious to your own feelings. How do you keep your numbness bar high? Each of us has our favorite ways: overeating, overworking, over exercising, over shopping, joking around, denial, avoiding self-knowledge, being righteous, consuming sugar, using alcohol or drugs, constant background TV noise, speeding, competing, fighting with the neighbors, self-hatred, trying to be perfect, and so on. We are extremely dedicated to – and creative about – staying numb.

Observing the level at which you typically hold your numbness bar may require the assistance of other people. You can ask for feedback from friends, relatives, or colleagues at work.

- Ask them to tell you from 0 to 100 percent how high you keep your numbness bar.

- Ask them to explain in detail exactly how you keep your numbness bar at that level, and why you must keep it there.

Ask for this feedback from a variety of people over a period of weeks or months. The suggestion for getting the most out of this experiment is to trust the feedback you get from people, even if you don't understand it, even if you think they are wrong.

Here are two more questions you can start living with now:

- In what ways am I blocking my feelings about what is happening right now?

- What do other people feel about this incident that I am not feeling?

SELF-OBSERVATION. PERIOD.

Through asking yourself questions and through requesting feedback from your friends, you may get views of yourself that don't match your long-held or most preferred self-image. The discrepancy between the way you imagine yourself to be and the way you are perceived by others could be vast. The vastness may be disconcerting enough to propel you toward wanting to take immediate actions to rectify the situation.

The invitation is to try not to change anything. Don't even try to change your knee-jerk reactions about making the pain of realization go away. Just observe the whole thing.

Trying not to move is like playing the game of Freeze! If you don't previously agree to freeze when the captain of the game shouts "Freeze!", then your first reaction to hearing someone yell "Freeze!" is to move!

In this game of self-observation, hold the intention that no matter what you observe during this observation period, you won't do anything about it.

Not doing anything can be an extremely difficult thing to do. Don't even carry the question around about what you *could* do. It is far too early for trying to make changes.

The strategy right now is to *not* make changes.

If you don't know what you are doing to stay numb, how can you be sure if you are doing something different from that? You can't.

Observing yourself requires consciously splitting your attention into two parts. Use half of your attention to do your normal life, and use the other half of your attention to neutrally observe what you are doing. At first you could get a bit dizzy from the simultaneous differing perspectives, but splitting your attention is normal. Remember a time when you were listening to an MP3 player while riding your bicycle, thinking about what to buy at the store, chewing gum, and watching the interesting people on the sidewalk all at the same time. You can already split your attention. The only difference now is you will be splitting your attention consciously.

It helps to imagine that you are living within a box of mechanical behaviors, completely identified with the box's behaviors as if they were your own true actions because you have no other perspective on your situation. When the box moves, you are moved by the movement. You can't help it. You are stuck in these mechanical reactions, and may be stuck there for the rest of your life. Perhaps you know someone like this?

Self-observation is like taking a new pair of energetic eyeballs into your hand, reaching your hand out beyond the edges of your box, and twisting your hand around so that your new eyes can look back at the box from the outside. By seeing from this perspective, you easily discover that the box is no more than an assembly of mechanical reactions triggered automatically by external stimuli. Keep your arm out there and just watch what happens for a long time.

When you first hold out your hand with the eyes it gets tired within a few moments and you bring it back inside the box again, often without even knowing it. Moments, hours, or even days go by before you wake up with a start and remember what you were trying to do. You see that you are no longer splitting your attention, but you have no memory of stopping. Even at those times do not judge yourself. Or if you do judge yourself, observe the mechanicality of your self-judgment and do not judge that. When you notice your lack of self-observation, simply extend your neutral eyes out beyond the perimeter of your box again and continue observing yourself.

Lee Lozowick identifies three conditions under which to pay particular attention to observing yourself:

1. When you are laughing.

2. When you are praying.

3. When you think nothing is going on.

Yes, especially observe yourself when you assume there is nothing special to observe.

Remain as neutral as a video camera.

You are familiar with the term *second sight*, having insights after the fact? During self-observation try to use *first sight* so you can observe what is actually happening while it happens without having any insights about it. *First sight* is seeing what is as it is rather than seeing what you expect or hope to see.

Observe with a crystal clear eye. No name-calling, no swear words, no inner vows, no self-flagellations, no justifications, no comments from the peanut gallery. Keep your opinions about your opinions to yourself. Simply notice.

As soon as you notice that you are not simply noticing, simply go back to noticing. It's that simple.

Observe yourself for an extended period of time so you can identify repeated patterns and the circumstances that trigger them. An extended period of time means months and months, years actually.

Observe . . .

- what you say.
- what you do.
- what you think.
- what you feel.
- your tensions.
- your intentions.
- your postures.
- your impostures.
- your accomplishments compared to what you promise.
- your sense of things.
- your incense about things.
- what offends you.
- what offends others about you.

- what in you gets fed by offending others.

- your layers within layers, games within games.

When you first begin self-observation you may have an attention span of only a few seconds before you get knocked unconscious and fall asleep. Work to build up your muscles of attention.

As your *modus numbness* becomes more and more apparent it will simultaneously become more predictable. When your own behavior becomes predictable to you then you see it is dead. Only then do you gain a new freedom of movement. Your mechanical commitment to staying numb can be avoided without sentimentality, because you will not be killing something that you still regard as being alive. It will take months of dedicated observation before you get to this point. That is not too long. The months will go by no matter what you are doing. You may as well be building your attention muscles.

DOCUMENTATION

In the meantime, do not avoid the impulse to write your observations down. I carry around a little black book in my pocket for making notes about myself. I call it my "Beep Book," a place to jot down what people tell me about myself, what I notice, wild ideas for things to try, phrases that lead to thinking in ways that are not in my present thought patterns, designs for new experiments, and so on. My little books fill up faster than I ever imagined.

Without writing things down you can easily become a victim of *blackouts*. Blackouts are when your psychological defense strategy (belief system, self-image, what I call "The Box") causes you to forget something that it would rather you didn't know about, such as particularly insightful pieces of feedback, or experiences that you do not have a name for. If a blackout can get you to forget about something one time, it can get you to forget about it many times. If you forget about a thing without knowing you have forgotten about it, that thing becomes invisible to you. Blackouts don't really protect you from anything. Just because you cannot see a thing does not mean it loses its power to damage your life. (Ask the captain of the Titanic.)

So get yourself a Beep Book and develop the practice of writing down your self-observations and feedback. Unveiling your technologies for staying numb is *your* job, no one else's. The problem is that you are an expert in avoiding disillusionment (like the rest of us). Here lies the value of working in a team. It is far easier to see someone else's denial mechanisms than our own. If you arrange to come together regularly with others in a men's or women's group, or in a self-development laboratory, you can establish a protocol for waking each other up when you are fogging yourselves.

There is a warning about group work, however. Making the group responsible for waking you up won't work. A reminder from someone else does not give you power. It keeps them alert but not you. The reminders from others serve as an interim step until you can catch yourself. Only when you can identify your own numbing techniques and can stop before using them do you gain the power to choose another behavior.

NEW MAP OF THE NUMBNESS BAR

Lowering the numbness bar is neither philosophical nor conceptual. It is experiential. You will physically detect each millimeter it goes down. When it goes up you won't notice it. But when it goes down it is like being in spotlights naked on stage, like scraping a knife on a china plate. The bar cannot be lowered for free—it takes work. As Swami Prajnanpad, a wise Indian teacher, bluntly put it, *You must pay full price.*

The price of lowering your numbness bar is to be more conscious of pain, more sensitive to your own feelings and the feelings of others. Lowering your numbness bar also makes you more aware of the consequences of your actions and the actions of others. Greater awareness brings greater responsibility.

MAP OF THE NUMBNESS BAR (NEW)

You can gradually and responsibly move your numbness bar ever lower. In doing so you become more vulnerable, perceptive, relational, and responsive. The intention in modern culture is: *avoid pain*. In next culture the intention is: *seek beauty*. Perceptions of pure beauty can be intense.

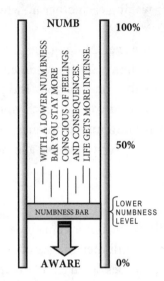

Lowering your *numbness bar* is neither philosophical nor conceptual. It is experiential. The bar cannot be lowered for free – it takes work and you must pay full price. The price of more consciousness is pain. The more you are aware of, both within you and around you, the more pain you feel. If you are not skilled in inner navigating the four feelings – if you do not live in the clarity that pain is just anger, sadness, fear or joy – then lowering the numbness bar may seem overwhelmingly intense. An adult human being is designed to be 100 percent conscious, and to experience and make use of 100 percent intense pure feelings. These skills and this knowledge are not provided by modern culture, but are basic to next culture. They can be learned in extraordinary trainings. It can help to remind yourself that the practice of gently but steadily lowering your *numbness bar* is less about being perfect and more about being human, present, and alive.

GIVE YOURSELF SOME SLACK

The journey from numbness to feeling is part of an archetypal rite of passage into adulthood. Such a journey may begin at childhood's end, but any true master will tell you that you must practice until your last breath.

Once the journey is begun it does not help to try to hurry things along. Also, do not be too disappointed if from time to time you recoil at the strength of your own feelings and temporarily recede into periods of numbness. When you notice that you have gotten numb again, simply return to your feeling practices and keep going. Do not beat yourself up about vacillations. Two steps forward and one backward seems to be how it goes.

Most people reading this book are old—at least older than fifteen. If we were prepared as adolescents the rite of passage shift from *un*consciously feeling to consciously feeling would be swift and sure. Formal rites of passage to adulthood over the past 100,000 years have shown that human beings are designed to leap into conscious responsibility for 100 percent maximum archetypal feelings at fifteen.

But the farther past fifteen we are, the creakier our psychological joints seem to get. Shifting from *un*consciously feeling to consciously feeling involves flexing in places that may have begun to crystallize. We may face rigid old beliefs, petrified interpretations, opinions that we have magically transformed into truth, and inarguable assumptions about who we are, who other people are, or how best to survive in this world.

Old beliefs have stayed in place long enough to become old because they never give up without a fight. Nothing has previously caused them to waver. Don't expect your beliefs to just politely bow, step off their pedestal, and walk away now that you have decided to lower your numbness bar. More likely they will laugh in your face.

Remember, laughing is one of the most important times to pay attention and observe. While the patterns are laughing at you, do not look away. It is an opportunity to notice minutiae. Fine, almost trifling details of structure reveal weaknesses and ways through the mind's clever maze defending its status quo. Be patient. Time is on your side. Even a defense strategy tires itself out by defending itself.

Seek to identify the phrasing of each of your self-defining limits as precisely as you can in terms of when and why you established it in the first place. Beginnings are the most delicate of times. A seed holds all the secrets of the thorny weed it is to become. By empathizing with a defense strategy's opening phrases (such as, "You never . . .," or, a sigh followed by a head shake and the phrase, "I don't know . . .), its original purpose is understood. Its original purpose was to try to protect you, to try to take care of you and arrange for you to survive.

It is here that you can admit that taking care of yourself is a noble purpose.

Let me say that again.

Figuring out ways to protect and take care of yourself is *noble*. It is no one else's job. It is *your* job, and you accomplished it! The ways you figured out to take care of yourself succeeded marvelously, because indeed you have survived!

MAKING A NEW CHOICE

As a child you could well see what was going on in your family or in the world with clarity and indignation. Perhaps you feared that if you spoke out against it, if you challenged your parents or other authority figures, you would be punished or destroyed. You could accurately assess the situation but you concluded that it would be safest to disempower yourself. So you did just that. Think what a powerful action it is to disempower yourself.

Boys with guns. It's time to grow up. Growing up begins with lowering your numbness bar so you feel the consequences of your actions. Consciously experiencing your feelings confers the authority to choose to do something completely different.

Perhaps you adopted a pattern of being shy, of doubting your instincts, or of confusing yourself rather than speaking out about what you saw. The pattern may have saved your life. But after all these years you may have forgotten the moment in which you chose to install your survival pattern. You may think that the self-doubting actually defines who you are rather than being merely a clever defense strategy that allowed you to make it through your childhood.

Your circumstances may have changed drastically since you made the life-saving decision, but the old decision remains actively in place, still influencing your life today. Taking conscious responsibility for having made the original survival decision is the point at which you gain the option to make a different decision. This time you have the power to choose to live instead of to merely survive.

Merely surviving may no longer be a sufficient response to the glorious and precious opportunity of having been born. Your essential being has grown to the point where what once served to protect you has now become your prison. The patterns that saved your life then now impede your life's onward journey.

Releasing yourself from outdated defensive limitations becomes a simple matter of letting them slip away, like outgrown snakeskin, while maintaining complete respect for them having accomplished a job well done.

Taking on a new way of being is actually a simple matter, but it may not feel that way. It may feel like losing your mind. In this case, it helps to learn how to learn.

THE FOUR STEP LEARNING SPIRAL

STEP 1: The first learning step is the hardest. That is because the first step is to recognize that what you already know is not working. You are faced with admitting your own incompetence.

How uncool!

The first times you practice a new behavior you are guaranteed to look bad, because by practicing a new behavior you admit to having used an old behavior for all those years.

How embarrassing!

This is often the biggest barrier to learning new skills—the fear of looking bad. The point is that, in any true learning, looking bad is unavoidable. It is the first step in the four step learning spiral, moving from Quadrant 1, *unconscious incompetence*, to Quadrant 2, becoming *conscious* of your present *incompetence*.

The shock of becoming conscious of your own incompetence can provide enough inspiration to practice new skills.

At the beginning every effort feels totally strange, bizarre even. There can be a majority opinion in your mind thinking *this whole thing is just stupid, a waste of time, and totally embarrassing besides.* Just observe it.

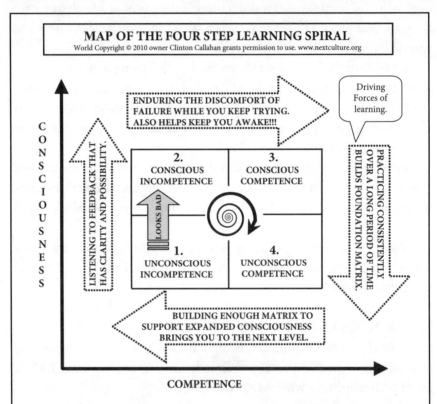

MAP OF THE FOUR STEP LEARNING SPIRAL
World Copyright © 2010 owner Clinton Callahan grants permission to use. www.nextculture.org

This map shows a spiral going clockwise round and round, circling straight up out of the page. Learning happens when any of the four driving forces actively takes you to the next level. This means that although you can learn by making different kinds of efforts, completing the learning cycle includes a balance of all four forces and goes through all four stages. The step from *unconscious incompetence* to *conscious incompetence* feels *awful* because everyone sees that you do not already know. *This step cannot be avoided.* It helps to decide ahead of time to go ahead and learn even if you look bad. Listen to feedback, because feedback guides you to the treasure of gaining new competence. Once completing a cycle, fierce learners do not hang out in *unconscious competence* for more than about fifteen seconds before seeking consciousness about a new incompetence. (The original source of this Map is disputed, possibly D. L. Kirkpatrick 1971, W. C. Howell 1977, or T. Gordon in the 1970s. This thoughtmap is also similar to the famous Johari Window. The driving forces of learning were added to the map by Clinton Callahan in 2006.)

STEP 2: To move from Quadrant 2, *conscious incompetence*, to Quadrant 3, *conscious competence*, requires persistent practice in the face of repeated failures. Even if you never seem to get it right, keep practicing.

Hints for improving the effectiveness of your practice include:

- Ask for (and listen to!) feedback and coaching.

- Select one feedback distinction at a time and practice making only that one shift.

- Make subtle changes in your posture and breathing.

- Pay attention to where you place your attention.

- Stay aware of what your purpose is.

STEP 3: Sooner or later (and probably not as soon as you might wish) you behave in the new way without so much pain, without having to plan, without having to remember what you are suppose to remember, without even thinking about it. Voila! You have entered Quadrant 4, *unconscious competence*.

STEP 4: You have achieved a stable new level of competence. The shocker is that no matter how hard you struggled to achieve the new way of being, the mind quickly adapts to it and soon transforms the remarkable new perceptions and benefits into a new normal. The honeymoon is over. Our miraculously tender and pleasing intimacies of infatuation are suffocated without effort by being taken for granted. And herein lies the value of continuing on in the spiral of learning. Success is the doorway to the next failure.

STEP 1 AGAIN: In the moment you become truly competent at one thing, you become truly incompetent at a whole new level of things that you could not be incompetent at before. The next cycle of learning begins in Quadrant 1, *unconscious incompetence*, again. You can never know the next thing you don't know until you are able to know it. As soon as you discover (or have it pointed out to you) that there is a next thing to learn, you again enter Quadrant 2, *conscious incompetence*, and the spiral of learning continues.

It can be useful to know that if you are to learn anything, you will be looking bad until you don't look bad anymore. That's all there is to it.

But it seems to help to know this. Then you can simply plan on looking bad, just like everybody else.

My friend Ken Windes used to say that we have a choice. We can be on the *learning team*, where it is guaranteed that we *will* look bad. Or we can be on the *looking good* team. Whenever he noticed me holding back, trying to save face, trying to keep safe, he would come over to me and say, "Looking good, going nowhere."

Along the path of shifting from *un*consciously feeling to consciously feeling, it is guaranteed that you are going to look bad. Welcome to the learning team.

BEGINNING THEORETICALLY

Do not think that anything should have happened for you already. This whole chapter has been theoretical. We haven't actually tried anything yet. We've been dancing around the *theoretical possibility* of lowering your numbness bar, but not actually doing it. We're just warming up. The next two chapters are additional warm-ups. When you are so warm that you are almost hot, then in Chapter 4 we will actually start some conscious feelings work. By then it will go almost as if by itself.

If you are thinking that it might be a good idea to jump ahead right now and go directly to Chapter 4, I have a different opinion about your idea: it won't do you any good. There is a lot that you don't know you don't know about feelings. Believe me, I had to learn the hard slow way that there is no way around the hard slow way.

2. EXPANDING INTO ALL FOUR BODIES

This chapter will present you with a series of thoughtmaps from beyond the understanding limits of modern culture. Looking at modern culture from the outside puts its limits into a new perspective. The *observer* perspective permits you to better see what modern culture is and what it is not, what it has provided for us and what it has not. Having new thoughtmaps where before there were few makes it easier to navigate into a culture of more significant responsibility than modern culture.

For example, modern culture provides the thoughtmap that a human being is no more than a body with a mind. If you conceive of yourself this way then you force yourself to stay numb to a rich array of inner intelligences and valuable personal experiences arising on a daily basis that don't fit the body-mind thoughtmap.

For instance, a wide range of subtle ongoing feelings naturally arises in a human being. These feelings are stimulating and satisfying from the archetypal perspective, but they don't fit into the picture when we only understand ourselves to be a mind with a body. Instead of embracing our personal experiences we cling to the commonly accepted model. In exchange, modern society sells us MP3-cell phone-camera-GPS-Internet-clocks, soap operas and game shows on cable television, mail order catalogs, and 24-hour online gambling.

Another example is our inspiration. Modern society keeps us busy, busy, busy. If we slow down below modern society's usual speed-of-mind action-packed days, we may sense an inner longing to fulfill a vision that sits deep in our soul. Sticking with the cultural model cancels having a vision that truly inspires us. In its place modern society sells us international sporting events, new-model cars, tropical vacations, and the unfulfillable longing to be a rich and famous movie star.

Living without authentic feelings and without inspiration may seem ideal for subsisting as an uncomplaining cog in an industrial machine, but it provides little foundation for exploring the magnificence of our innate human potential.

Permit me to offer a slightly more complex model of what we human beings are.

On September 3, 2005, I saw the original Map of Four Bodies spontaneously drawn on a flip chart by Possibility Manager Wolfgang Köhler during a three-day Possibility Lab. The new thoughtmap splashed into the training space like a boulder in a puddle. As the tsunami settled down we found our perceptions sparkling with many new facets of clarity.

The Map of Four Bodies starts like this. Rather than imagining yourself as merely a physical body with a thinking mind, imagine yourself as having four distinct bodies layered one on top of the other, all in the same place.

The foundation body is your *physical body* with sense organs that experience touch, sight, sound, smell, taste, instinct, and centeredness.

Layered on top of the physical body are three additional bodies, each with its own unique properties.

One layer is your *intellectual body* with your *mind* that generates thoughts and holds knowledge, opinions, beliefs, reasons, expectations, interpretations, memories, conclusions and insights.

Another layer is your *emotional body* with your *heart* that generates feelings of anger, sadness, joy and fear, can sense those same feelings in others, and resonates and expands with love.

And another layer is your *energetic body* with your *being* that has presence and will, directs your attention and intention, accesses imagination, and is inspired by your destiny principles and your vision of what is possible.

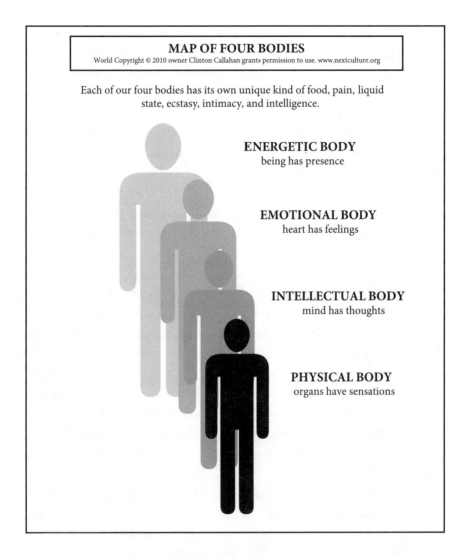

MAP OF FOUR BODIES
World Copyright © 2010 owner Clinton Callahan grants permission to use. www.nextculture.org

Each of our four bodies has its own unique kind of food, pain, liquid state, ecstasy, intimacy, and intelligence.

ENERGETIC BODY
being has presence

EMOTIONAL BODY
heart has feelings

INTELLECTUAL BODY
mind has thoughts

PHYSICAL BODY
organs have sensations

STARVING HEARTS AND SOULS

Without distinguishing four bodies you miss out on a wealth of experience and understanding that would add deeper appreciation of the quality of your daily life. For example, each of the four bodies requires its own unique kinds of food, experiences its unique kinds of pain, liquid state and ecstasy, and enjoys unique forms of intimacy. Clarity about these added dimensions opens the doors to perceiving and entering new depths of relationship with other human beings and with what is possible to create in life. Viewing yourself and others as having four bodies instead of just one, provides expanded opportunities for self-expression, satisfaction, relationship and community. Without distinguishing the four bodies these added dimensions are often blocked from nourishing you.

Since mainstream culture's standard education does not include the four bodies you probably haven't noticed that something is seriously missing. The single-bodied life seems normal to you.

To understand the new model you can begin by thinking of food groups. If you do not recognize the four basic food groups then you might eat only your favorite brand of fast-food fried chicken and starve yourself to death, all the while thinking you are well fed. This is an exact metaphor.

Modern education force-fed your mind a massive overdose of information. To round out the program you were instructed how to kick a ball around twice a week for physical exercise. If you were lucky enough to receive any lessons in art or music, they were most probably directed exclusively toward your intellectual body. Modern education completely ignores your emotional and energetic bodies so they remain underdeveloped and immature, wasting away from malnutrition. Because the whole of modern society is distorted in this same way, your hideous deformity is only vaguely apparent until you become aware of the Map of Four Bodies.

Well before completing twelve years of schooling you were twisted into an intellectually enhanced monster with a horribly swollen head, shriveled heart and withered being. If you do not step beyond the limits of modern culture and find books, talks, workshops, practices and transformational processes to reeducate yourself, then modern culture's imbalance hardens into crystallized habit. Your heart and soul starve while your mind eats your life. Since this same ailment plagues almost everyone you know you have little reason to question it. Yet here you are reading this book. There must be at least one little question motivating you . . . ?

If you allow that question to move you to look in the mirror in certain quiet moments searching for your own authentic presence, your preference for numbness may acquire a sudden crack in it.

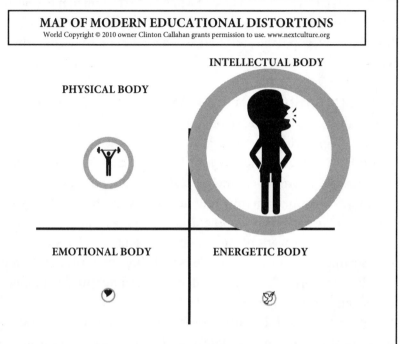

MAP OF MODERN EDUCATIONAL DISTORTIONS
World Copyright © 2010 owner Clinton Callahan grants permission to use. www.nextculture.org

INTELLECTUAL BODY

PHYSICAL BODY

EMOTIONAL BODY

ENERGETIC BODY

Viewed from within modern society the gross imbalances of our educational programs are not visible. When seen more objectively the imbalances verge on abuse. The intellectual body is force-fed verbal-reality information until it distends abnormally, while the emotional and energetic bodies atrophy from disuse. Addressing these imbalances begins with stepping beyond modern society limits and finding books, workshops, practices and transformational processes to reeducate ourselves in the skills of conscious feeling and conscious presence. Rebalancing takes time and effort.

If you allow your question to cause you to ask your friends and colleagues about the purpose of their lives and their answers do not inspire you, the crack in the numbness widens.

If you allow your question to move you to observe your neighbors frenetically distracting themselves with gossip, problems, overconsumption, and mass-produced entertainment, and you see yourself in them, the crack in your numbness gets bigger than the numbness itself. Your smart justifications dissolve into mere word salad, replaced by a direct experience of your own aching heart and starving soul.

It is the ache that you may have desperately been trying to avoid, and yet the ache itself is the way through to expanded dimensions of feeling.

As the sixty-year-old man said when he first shuffled into one of our Expand The Box trainings, "My wife said I should learn to feel something." It may be pitiable, but here is where we are, so here is where we begin.

NEW DIMENSIONS OF ECSTASY AND INTIMACY

Let's further explore the Map of Four Bodies.

Let's begin with the physical body. *Physical food* includes water, air, sunlight, exercise, and the four food groups with proper vitamins and minerals. *Physical pain* includes too loud sounds, too bright lights, dropping a hammer on your toe, hunger, headache, or creaky joints. *Physical ecstasy* includes sipping a hot latte macchiato on a crisp fall morning in a café overlooking a valley full of autumn leaves. It includes body surfing in Pacific Ocean waves, snorkeling on tropical reefs, mountain climbing, orgasm, running full out, sword fighting, galloping on a horse, dancing, and yoga.

Intellectual food includes ideas, entertainment, plans, designs, knowledge, art, and music. *Intellectual pain* includes confusion, disagreement, forgetfulness, being lost, losing an argument, figuring something out wrong, or losing your car keys. *Intellectual ecstasy* includes clarity, agreement, remembering, creating solutions, entertaining others, solving a puzzle, or finding the car keys.

Emotional food includes communicating both the information of a message as well as its carrier-wave, the feelings, delivered and understood with simplicity, clarity and responsibility. It includes respectful listening as well as respectful speaking, an exchange that can be called *sharing*. *Emotional pain* is feelings that are suppressed, denied, withheld, swallowed, feelings that are mixed confusingly together, or feelings that are expressed but heard by no one. *Emotional ecstasy* is completely unhindered expression of feelings with confirmation about what is being shared, and also using the energy and information of feelings to fulfill one's destiny by taking bold actions in the moment.

Energetic food includes being in the company of saints, being in the presence of sacred artifacts, objective art, shrines, or holy spaces, facing certain kinds of stresses and challenges with commitment even if you don't know how to do it. *Energetic pain* includes lack of vision, poor leadership, despair, existential angst, feeling as if you have fallen off the path of evolution, as if your love of the path has been subsumed by ego. *Energetic ecstasy* includes serving something greater than yourself, getting confirmation that you are well footed on the path, being in the company of fellow travelers, being in resonance with the flow of the universe, being the space through which the principles that you serve can do their work in the world, being present and in contact with someone else who is present, being in Countenance.

These descriptions are clear about food, pain and ecstasy, but what about intimacy? Humans do not in general live alone in caves. We live in groups, families and tribes; we work in teams, projects and departments. Human beings thrive on intimacy. We seek to be in love, to be in working relationships.

In those times when your main relationship is hurting nothing else in life seems to matter much. With relationship being so important to human satisfaction you would expect to have been born into a society that endows each of us since childhood with an abundance of education and support in the domain of relationship. But you definitely were not. Modern citizens are paupers, not even beggars, when it comes to understanding relationships. You were given no education, no training, no practices, no distinctions to implement. You were left to imitate what your parents demonstrated to you, or what you fantasize that movie stars might do when they are off camera.

In the modern culture context it is common to think that relationships depend on love. You learned this from pop songs on the radio. But radio songs only teach about ordinary love, leaving extraordinary love and archetypal Love completely off your thoughtmaps. (For more about navigating the space of your relationship through three domains of love, please refer to my book *Radiant Joy Brilliant Love—secrets for creating an extraordinary life and profound intimacy with your partner.*)

In the ordinary context it is common to think that relationships die from a lack of love, and they do not. There can be a wealth of love and a very crippled relationship, because relationships do not die from a lack of love. Relationships die from a lack of intimacy. It is intimacy that

MAP OF FOUR KINDS OF INTIMACY

Relationships do not die from a lack of love. Relationships die from a lack of intimacy. Distinguishing four bodies opens whole new dimensions for experiencing profound intimacy in your everyday life.

1. **PHYSICAL INTIMACY:** singing, eating, washing dishes, walking, holding hands, sauna, sports such as roller-skating, biking, tennis, skiing, swimming, etc., martial arts, dancing, massage, being held without caresses, brushing your partner's hair, brushing their teeth, cutting their fingernails, bathing them, dressing them, a private fashion show, traveling, making art together, body painting, gardening, playing with the children, action games such as charades, going to the zoo, remodeling the house, cleaning out the garage, and so on. Also foreplay (what isn't foreplay?) and sex.

2. **INTELLECTUAL INTIMACY:** talking, discussing, philosophizing, debating, writing poetry, writing proposals, running a business, meeting, planning, strategizing, designing, creating, learning together (such as languages), taking classes, lessons or workshops, attending conferences, playing games (cards, chess, Scrabble, Twenty Questions), entertainment (opera, theater, concerts, shows, movies), going to museums, reading articles out loud, telling stories, telling jokes, humor, sharing memories, collaborative writing, creating possibilities, and so on.

3. **EMOTIONAL INTIMACY:** sharing the experience and the expression of feelings with 1000 percent trust, saying "I feel mad, sad, glad or scared because...," vulnerability, openness, acceptance, deep listening without discussion, grieving, contact, simplifying, revealing wounds, sensitivity, warmth, compassion, generosity, kindness, weakness, confusion, consciously separating the mixed feelings of depression or jealousy, expressing ecstasy, joy, delight, passion, and so on.

4. **ENERGETIC INTIMACY:** being present, *being-with* the other, praying together, ritual, meditation, appreciation of experiences, being in the company of saints or sacred artifacts, respect, dignity, nobility, being in the space of Love, moving at the speed of Love, communion, oneness, Countenance, evolution, transformational processes, development, expanding the Box, radiance, teamwork, family, community, holding space, serving Bright Principles as a couple, and so on.

feeds the body, mind, heart and soul. A diamond mine full of brilliant possibilities for intimacy opens up when you distinguish four bodies and consequently four kinds of intimacy.

The Map of Four Kinds of Intimacy lists dozens of opportunities for intimacy. I encourage you to consider each idea as a unique invitation to do personal experimentation. Sure, you have tried a couple of intimacies in each of the four categories. All of us have. Limiting yourself to those known few intimacies may at the time seem intelligent. (*Oh, but I can't dance. I can't wear things like that! That's silly. That's ridiculous. I don't know how to do that. I can't do that with you. It's too embarrassing to try. I'd feel like an idiot.*) To you, your own Box sounds so reasonable. But I would suggest that the abundance of excuses generated by your Box is, in effect, strangling an endless flood of unexpected joys from gushing into your life day after day. Are you sure you want to insist on staying the same?

Most of your blocks to intimacy hinge on your inexperience with feelings and with sharing your feelings. All this is about to change for you. By studying this book and trying the exercises you are learning to consciously feel. Then experiencing and expressing your feelings will itself become a cherished form of intimacy.

RESISTANCE TO CHANGE

Learning something new changes your life. A change in your life affects the people and environment around you. Here's how. Imagine that you are an egg in an egg carton. When you read this book or take a training, you step out of the egg carton. Because of what you learn your volume of presence expands. You change from a chicken egg into a goose egg. Then as you return to your life in the egg carton it becomes obvious that you have changed but your life has not. The space is too small for you. As you snoozle your way back into everyday relationships the people closest to you must jostle around to give you more room. They need to change to adjust to your new shape—and it wasn't their idea to change! It was *your* idea! So it is understandable if they get a little upset about the forced inconvenience.

In fact, your friends and relatives may get upset even if you hint that you wish to learn something new. They could say that you are crazy. "It's probably a sect or something," they say. "It might not be so wonderful here, but at least it's familiar. Out there you don't even know if you will survive."

On April 26, 1986, a nuclear reactor exploded in Chernobyl, a Russian town now listed as one of the ten most toxic cities of the world. The unbelievable thing about this disaster is that *people still live in the town of Chernobyl!* Nuclear contamination of Chernobyl's dust, food, air and water has caused multiple cancers, horrible birth defects, mental retardation, and a life expectancy reminiscent of the Dark Ages. Why don't people leave the town? Chernobyl is not an island! People could walk to anywhere in Europe, Asia or Africa. Why stay in a place where you and your family's lives are almost guaranteed to be unnecessarily miserable? What is so resistant to change? The answer is, *the Box.*

While growing up you collected an assortment of behaviors and attitudes for the purpose of finding a way to survive. This collection becomes your worldview, psychological defense strategy, personal identity, belief system, comfort zone . . . in short, your *Box.* The Box is made of very real things: thoughtmaps, assumptions, expectations, opinions, rules, beliefs, decisions, interpretations, memories, meanings, etc. Everyone has a Box made out of similar structural components, and yet each Box is unique, custom designed by the owner, you.

Your Box stands between you and the world as a giant filter that edits everything you can perceive and everything you can express. Its purpose is to assure your survival. Since the Box has so far succeeded in its defensive purpose—demonstrated by your being still alive—the Box makes its top priority to defend itself first. It figures that if it can defend itself, it can then defend you. So the Box is one of the hardest things in the universe, far harder than diamonds.

The Box does everything it can to control and shape your surroundings to fit its survival techniques—including where you live, who you marry, what kind of job you do, how much money you make, how you dress, how you take care of your health, how much happiness you experience, and the limits of your future possibilities. Changing even one tiny aspect of your life condition threatens the Box's ability to assure your survival, and against this event the entire defenses of the Box are automatically directed.

It can be shocking to realize that your actual survival could be threatened by submitting to your Box's standard techniques of survival. For example:

- People live in toxic environments, assuring themselves an early and agonizing death, so their Box does not have to feel

---

MAP OF THE BOX (BOX TECHNOLOGY)
World Copyright © 2010 owner Clinton Callahan grants permission to use. www.nextculture.org

THE BOX DISTINCTION:
YOU HAVE A BOX. YOU ARE NOT YOUR BOX. NEITHER ARE THEY!

VAST UNLIMITED EVERPRESENT POSSIBILITIES

OTHER NAMES FOR THE BOX: worldview, belief system, ego, comfort zone, psychology, mindset, identity, survival strategy, defense mechanism, personality

THE BOX
The Box stands between you and your vast potential.

BOX'S PURPOSE
Survival
Comfort
Protection
Control

The Box is a giant filter that controls everything you can perceive

and everything you can express.

BOX IS MADE OF
Beliefs
Attitudes
Conclusions
Expectations
Culture
Rules
Opinions
Assumptions
Habits
Prejudices
Interpretations

New functionality comes from changing the shape of your Box.

The Box explains, *If I am safe, you are safe, so I will control your environment to block all changes. It's for your own good!* But, is it really? The Box can take on a new purpose. Through an authentic rite of passage it can shift from defensive to expansive.

The Box is dedicated to your survival. The Box asserts that if it can defend itself first, then it can defend you. This is true throughout childhood, but at some point, what once defended you has now become your prison. Your full potential is accessible through becoming less identified as a thing and more as a flexible space of possibility. At about fifteen years of age your Box is prepared to shift from defending itself to expanding itself. Through a formidable rite of passage into adulthood you take over responsibility for your life from your Box. Then instead of merely surviving you shift to fully living. Your rite of passage begins with being no longer numb.

---

uncomfortable moving to the strange surroundings of a healthy environment.

- A woman stays with a physically violent man because being battered and terrified is more familiar to her Box than leaving the man to live a joyous adult life with someone who respects her.

- A man works long years in a job that does not fulfill his heart's desires because depression, despair and secret outrage are more comfortable for his Box than the risks of creative self-expression. The man's Box feels more comfortable following society's plan than it would feel if he chose to use the intelligence and energy of his feelings to do what he came here to do: reinvent society.

- A student remains in a school that wastes the years of his youth teaching him things that won't help him live well in rapidly disintegrating conditions, financial collapse, peak oil and climate change. He stays because leaving school would give him new problems that his Box does not already know how to manage.

- A soldier faces a nameless enemy who is scared and fanatical, doing everything to end this soldier's life. The soldier has seen too much to believe the deceptions parroted by government officials. His future passes before his eyes: DU (Depleted Uranium) contamination, PTSD (Post Traumatic Stress Syndrome), Gulf War Syndrome, drugs, suicide. He could just stop being a soldier. He could go home to his wife and kids. But what would his buddies think? They're sticking it out. He will too.

Locking yourself into the prison of your Box's limitations *so you can survive* is made all the more ludicrous through acknowledging that survival is the *one* thing you can never attain—because in the end you will die. The final scene of your present existence is already known.

You cannot change the end of your story; however, you *can* change the middle chapters. But your Box is fast and clever and offers every reason for you to avoid change.

Most people stay captured by the reasons of their Box. You do not have to. Freedom from your Box's imperatives comes through breaking the weld between you and your Box. Replace the bond with a gap, a paper thin friction-free space so your Box can react in whatever way it needs to and you don't have to. Then set about learning more about your Box's various operating modes.

It is unbelievable, but examples of the Box's ability to threaten your life in the name of saving your life are as endless as human creativity. The same creative force can be used unconsciously to stay numb, or consciously to stay alert and creative.

Consciously directing your creating comes through consciously feeling, which begins by becoming painfully aware of how, when, where and why you block yourself from feeling. Thus you commence the journey into your own shadowlands.

MAP OF THE BOX'S RESISTANCE TO CHANGE

World Copyright © 2010 owner Clinton Callahan grants permission to use. www.nextculture.org

The Box's resistance to change is stronger than common sense. Here are four typical traps your Box may use to interfere with your natural impulses to learn something extraordinary.

1. Friends' and relatives' Boxes will attempt to dissuade you from making any changes because through your changes they are forced to change. They will use their fears, doubts, insecurities, victimhood, love and care for you as ropes to bind you to the limits of their world.

2. Your own partner may want to stay locked into their life as it is. This only becomes a problem for you if you catch yourself thinking that to love someone means to block your own development so as to not upset the world of your partner, their friends and family.

3. Society promotes the idea that you should have a strong image of who you are. But change starts with entering *the liquid state* where you cannot have a solid identity for a while, a state that society labels as crazy. Society markets the belief that it is definitely safer to avoid change.

4. The process of entering and owning your shadow world adds awareness but undermines your Box's old self-image. Nothing much from your Box will help you through your underworld journey, but if the Box feels useless it can freak out. Having a hysterical Box can seem threatening enough to give up this whole wish to consciously change. Perhaps it's better to stay in normal life.

These and other forces stand between you and going through the changes involved in learning to consciously feel. The obstacles to begin and the obstacles along the way can seem formidable. That is because they *are* formidable. They need to be formidable. The power involved in authentic change needs to be greater than the Box's power to keep things the same or there would be no such thing as growing up. The question that stands before you is, do you choose the challenge of growing up?

VERBAL REALITY AND EXPERIENTIAL REALITY

Another of your first steps in learning to consciously feel will be to make a particular distinction in your relationship to the world. The distinction is between *verbal reality* and *experiential reality*. You make the distinction by separating your physical body from your intellectual body, or more precisely, loosening your intellectual body's grip over your physical body's interaction with the world.

Without your consent, modern culture hammered you into a tiny section of the universe called *verbal reality*. You were bombarded with words from your very first days. Loud talking heads loomed close in your visual field, radio and television pestered your ears. Advertisements, media, and the printed word surrounded you wherever you were. Everyone important to you was impatient for you to break off the being-to-being contact and enter their world of verbal communications. People weren't willing to relate to you unless you started using the names they gave you for things. Instead of sharing in your wondrous, wordless, wide-open perspectives, people pushed objects into your face and said, *This is a ball. See? Ball! B-A-L-L. Can you say that? Ball!* As soon as you speak your first words you are finally recognized as joining the human race.

Reading, writing and arithmetic, the focus of school, the focus of civilization itself, all involve diminishing your four body experience of the world to symbols of your experience of the world.

Incessant external conditioning forces your intellect's vocabulary to supersede your direct physical experience. At some point you surrender and are trapped. You might even remember the moment when your innocence was stolen away, when you gave up the real world in exchange for being accepted by your parents, older siblings and teachers. Within a short time you hardly experienced anything you did not have words for, and experiential reality drifted away.

Since the vast majority of people in modern civilization were also reduced to living in the same verbal desert as you were, the dreadful price you have paid goes unrecognized. You are thus cut off from the nuance of your feelings, separated from your instinct, made stranger to your amazing knacks and natural talents, sapped of your passions, stolen from your true destiny, made fearful of your imagination, intu-

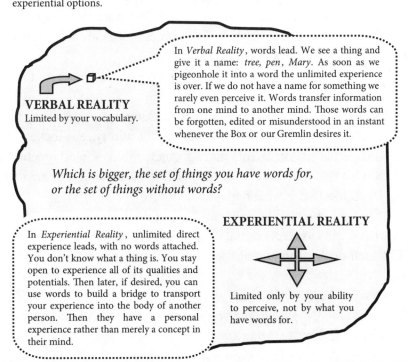

MAP OF VERBAL REALITY vs EXPERIENTIAL REALITY
World Copyright © 2010 owner Clinton Callahan grants permission to use. www.nextculture.org

What is bigger, the set of things you have words for, or the set of things without words? Obviously, the wordless world is far greater. Limiting yourself to the miniscule territory of *verbal reality* excludes you from vast areas of experience for which you have no words. Reclaiming the ability to enter *experiential reality* is monumental. For example, women confide with dismay that it is almost unheard of in modern culture for a man to actually experience his experience. Men have retreated into their heads instead. With guided practice it is possible to have both verbal and experiential options.

VERBAL REALITY
Limited by your vocabulary.

In *Verbal Reality*, words lead. We see a thing and give it a name: *tree, pen, Mary*. As soon as we pigeonhole it into a word the unlimited experience is over. If we do not have a name for something we rarely even perceive it. Words transfer information from one mind to another mind. Those words can be forgotten, edited or misunderstood in an instant whenever the Box or our Gremlin desires it.

Which is bigger, the set of things you have words for, or the set of things without words?

EXPERIENTIAL REALITY

In *Experiential Reality*, unlimited direct experience leads, with no words attached. You don't know what a thing is. You stay open to experience all of its qualities and potentials. Then later, if desired, you can use words to build a bridge to transport your experience into the body of another person. Then they have a personal experience rather than merely a concept in their mind.

Limited only by your ability to perceive, not by what you have words for.

ition and innovation, and blocked from the direct experience of both extraordinary and archetypal love.

The unspeakable mystery of life has now been squeezed into a wiki website, guarded by jealous computer-smart intellectuals who claim possession and dominion over their particular bit of correct knowledge.

Verbal reality creates the wall of your numbness. The question I am asking is this: Are you ready to come back to life? Are you willing to tear down the wall?

Imagine the following demonstration. A courageous but somewhat anxious man volunteers to step to the front of the training room. I ask him to face the audience and pay close attention to what happens next. He is keenly alert as I gently press my fist into the side of his upper arm.

After a moment I ask, "What happened?"

He says, "You touched my arm."

I wait a moment to see if anything else comes from this shining exhibition of twenty-first century intelligence. I have waited a hundred times during this same demonstration. Nothing more ever does.

The man has been to school. He assumes he has found the correct answer and waits for the teacher's confirmation.

I turn to the audience and say, "This is a perfect demonstration of verbal reality."

The audience has no idea what I am talking about, yet. They have also been to school. Each person sitting in the audience is locked into the same verbal prison as this man. To their mind, what happened is exactly what the man said. I touched his arm. How could it be anything else? Of course that is what happened.

Then I ask the man to stay with me as I draw and explain the Map of Verbal Reality vs Experiential Reality on a flip chart board. I carefully make each distinction and at the end I ask him if he understands the map.

He says, "Yes."

I say, "Good. I would like you now to shift from verbal reality to experiential reality. Are you ready?"

He considers this for a moment and then says, "Yes." His answer is tainted with no small amount of uncertainty. That uncertainty creates the possibility of the shift. The secret of making shifts is to commit before you know how.

I have the man face the audience again. After a moment I press my fist into his arm *exactly* as I did a few moments before.

There is a pause. He seems to be noticing something. His eyes slightly glaze over, wandering off in a manner that is unusual for him. His attention goes inward. He sinks into his body, falling away from the hypnotic grip of his intellectual vocalizations.

There aren't thoughts in this man anymore. He has gotten out of his head. The shift to experiential reality has occurred. In this very moment he is experiencing his experience and the space of the entire room shifts.

The audience feels it. There is awed silence. People look on in wonder. A new man is standing before them now where the verbal reality man used to be. Especially those who have known this man for years are touched.

This new man seems somehow deeper and richer, more sensuous, less defined, more flexible, less confined, more alive, less predictable. This new man clearly accesses a vaster world of possibility than he did before. He is no longer straight jacketed by his vocabulary. One by one the audience members regain a long-forgotten hope for themselves. If this man can reclaim his direct experience of the world, perhaps they can too. All of this happens in a sustained wordless moment.

Then I gently ask the man, "What happened?" It is the identical question I asked him before.

He does not answer immediately. His intellectual body is no longer in charge so he does not have to answer according to the logic and timing of his mind. He can wait and answer the question if and when and how he chooses. He has his power back, having repossessed it from the tyranny of his intellect.

He seems slightly perturbed by my request for words, but then something happens. A new function emerges in him—a function whereby he can stay centered in the wordlessness of his direct experience while at the same time he can use a portion of his intellect to grope around for some sort of words. He will use the words as building blocks to construct a bridge directly from his body to the audience's body so they can share the experience of his experience.

He takes a four-bodied breath and says, "An impulse started in my right arm and flooded into my chest like a swarm of happy honey bees, humming and vibrating around in there. Pressure waves echoed down through my abdomen, waking up my inner cells, tingling down my legs and arms. Ripples are bouncing back and forth through my features, like a song sung free and loud in the mountains. There is orangeness and sweetness in my fingertips. Also in my toes. I still feel it. My earlobes are warm. My hair is electrified with aliveness charge. I can see more clearly, as if a fog has melted away, as if my eyes perceive in new sorts of frequencies. I can see love in you people who are looking at me now. We are in this experience together and it is okay for me to share about it, even if what I say sounds completely crazy."

Tears are rolling out of the man's eyes. It does not bother him. He could keep painting the experience but he chooses not to. He stands there vulnerable and delighted in his experiential wonder, looking at the people as if he had never seen faces before. He has missed this for so long. The door is again open wide to a world he has not explored since childhood, a world that was almost forgotten. He takes slow deep breaths and can't stop smiling. He looks over at me with gratitude, not for me but for the experience he is having, and the audience spontaneously starts clapping with joy and appreciation.

This is experiential reality. Are you ready for this?

3. UNCONSCIOUSLY FEELING

Modern culture asserts that it is not okay to feel. You are told and shown in both subtle and overt ways that feelings are as improper as farting in public. Feelings may accidentally burst out sideways from time to time and hurt the people dearest to you, but even if that *accident* happens regularly you are permitted to apologize for your impoliteness.

Having a feeling means there is something wrong with you. Modern society solves the problem of feelings by sending you to a doctor or psychiatrist who is more than willing to add you to the list of millions of men, women and children agreeing to take mood-altering drugs.

The conflict between having a body full of feelings and yet having it not be culturally acceptable to feel creates physical, intellectual, emotional and spiritual confusion. It can fill you with self-doubt, even self-hatred, and produces profound hesitation about daring to be yourself. This uncertainty makes you weak and confused, assuring that the patriarchal empire of modern culture can continue unhindered. You acquiesce, and teach your children to do the same.

Animals have feelings. You can detect when a dog or cat or horse feels scared, angry, glad, or sad. As zoologist Desmond Morris observed in his 1967 book *The Naked Ape*, human beings are animals, too. Just like other animals, you have feelings. Feelings come with the body.

But modern society promotes the myth that human beings are superior to animals. This myth has been integrated so deeply into your worldview that you forgot it is a myth. You believe it to be true. Modern culture mass-produces chickens, pigs and cows just like it mass-produces toasters, cars and mobile phones. Animals are regarded as little different from things. If we did to humans the horrific things we do to animals, we would be locked away.

A high dose of numbness is needed to maintain the assertion that humans are not animals.

NOT OKAY TO FEEL GLAD

Modern education about feelings is so distorted that we equate *feeling good* to *feeling numb*. We don't actually want to feel happy. We want to feel numb. Numbness is good. This is what we encourage the teachers to teach our children. This is what you communicate to a child when you say, "Shhhh! It doesn't hurt! Nothing happened!" Or when you act as if children should be seen and not heard. You communicate that it is better to have no feelings.

After all, this is the age of science, the age of reason, the modern age of a great civilization, that has, by the way, overpopulated the planet, systematically exterminated and enslaved diverse cultures, ravenously consumed nonrenewable resources, contaminated the environment, and is on the fast track to self-extinction—not so much to be proud of, actually.

This same civilization has taught you that it is not okay to feel angry because anger is dangerous, loud, and threatening. You might hurt someone or break things. You look bad when you express anger. You are out of control and uncivilized.

You were taught that it is not okay to feel sad because sadness is weak, childish, emotional, and sappy. Sad people are pathetic. They are not "with the program" of being happy. There is something wrong with them. And besides all that, men don't cry.

You were taught that it is not okay to feel scared because fear is irrational. Fear causes panic, so you cannot be a leader. Fear shows immaturity, ignorance, incompetence and instability. Besides, James Bond feels no fear!

You were taught that it is not okay to feel glad because people will become jealous. Being glad is childish, silly, loud and embarrassing. If you are glad, how can you be taken seriously? If you feel glad people will think you don't have enough work to do. Or that you are on drugs. If you express true joy you appear ridiculous, pretentious, irresponsible, and foolish.

What is this? Not even happiness is okay?

In the back of your mind you have held the idea that there are three bad feelings (anger, sadness and fear) and one good feeling (joy). But when you actually examine what society has taught, feeling and expressing joy is as unacceptable as anger, fear and sadness!

What happens if you walk down the street feeling extraordinarily glad? What is there to be glad about? Haven't you read the news? Being glad is naïve. You must be an airhead, and stupid besides. Joy has no place in the real world. Do you think you are on holiday? Why bother feeling glad anyway? It will just go away.

You have learned your lessons well. It is not okay to feel. Where does that leave you?

OLD MAP OF FOUR FEELINGS

World Copyright © 2010 owner Clinton Callahan grants permission to use. www.nextculture.org

ASSUMPTION: IT IS NOT OKAY TO FEEL

BECAUSE **ANGER** IS:
uncivilized, loud, destructive, unpredictable, impolite, might hurt someone, out of control, dangerous, insulting, immature, not taken seriously, chaotic, embarrassing, makes others angry, invites revenge, creates a mess, and starts wars.

BECAUSE **SADNESS** IS:
weak, emotional, childish, too soft, not fun, pathetic, victimy, unprofessional, not creative, too vulnerable, makes you look ridiculous, ruins other people's day, is discouraging, not inspiring, not part of modern happy society life, and no matter what men don't cry.

BECAUSE **JOY** IS:
unrealistic, childish, giggly, not serious, pretentious, naïve, arrogant, temporary, means you are doing too well, not intellectual, not real world, blind to the problems of life, makes other people jealous. What do you have to be glad about anyway? If you are smiling people will think you are on drugs or do not have enough work to do.

BECAUSE **FEAR** IS:
cowardly, irrational, unstable, Chicken Little, impulsive, hysterical, nerve-wracking, paralyzing, powerless, stuck, weak, incompetent, childish, untrustworthy, and over reactive. It fogs decisions, cannot protect, cannot lead, gets out of control and can quickly cause general panic.

LOW DRAMA AND GREMLIN

Since you have a body, you actually do have feelings. But since it is not okay to feel you are in a bit of a bind. What are you actually doing with all this feeling energy coursing through your nervous system if you are not permitted to admit that you feel? How do you manage to stay unconscious of your feelings to give the appearance of being civilized? What happens with all of the energy tied up in your unconscious feelings?

The answer to these questions is not generally known in modern culture. The answer is a radical piece of information.

The answer is that the energy of your unconscious feelings feeds your *Gremlin* through *low drama*.

What is *low drama*? Low drama is any action designed to avoid responsibility.

What is *Gremlin*? Gremlin is the part in each of us that thrives on low drama.

The Map of Low Drama distinguishes three roles that are played out in any dramatic interaction. The three roles are the *victim*, the *persecutor*, and the *rescuer*, each role being an aspect of *Gremlin*. Low drama is the unconscious expression of feelings.

The most powerful position in a low drama is the victim. The victim's power is clear: if no one plays the role of victim, there can be no low drama.

The victim is the one who sets the stage for the persecutor to persecute and the rescuer to rescue. A skilled victim can make a persecutor or a rescuer out of anybody.

All the victim needs is one small piece of evidence to prove that a person is hurting them and they can evoke a persecutor ("It was in your tone of voice! You didn't even look at me! You should have been more human! You did not say goodbye when you left! You didn't wait for me! You hurt my feelings!").

All the victim needs is one tiny reason to give away responsibility for themselves and they have created a rescuer ("I don't know how to do it! I am so overwhelmed! You are better at this than I am! I don't have enough time! I can't find it! I can't figure this out! I've been working so hard! My feet hurt! I'm so tired!").

MAP OF LOW DRAMA

World Copyright © 2010 owner Clinton Callahan grants permission to use. www.nextculture.org

Low drama is any action designed to avoid responsibility.

PERSECUTOR

The persecutor uses
anger unconsciously.
The persecutor says:
I am okay.
You are not okay.
I must get rid of you.

RESCUER

The rescuer uses **fear**
unconsciously.
The rescuer says:
I am okay.
You are not okay.
I must do it for you.

▶GREMLIN

Gremlin is king or queen of
your shadow world, CEO of
your low drama department.
Gremlin uses **joy** unconsciously
to feel glad when other people
feel pain.
Gremlin says:
Ha! Ha! I got you!
I win. You lose.
If you don't consciously own
your Gremlin, he owns you.

VICTIM

The victim uses **sadness** unconsciously.
The victim says:
Poor me! I am not okay.
You are hurting me. I must go away.
It's too much for me. I can't do it myself!

All three low drama roles serve Gremlin's purposes. Notice the similarity between the *persecutor* and *rescuer* positions: both think that they are okay and the victim is not okay. The most powerful player in a low drama is the *victim*: if there is no victim, there can be no low drama! *A skilled victim can make a persecutor or a rescuer out of anyone!* Low drama seems real when you unconsciously change positions on the triangle. Anytime you are blaming, resenting, justifying, being right, complaining, or making someone wrong, it is low drama. The only thing that happens in low drama is you get older. Nothing changes for the better because *responsibility is the procedure for change*, and low drama is about avoiding responsibility. (Note: This thoughtmap is used with permission from Dr. Stephen Karpman <www.karpmandramatriangle.com> who created the original *drama triangle* in 1965 and brought it into Transactional Analysis (TA) originated by Dr. Eric Berne <www.ericberne.com>. In 2000, Clinton Callahan connected the four feelings to the drama triangle and renamed it *low drama* so as to reveal its relationship to *high drama* on a bigger thoughtmap called The Map of Possibility, shown in Appendix C, and further explained in my book *Radiant Joy Brilliant Love*.)

One particularly pernicious sort of victim is the victim who does ostensibly responsible things but does them *as a victim*. This is when you take out the garbage—which looks like a responsible thing to do— but you don't truly choose to take out the garbage. Instead you take out the garbage because "no one else is doing it," because "*somebody* has to

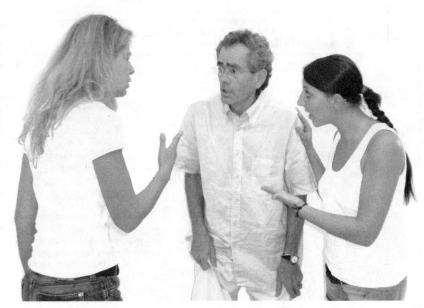

LOW DRAMA The classic persecutor, victim and rescuer roles in low drama are so exciting we imagine them to be life. But low drama is not life—it is only low drama. The possibilities of high drama cannot be explored until you get nauseatingly clear about your ongoing participation in low drama. Only after you feel the pain of how much low drama costs in terms of integrity, clarity, and authenticity will you have any chance of relating differently.

do it," because "it hasn't been taken out for a really long time"; you get the idea. This sort of victim is called the *responsible victim*.

Then, while you are taking out the garbage, you run certain low drama conversations in your mind. You take on a kicked-dog attitude. You start building up a charge about the whole thing. "It's not really my job. I did it last week. I always have to take out the garbage. I have other things to do, too!"

Then you march back in with the empty garbage can (and your hungry Gremlin) and use your fresh victim story to find and persecute the person whose job it is to take out the garbage. "Where were you all week? Why do you always avoid your responsibilities? Do you think I don't have other things to do? Your life is so important that we slaves can take out the garbage for you?" Isn't this a *glorious* time (for Gremlin)?

Or you use your victim story to get sympathy from some willing rescuer. "It wasn't my job, you see, but I thought I could help out a little. So I took out this stinking garbage can full of fish scraps and chicken fat and the grease got all over my new pants! Look at that! My good pants! Ruined! And it was raining outside, and I slipped in the mud. But the neighbor's dog had been over in our yard, so it wasn't really mud that I slipped in . . ."

Do you know anyone who has ever been a responsible victim?

Have *you* ever been a responsible victim before?

GREMLIN FEEDING TIME

The persecutor holds the position of "I am okay. You are not okay, so I will get rid of you." Examples of famous persecutor characters include Adolf Hitler and George W. Bush. The rescuer holds the position of "I am okay. You are not okay, so I will do it for you." Examples of rescuers are the Boy Scout who brings the old lady across the street even though she doesn't want to cross the street and the father who interferes with his child trying to learn something by doing it for him.

It can be difficult to see rescuing as low drama because we think we are just trying to help. But the rescuer holds the same respectless position towards the victim as the persecutor, namely, "I am okay. You are not okay." Holding this position is a kind of insanity, because every person is unconditionally okay.

The victim's position is, "Poor me! I am not okay," which is *also* a kind of insanity. Healthy relationship begins from asserting, "I am okay, and you are okay," a position in which there can be no low drama.

Low drama is Gremlin feeding time.

For example, if I walk through a room and smash my knee on a chair, my Gremlin creates a low drama when it says, "Who put this chair here?" Gremlin is the one who swears out loud and kicks the chair, blaming the stupid chair itself for being in *my* way. Low drama is how I avoid taking responsibility for smashing my own knee into the chair. Gremlin has used a completely neutral incident to create low drama food for itself to eat.

The low drama is not automatically there. Gremlin created it out of nothing, as a piece of unconscious theater. There was no low drama until Gremlin made one. I could have simply rubbed my knee, moved the chair so someone else didn't bump into it, and gone on my way. But Gremlin didn't let me. Gremlin was hungry and whipped it up into a low drama to feed on.

WHICH "I" IS SPEAKING NOW?

It can be quite enlightening to be careful when you use the word *I*. This is because your Box has parts. When you are meticulous about your use of the word *I*, you gain experiential clarity that your Box has more than one *I*, each with its own purpose and style.

Soon you will discover that you live in a rapidly changing circus of "I's". "I am a man. I am a father. I am a computer programmer. I am a husband. I am a SCUBA diver. I am an artist. I am Irish. I am Taoist Orisha Muslim Rasta Shinto Baha'i Sufi. I am . . ." (fill in the blank).

As each particular *I* takes over, you slip into identification with that *I*, as if this is the only possible *I* that you could be. You easily assume that you are a single *I* when in fact you are a rather ill-tempered schizophrenic committee. You can observe this easily in another person when, for example, the phone rings and it's the person's mother, or the police, or their kid. Suddenly they slip into a completely different *I*, with different speech patterns, different tone of voice, different postures. When the phone call ends they pop back into the *I* that talks to you, and they don't notice that anything ever changed. You see it in others, of course, but you might hesitate to admit it of yourself (your*selves*). Admit it or not, it is still true. Within you is a complex underworld ecology of characters and roles to play out. Lording over them all is your Gremlin, the king or queen of your shadow world.

LOW DRAMA IS SO EXCITING WE THINK IT IS LIFE

Whatever part of your Gremlin you do not consciously own, owns you. That is, Gremlin will feed himself on every part of your life that you do not restrict him from feeding on. The process of becoming more and more conscious of the deeds and intentions of your own Gremlin may constitute the most painful experience of your life. After a while you may come to agree that it is better to know the scandalous truth about yourself than to remain a deluded victim of your Gremlin's unconscious intentions.

Let's go back to the example of bumping into a chair. Suppose you bump your knee and your Gremlin is hungry for a low drama. Using the chair as his opportunity for a "meal," your Gremlin takes on the low drama role of victim. If your Gremlin can find the *evil* person who put that chair in your way, then Gremlin has proved that this person persecuted you. Gremlin then feels instantly justified changing roles in the low drama and getting revenge by persecuting the persecutor who sabotaged your whole life with that chair.

Only a hungry Gremlin will accept being put in the role of persecutor in someone else's low drama. When you are clear about what low drama is and can detect when a low drama is being generated, you won't accept the invitation to join the low drama. Your hungry Gremlin might very much want to, but you don't have to. You can provide food for your Gremlin in other ways. By cultivating a conscious relationship with your Gremlin you can elegantly sidestep low dramas the way a bull-fighter sidesteps a charging bull. You let low drama charge past without being hooked by its horns. Letting low dramas pass you by without being hooked is called *high drama*, but we are getting ahead of ourselves here. We will get to high drama in a later chapter. Right now we are still discovering how hungry Gremlins periodically change our lovely lives into low drama feeding frenzies.

As soon as your Gremlin has identified another person's Gremlin as one that is willing to play the role of persecutor in your Gremlin's low drama, then your Gremlin is justified in instantly switching roles and taking revenge on the persecutor. Your Gremlin becomes the new persecutor and their Gremlin becomes the new victim.

Then some other hungry Gremlin can come along and say, "Oh, what happened to you? Are you all right? Oh, poor baby! Let me get you some ice to put on your knee, some cream and a Band-Aid. How could this happen to you? That's not fair!" Now the rescuer has arrived and the low drama is in full action.

But the hungry rescuer Gremlin can go even further in this low drama. The rescuer can attack the persecutor for hurting the poor victim.

LOW DRAMA It seems so real but low drama is just Gremlins devouring your life energy. In this low drama exercise, the objective is to not change roles—difficult—because as soon as the victim can prove that someone is hurting her she can instantly change roles from victim to persecutor and take revenge. Resisting the shift of roles brings the low drama into the light of consciousness.

"You idiot! That chair doesn't belong here!" The rescuing Gremlin changes role from rescuer to persecutor! "Can't you *ever* put things back where they belong?" The persecutor becomes the victim Gremlin! "I didn't know! Nobody told me! It was an accident! The phone rang and I had to answer it right away so the baby didn't wake up. I just forgot to put the chair back!"

This is so exciting! Low drama is so exciting that it is easy to assume it is life. But low drama is not life. Low drama is low drama, a Gremlin feeding frenzy. On and on, around the triangle they go, each Gremlin taking its turn playing its favorite roles until the Gremlins have had their feast and the low drama comes to a stop.

Low dramas do not end because something has been resolved. Low dramas end because the Gremlins have full stomachs and have gone to sleep. You may think, "Hmmm . . . I wonder what that was all about? Silly me." You may even go apologize. Peace reigns. There are no more low dramas . . . until your Gremlin wakes up hungry again.

Some Gremlins have a feeding schedule of one big low drama each month for seven days straight. Some Gremlins eat once a week for one or two days. Some Gremlins feed themselves on one solid low drama a day. And some Gremlins are *snackers*, creating little low dramas here and there with anybody who crosses their path all day long. What is the feeding schedule of your Gremlin?

Low dramas don't change anything. That is not their purpose. The purpose of low dramas is to feed hungry Gremlins. The tastiest Gremlin foods are innocence, tenderness, vulnerability, joy, success, order, love, and trust. Each Gremlin serves a set of three, four or five Shadow Principles, such as betrayal, deception, being right, superiority, manipulation, domination, control, or revenge. The Shadow Principles of your Gremlin are your *hidden purpose*. It is what you serve when you are unconsciously feeling.

It does not matter how right you are, how good your justifications are, how loudly you blame someone, how artfully you complain, how resentful you are, or how clearly you can prove someone else wrong. Nothing changes in low drama. The only thing that happens during a low drama is that you get older. The procedure for change is taking responsibility. Low drama is taking actions that *avoid* responsibility.

It is crucial to disconnect the idea of *Gremlin* from the idea of *bad*. Gremlin is not bad. Gremlin is simply Gremlin: irresponsible, the part of each of us serving unconscious purposes.

Judging something as good or evil, right or wrong (in a moral sense), positive or negative (as in good or bad) is itself a significant Shadow Principle, an irresponsible game.

Judging something as bad or evil is a clever way for any Gremlin authority figure to create a nearly endless supply of Gremlin feasts. Think of the almost seven hundred years (1184–1860) of first-rate tortures contrived and feasted upon by Catholic Inquisitors as directed by an unbroken series of seventy-five Popes! Think of the two hundred years of governmental witch-hunters testing and burning people in Gremlin feeding frenzies to gain property and riches. Think of modern government and corporate leaders collecting information, assembling armies, growing and selling opium to buy clandestine weapons, imprisoning, torturing and killing so-called terrorists, starting wars and stealing oil. It is not democracy or capitalism. It is all Gremlins.

Gremlin behavior creates certain kinds of results. Until you recognize your own Gremlin and make his unconscious behavior painfully conscious your Gremlin will continue running your life and feeding on the people closest to you. This happens outside of your awareness. Gremlin is only outside of your awareness because you are numb to the consequences of your Gremlin's actions. As soon as you lower your numbness bar to the point where you feel the pain of the consequences of your Gremlin's actions you will no longer be able to permit Gremlin to feed in his usual ways. Your behavior will change by itself.

Split your attention and neutrally observe how your Gremlin feeds. Become almost neurotically sensitive to discerning low drama actions. Start with yourself. Start with tracking your own wish to hurt others, to be a victim, to make excuses, to complain, and then to switch to persecutor. Ruthlessly notice how glad your Gremlin feels when certain people lose and you win. Notice each little revengeful joke and comment that your Gremlin makes to destroy people around you. Notice all the times your Gremlin triangulates by talking about someone when they are not there, talking behind their back. This is pure Gremlin food and this is the way you keep your Gremlin fat and unconscious. Find out exactly what you are doing or you will have no chance to do something different.

You are right. This is not fun or pretty stuff we are talking about here. Gremlin activity has been swept under the carpet for most of human history. The majority of people in official institutions, government, politics, corporate businesses, schools, or the church will never learn how their Gremlin dishonors their leadership position just to feed himself. Why not?

I don't know why not. I can't understand it. I think it is *fantastic* to learn about low drama. Learning to avoid low drama gives you direct access to creating and entering the fabulous world of high drama. In high drama there are glorious moments, ecstatic sensations, wondrous experiences, archetypal love, trust, friendship, inspiration and respect. True joy flows freely and abundantly.

Why don't we people want this? I think we actually do want this. I think we *do* want to turn on our conscious archetypes and create an ongoing series of responsible gameworlds for fulfilling our Bright Principles together. I think we do; we simply were never told it was possible. We see no role models. We do not yet realize we have this option. We haven't been educated about this yet. This is cool new stuff.

The experiments you try while learning how to feel are at the cutting edge of human evolution. *You* are the role model. Each effort you make launches new forms of consciousness that others can then more easily follow. Each connection you establish with people who are also seeking to lower their numbness bar and gain their conscious feelings weaves strands in a network of critical connections. Resilient connections establish the basis for the emergence of a sustainable next culture that replaces patriarchal empire. This mirrors the high drama of you learning to consciously feel.

OWN YOUR GREMLIN

Certain experiments change your relationship to your Gremlin. Previously, Gremlin knocked you unconscious and did whatever it wanted to feed itself on your life. In these experiments you make Gremlin your ally instead of your owner.

At first Gremlin will hate you for your efforts. Gremlin hates you because you represent responsibility. Responsibility to Gremlin is like water to the Wicked Witch of the West. If you douse Gremlin with responsibility he fears he will dissolve. Gremlin is terrified that you seeing him means he will soon starve to death from lack of irresponsible, low drama food. Your job is to put your Gremlin on a regular feeding schedule so that starvation is no longer an issue for Gremlin.

GREMLIN Each of us has an inner Gremlin actively serving irresponsible Principles. Gremlin is neither good nor bad; he is simply Gremlin. Whatever part of your Gremlin you do not consciously own, owns you. Artwork © Copyright 2010 by Timo Wuerz, all rights reserved. <www.timowuerz.com>

There are certain foods that your Gremlin loves to eat—foods that regularly deplete your energy reserves—and other foods that will feed your Gremlin without costing you so much in terms of the quality of your life. Your task is to distinguish between these two kinds of Gremlin foods. Then you feed your Gremlin the foods that *you* choose on a schedule set by you rather than letting Gremlin eat the foods he chooses on his schedule.

To start, make a list of what your Gremlin loves to eat whenever he has free rein. For example, your Gremlin might love to devour the following:

TYPICAL GREMLIN FOODS

- Creating the story that your boss, companion, or child is an enemy and having regular low drama confrontations.

- Weekly social gatherings with alcohol, coming home late and drunk.

- Eating an ice cream a week.

- Incessantly talking to fill up any empty space with the sound of your own voice.

- Staying up until 3 A.M. on business trips watching porn films.

- Not paying your telephone bill and having the phones almost cut off.

- Finding fault with your mate as an excuse to throw dishes and lamps against the wall.

- Wearing funny, strange or mismatched clothes to get attention.

- Behaving insanely to shock people.

- Interrupting other people to blurt out whatever you want to say.

- Teasing your mother-in-law so she is too flustered to criticize you.

- Bingeing on videos every other week.

- Drinking colas or coffee every day, or all day.

- Complaining.

- Changing everything into something to laugh at.

- Eating doughnuts, cookies, candy, or cake daily.

- Smoking (anything).

- Gossiping; speaking about someone when they are not there (triangulating).

- Putting attention on and believing what you see on TV or read in newspapers and magazines.

- Watching horror films; reading murder mysteries.

- Holding resentful grudges and plotting revenge in the bottom of your heart.

- Eating chocolate.

- Thinking about eating chocolate.

- Thinking that you shouldn't eat so much chocolate.

- Sleeping past your alarm.

- Devouring greasy, salty junk food, such as hot dogs, burgers, chips, pretzels, popcorn, peanuts, and fries.

- Catalog shopping to the maximum limit on your credit cards.

- Biting your nails, scratching your face, twisting or pulling your hair, picking your nose.

- Having internet sex here and there.

- Having an ongoing feud with your neighbors and feeling right about your position.

- Eating so much pizza and ice cream that the endorphins kick in.

- Having power struggles with your mate; proving they are wrong in public.

- Manipulating relatives, colleagues and authority figures with your illnesses.

- Leaving messes around the house that drive your partner crazy, or ranting about their messes.

- Flirting with the guys or gals at the exercise club.

- Swearing at other drivers.

- Paying your taxes late.

- Blaming the government.

- Keeping your desk buried in an almost nonfunctional pile of papers.

- Kicking the dog.

- Add your favorites . . .

It might take you a couple of weeks to collect the details for your list, but then again, maybe you can make the list immediately. Once you have your list of favorite Gremlin foods, develop a reasonable strategy for a regular feeding schedule. A strategy that works well is to choose one day during the week, for example Saturday, and promise your Gremlin that on this one day, from 6 A.M. Saturday until 6 A.M. Sunday, he can feast as much as he wants on the specific five items that you have selected from your list. Write out the five available Gremlin foods on a paper and keep it in your wallet. Then for the other six days of the week go completely *cold turkey* on all Gremlin foods.

In the beginning you might make it through one day of no Gremlin food before Gremlin knocks you unconscious and you wake up on the far side of a binge or a quarrel. Do not feel guilty. Do not beat yourself up. Do not punish your Gremlin. This is just more Gremlin food. Simply remake your commitment and keep your promise of maximum feeding on the specified day only.

After a while you might make it through three days before getting knocked unconscious. In the meantime Gremlin might put a constant stream of voices in your head, "This is stupid! This is *really* stupid! I hate this! Mmmm, look at those tits! Just a little piece of chocolate would be okay. Then I'll be satisfied. What a jerk! Let's stop this nonsense. I can't do this anymore. Where's all the fun in life? I'm a failure. I'm not good enough. I'll never make it. Whoa, this is too much for me. I can't stand it! Whose idea was this anyway? Not mine. Fucking book!" And so on. These are only voices. You may wish to keep in mind that you own a fully loaded *Voice Blaster* strapped to your hip. Blast away! (We'll get to the Voice Blaster in Chapter 5.)

Gremlin might lose a little weight, but he will soon start feeling more fit and alive without so much fat around his belly. He will appreciate his new trim feeling and will recognize that you respect him and are treating him well. After a few months you and your Gremlin might get through an entire week with no snacking. Stay on this regular weekly feeding schedule for the rest of your life.

GREMLINS These are slightly exaggerated Gremlin faces, often seen on others, sometimes seen in your own mirror . . .

At some point you might notice that a feeding day went by and your Gremlin forgot to feed. Do not change the feeding day that week. If Saturday slipped by with no feeding, do not feed him on Sunday or Monday. Just wait until Saturday comes around again.

You might also notice that a feeding day arrives and none of the five special Gremlin foods appeal to Gremlin. This is okay. You do not have to force-feed your Gremlin. But also do not let it graze on the banned Gremlin foods. Stick to your feeding schedule.

Being accountable to your Gremlin for providing it with a regularly planned feeding schedule establishes a relationship with him like an owner has with his Doberman pinscher. Your barely tamed, potentially vicious beast is willing to sit at your feet on a short leash whenever you say *SIT!* because he knows that he is respected, he is taken care of, and in particular, he is regularly fed. This really works.

THEN PUT YOUR GREMLIN TO WORK

Contrary to what you might expect you will use Gremlin more in high drama than in low drama. In low drama Gremlin is starving, sneaking around as a *ronin*, a lone samurai without a master, devouring whatever he can steal just to survive. In high drama the rightful place of Gremlin is established: awake, attentive, sitting at the feet of Archetypal Man or Woman with a short chain around his neck, ready to serve.

At first, when discovering the true nature and intention of Gremlin, it is quite difficult not to simply declare with disgust that Gremlin is bad and must be imprisoned or banished forever. Such thinking serves the Good/Bad Shadow Principle and will leave you with your Gremlin invisibly at work, busily creating his usual unconscious horrors in your life, just like the priests at a parochial school justifying violence and sexual intimacies with the boys in their care.

Gremlin is Gremlin. Gremlin does what Gremlin does. We all have Gremlin and no matter what you think or try to do, Gremlin will never go away. Gremlin is a force, like sulfuric acid, like plastic explosives, like a laser beam, like a crowbar or lock picks, neither good nor bad, but definitely capable of producing certain results. As with all tools, Gremlin can be used to fulfill responsible or irresponsible purposes.

This is a wild world. It helps immensely to have direct access to an intelligent inner wildness for taking care of yourself, your community and your destiny. The source of that wild intelligence is Gremlin. Once you have possessed your Gremlin a source of wild intelligence sits at your feet, a trained attack animal, ready to do what it always does but doing it as you responsibly and maturely direct.

Gremlin is an exceptional tool of nonlinearity, particularly suited for creating high drama where only low drama existed before. The application of this tool is counterintuitive. You use Gremlin's ability to destroy anything at any time for no reason as the force to dismantle the mechanicality of your own Box. Gremlin is the only one who knows the secret ways to get through your own defenses, the only one clever enough to free you from being trapped by your own tricks.

The first use of Gremlin is very exact: use Gremlin to monitor itself to *not do* the Gremlin thing. It takes a thief to catch a thief, and Gremlin is the ultimate thief. Only Gremlin knows exactly how devious, cunning, and shrewd Gremlin is. Only Gremlin is sensitive and fast enough to catch itself before he steals your dignity with his shenanigans. Conscious use of Gremlin involves giving your Gremlin productive yet impossible jobs to do.

PRACTICAL APPLICATIONS OF GREMLIN

- Use Gremlin to sharpen your self-discipline.

- Use Gremlin to stop overly judgmental thinking.

- Use Gremlin to keep your attention free from being hooked and your heart free from emotionally reacting.

- Use Gremlin to hold your tongue when all it wants to do is lash out and destroy.

- Use Gremlin to not snicker, not sneer, not sigh, not yawn, and not roll your eyes.

- Use Gremlin to not speak the hurting cynical words, not make the cutting-tone-of-voice insinuations, not tell the nasty, stupid, degrading little jokes that hurt people.

- Use Gremlin to keep your center when everyone around you is giving theirs away.

- Use Gremlin to stay awake and pay attention when everyone around you is sleeping and hypnotized.

- Use Gremlin to look in shadowy places at what is normally ignored.

- Use Gremlin to not throw stones at the adulteress.

- Use Gremlin to stay still when other people move and to move when other people stay still.

- Use Gremlin to do the right thing even when the consequences are frightening.

- Use Gremlin to make and hold necessary boundaries even when the kids, customers, or lobbyists are screaming at you to give in to their demands.

- Use Gremlin to ask dangerous questions that no one else can even think of because the forces rigidly holding certain previously made conclusions are so strong.

- Use Gremlin to break the rules that minimize expressions of kindness, generosity or compassion.

- Use Gremlin to distinguish subtle details that make invisible things distinct from their camouflage.

- Use Gremlin to dismantle your own denial, walk directly into your own pain, and let your assumptions and beliefs go up in flames, burning to a cinder without your knowing what is next.

- Use Gremlin to remain alert and communicative and to avoid being sentimental, hysterical, isolated, or nostalgic while some element of your reality construct unexpectedly transforms.

- Use Gremlin to let yourself be seen raw, naked, stupid, crippled and wounded—exactly as you are—and not care about other people's opinions or judgments.

- Use Gremlin to energetically *spin* so that you hold no position and stay a moving target to other people's positive or negative comments.

- Use Gremlin to wait patiently through the unknown until the next thing can effectively be done.

- Use Gremlin to have the courage to commit to creating a result you want to create before you know how to do it, even if this thing has never been done before.

It is Gremlin who can stand completely revealed and vulnerable and not care. It is Gremlin who can allow chaos and destruction to rain upon you with the same neutrality that he allows blessings, appreciation, respect and love to rain upon you, neither attracted nor repelled, not making any sudden moves. And it is Gremlin who can feel deep compassion for other people whose Gremlins still own them and keep them living (if you can call it living) in an underworld created by their still unconscious and all-powerful Gremlins.

GIVING YOUR CENTER AWAY

Another typical characteristic of unconsciously feeling is adaptive behavior. Adaptive behavior is a childhood survival strategy incorporated into the design of your Box. There are certain authority figures who do not take well to being challenged. If one of these Gremlin authority figures is confronted with someone who sees what is going on and asks pointed questions about it, or who has their own ideas for alternative solutions, the Gremlin authority cannot stand it. The Gremlin authority is so frightened of being out of control that unconscious anger starts sputtering out of them every which way, like a Roman candle.

The Gremlin authority may have been one or both of your parents, your relatives, or your teachers. The person who could see what is going on and had dangerous questions to ask may have been you as a little person. You presented such a threat to the authority figure that you called down upon yourself their merciless wrath.

Suddenly you had to make a life-or-death decision. Should you continue with your outspokenness and desire for fairness and responsible actions, furthering your disturbing invasion into the Gremlin authority's domain? Or should you instead develop a technique for fogging yourself, disempowering your awareness, playing small and adaptive, giving away your center of responsibility and creative imagination so you become less dangerous and the Gremlin authority does not have to *kill* you?

The choice you made is obvious. You still live.

You learned to give your center away to Gremlin authority figures. This technique may have saved your life as a child, or at least made things more manageable for you, but now, as an adult, this same behavior may be sabotaging your life and relationships. What worked as a child might not be so valuable now.

What if you took your power back? What if you took your voice back, your imagination back, your sword of clarity back? What if you became dangerous again because you can perceive, you can feel, you can speak, you can take creative self-directed actions?

This all begins with taking your center back and learning to be centered. What does this mean?

A human being has two kinds of centers, a *physical center*, and a *center of being*. Your physical center is the center of balance of your physical body. This point is located about three fingers' distance below your navel, approximately behind your belt buckle, and halfway back through your abdomen. It is in the center of your physical body.

Another way to find your physical center is to draw an imaginary line between your hip bones, then go straight back into your body from the middle of the line. There is your physical center. It is a location that stays there.

In addition to this you have your energetic *center of being*. Your center of being starts out about the size of a grapefruit and it is mobile. It can move around. In modern culture we have been trained to keep our center of being in a certain place in our body. Where is that?

Think of Rodin's astonishing statue *The Thinker*.

Where is this man's center of being located?

Yes. He has put it in his head. This is what you were trained to do too. This is your role model for modern man (also modern woman!): put your center in your head and think.

Either you give your being center away to Gremlin authority figures, or you put your center of being in your head. Both are more socially acceptable than putting your being center on your physical center and being present as your true, powerful and fabulous self.

Why would you give your center away to a Gremlin leader? What are you thinking when you do that? You think, "I am safe. The leader

THE THINKER Modern society has adopted Auguste Rodin's *The Thinker* (1902) as its icon, compelling us to defer to the intellect. Over thirty casts of *The Thinker* sit prominently in modern universities and museums around the world.

will take care of me because I'm no longer a threat to him." This is why many people choose to work for governments or corporations. They think they can find a Gremlin leader with whom they can exchange their center for lifelong security and good retirement benefits.

What does the Gremlin leader think when he has your center? Oddly enough, he thinks the same thing you do: "I am safe." He thinks he is safe because you are no longer a threat to him. He thinks he owns you.

It is important to recognize that no one can take your center away. They can invite you to give them your center through subtle threats of retribution or rejection, but they cannot *take* your center. If someone else has your center, you gave it to them.

This is good news. It means you can always change your mind and take your center back.

What happens if you try to give your center to a true leader?

They don't want it. They say, "What are you trying to do? Where are you? I don't want your center! I want you to have your center so that you can take responsibility for yourself and for this project. I want you to ask questions, create solutions, make decisions, take intelligent risks, execute actions, check your results. I want *you* to have your power. My intention is to surround myself with leaders."

True leaders are leader makers. Have you ever had the honor of working for a true leader?

Have you ever worked for a Gremlin leader?

Which kind of leader do you tend to be?

Unconsciously felt fear causes you to give your center away so you are no longer a threat to the authority figure and they do not have to energetically *kill* you. Unconsciously felt fear causes a Gremlin leader to surround himself with people who give him their center so he feels safe and all powerful. In neither case is the feeling of fear felt consciously. If it were, it would be used for an entirely different purpose than seeking the illusion of security.

To get your center back, or to keep your center so that you don't give it away in the first place, you will need to develop a couple of skills. The first skill is to place your attention on your *being center*. The other skill is to keep your *attention* on your *being center* and at the same time use your *intention* to move your *being center* onto your *physical center*. These are precise instructions.

Learning to place your attention on your being center is like learning to place your attention on any one particular thing. You can place your attention on this dot (●), then you can place your attention on the center of a clock in the room or on a leaf on a plant outside. Then you can place your attention back on that dot again, then on the clock or leaf again. Slowly and deliberately move your attention back and forth between the dot and the clock (or leaf) until you know what it feels like to consciously place your attention on something. Then place your attention on your center of being. Learn what that feels like.

Now develop your intention muscles. Hold your open hand out in front of you with your fingers together and your palm facing upward. Hold it that way.

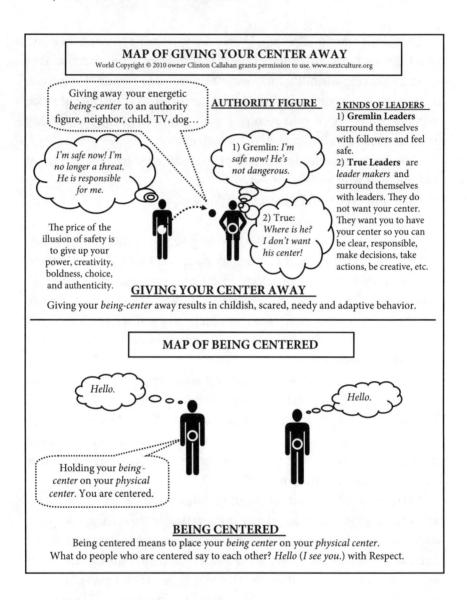

MAP OF GIVING YOUR CENTER AWAY

World Copyright © 2010 owner Clinton Callahan grants permission to use. www.nextculture.org

Giving away your energetic *being-center* to an authority figure, neighbor, child, TV, dog...

AUTHORITY FIGURE

I'm safe now! I'm no longer a threat. He is responsible for me.

1) Gremlin: *I'm safe now! He's not dangerous.*

2) True: *Where is he? I don't want his center!*

The price of the illusion of safety is to give up your power, creativity, boldness, choice, and authenticity.

2 KINDS OF LEADERS
1) **Gremlin Leaders** surround themselves with followers and feel safe.
2) **True Leaders** are *leader makers* and surround themselves with leaders. They do not want your center. They want you to have your center so you can be clear, responsible, make decisions, take actions, be creative, etc.

GIVING YOUR CENTER AWAY

Giving your *being-center* away results in childish, scared, needy and adaptive behavior.

MAP OF BEING CENTERED

Hello.

Hello.

Holding your *being-center* on your *physical center.* You are centered.

BEING CENTERED

Being centered means to place your *being center* on your *physical center.*
What do people who are centered say to each other? *Hello* (*I see you.*) with Respect.

Then, using your intention, slowly turn your hand over so it is facing palm down. Now hold it *that* way. Hold your hand palm down until you change your intention to turn it palm up again. Then turn your hand palm up. Slowly and deliberately rotate your hand one way and then the other way, but only in the moment when you intend that it face a certain way. And in between, use your intention to hold it the way that it is.

Now place your attention on your being center, follow your *attention* with your *intention*, and intend that your being center moves to your physical center. When your being center is on your physical center you will stand differently, move differently, breathe differently, and interact with the world differently. It feels nobler, more relaxed, more light-footed, more flexible and balanced. Stay centered by using a portion of your intention to keep your being center on your physical center, preventing it from drifting away.

This is what it is to be centered.

When two centered people meet each other, they exchange a certain kind of greeting, something similar to the respect implied in the Na'vi greeting, "I see you" and in the Sanskrit word *namasté*, which means approximately "I salute in you that which is divine" or "I recognize the place in you where the whole universe resides, and when you are in that place in you and I am in that place in me, then we are one."

To be centered is to locate yourself here and now in the present moment, in your body. One reason centering is not a standard teaching of modern culture is that when you are centered here and now in your body, you will begin to feel all of the feelings that have been held back deep in your guts for all the years of your life. The feelings didn't go anywhere. They have been held in stasis, unexpressed. They have accumulated as silent things within you, incomplete communications. You may have an entire volcano of them.

If you are going to practice being centered, now would be a good time for you to learn about how to consciously experience and express your feelings. The dam is about to break, and then the flood will come.

4. CONSCIOUSLY FEELING

NOTE TO THE READER: If you have skipped ahead to this chapter without carefully studying the previous three chapters, it's a clever idea but I don't recommend it. Learning to consciously feel has similarities to learning to SCUBA dive, which is actually quite simple. Strap a tank of compressed air onto your back, push a regulator into your mouth, jump in the water and swim away. But they make you take lessons and get a license before letting you go SCUBA diving. It's for your own good. That's because if you hold your breath underwater and swim upward your lungs explode. If you stay down too deep for too long you get nitrogen narcosis. Come up without decompressing and you get "the bends." I am not saying anything like this will happen if you skip over the previous chapters. But I am saying that the world of conscious feelings operates under different laws than the world of numbness, just like SCUBA diving is different from walking on dry land. Before you dive into consciously feeling, I strongly encourage you to study the first three chapters of this book. It's for your own good.

THE POWER OF BEING CENTERED

Consciously feeling begins with being centered (as described in Chapter 3). It is simple to understand why modern culture avoids teaching you to be centered in your body, here and now in the present moment. The reason is this: if you are centered, then you have power—more power than can be suppressed by the modern methods of hierarchical governments, institutionalized religions, and corporate marketing agencies *combined.*

When you are centered you have power to consciously choose among more options than are presented, power to declare what is so and what is not, power to ask questions whose answers are not contained in current reality, and power to take unprecedented action. These are standard human powers.

When you are centered you have the kind of power that Andrew Jackson meant when he said, "One man with courage makes a majority." (Note: I am certain that Mr. Jackson phrased his observation in this particular vernacular merely as a linguistic convenience and that if asked he would heartily agree that it applies equally well to women!)

Modern society is so lacking in references to the noble qualities and nearly unimaginable powers of the adult man or woman that trying to compensate for this deficiency through a mere book is neither dignified nor substantial enough to rectify the condition. What is called for is an entirely new society, a society that supports each person to realize the fullness of their humanity through embracing their archetypal destiny.

If you have the same temperament as I do, then when faced with the question of creating the next evolutionary step in society the only answer is, *Yes! Let's go!*

But there is a price that you pay for your enthusiasm about change. It is what my friend Bandhu Scott Dunham calls, *the burn* <www.salusaglassworks.com>.

Bandhu says that when you clearly perceive the possibility of an extraordinary new culture while at the same time recognizing in detail how far away you are from experiencing that vision in your daily life, a conflict ignites deep in your soul. It is a burning tension between what could be and what is, flashing like lightning, roaring like thunder, intensifying the experiential impact of each moment.

This gut-wrenching dynamo is strong enough to tear me away from a summer afternoon of coffee and card playing on the back patio with my gorgeous and delightful female companion, and propelling me upstairs into my chair to wrestle these words into sentences with a fierce intention.

I fantasize that the burn in me would ease up if I had certainty that these words encouraged you, in Andrew Jackson's terms, "to become an irresistible majority," making life choices not offered on the McMenu of globalized society.

If I was convinced that you would take actions that bring next culture to life *now*, I would be certain of a bright future.

But such "certainties" are rare, fleeting and frivolous. Instead, like you, I burn every which way while pushing a doubt-ridden present over the cliff into an unknown future. Then we wait and see how she flies.

Seeking certainty is merely ego trying to avoid the intensity of continuously coaxing out of nothing that which does not yet exist. Creation doesn't happen except within the terror of the uncreated, so here we go. Let us address the central question of this book: what is it all about, this stuff called "conscious feeling"?

In the previous chapter we distinguished low drama and other discouraging consequences of living on a flat-world map of unconscious feeling. It is time now to consider what a round-world map might look like.

SOME GENTLE PRECAUTIONS

Upgrading the way you think about feelings is just as revolutionary today as it was five hundred years ago to adopt Galileo's outrageous ideas about the orbit of the Earth. It is something you would only talk about while being mindful of who is listening at the next table preparing to report you to the authorities.

While you study these next pages please give yourself time and space to permit the internal reordering of your other three bodies to keep pace with your mind. Giving yourself time and space might involve not skimming through the pages so fast that the ideas only brush your brain cells, never caressing your heart. Giving yourself space might mean not squeezing everything you planned into your daily schedule this week. It might involve drinking a little extra water, taking a few slow walks in the woods and a long hot bath, going to bed earlier, or having daily naps.

If you get a headache, catch a cold, drop a dish on the floor, or forget your dentist appointment, please don't rush off to get a brain scan! Nothing is wrong with you.

If you get overwhelmed with deep grief and suddenly need to cry for a few hours, go ahead and enjoy the crying. You are not psychotic. When was the last time you sobbed deeply anyway?

If fear comes up your spine, more fear than you ever remember feeling, or anger takes you by surprise like a herd of stampeding buffalo, it is not lethal. It will pass. Let yourself have these experiences.

These symptoms as well as others reflect that learning is happening. Conditions are simply readjusting themselves inside of your four bodies to accommodate your modified view of the world. Reading this book could be like watching someone you love sail beyond a horizon which you believe to be the edge of the world, and then sail back again transformed . . . only that someone is you!

Allow yourself an extra dose of patience while old attitudes and preconceptions detach themselves from you and float away. You can't rush these kinds of changes, even when they seem inevitable, just as you can't rush a cherry blossom's opening.

Would it help a butterfly to surgically extract it from its chrysalis? No. The struggle to escape the confining shell helps force fluids into the butterfly's unfolding wings. Eliminating the struggle would leave the butterfly with tiny shriveled wings, crippled for life. Your own evolutionary struggle will take months, years. The struggle is part of the process.

It is true that using a year or two to learn to feel is a long time, but think of how many years you dedicated yourself to *repressing* your feelings, to avoiding being authentic . . .

EXPANDING CONSCIOUSNESS HAS A SPEED LIMIT

Expanding your kindness and generosity are side effects of expanding your consciousness. Consciousness is not in your mind. Consciousness is in your being. If consciousness existed in a person's mind then we could simply explain the consequences of the corporate strategy of externalizing costs and people would instantly stop working or investing in any corporation forever. We could explain the horrors of overpopulation and Indian and African villagers would instantly and forever stop having more than two children. But it does not work that way. Adding information to the mind is not enough to create change. Expanded consciousness is required.

Consciousness expands at a certain speed limit. It can only increase as fast as you can build the energetic matrix to support it, and building matrix takes time. It's like building good soil. Without good soil, plants won't grow. If you start out with rocks, sand or clay, building good soil requires consistent hard work over a long period of time. Pull out the stones, break up chunks of clay, mix in compost, balance the acidity.

Similar time and effort is required to build the energetic matrix upon which consciousness can grow.

Just as a good strong trellis supports a vibrantly healthy climbing rosebush, so too a good strong energetic matrix supports a vibrantly healthy growing consciousness.

Diligently practicing the exercises in this book, even if they seem embarrassing or confusing at first, is a proven approach for building matrix.

Matrix can also be built through persistently engaging other constructive stresses, such as:

- Living in foreign cultures, eating unfamiliar foods, communicating in foreign languages, adapting to different customs, etc.

- Being in the company of saints.

- Building a consistent practice involving skills or lifestyle choices such as physical exercise, vegetarianism, study, meditation, martial arts, singing, music, etc.

- Exposing yourself to radiations from sacred artifacts, holy tombs and sanctuaries.

- Having integrity, which means doing what you say you will do (e.g., spending time with the kids, being on time to appointments, paying the bills on time, taking out the garbage).

- Giving improvised public talks with feedback and coaching from the audience.

- Being radically honest.

- Regular fasting for one to three days.

- Making a fierce commitment to complete a worthy project.

- Observing periods of silence.

- Staying alert to the responsible or irresponsible purposes of your interpretations about what is happening.

- Cleaning your house of extraneous material possessions.

- Asking for, and listening undefendedly to feedback from your enemies.

- Changing small habits of behavior (e.g., putting your jacket on starting with the opposite sleeve from usual, clasping your hands with the other thumb on top, not scratching a particular small itch, ordering food you would not normally order at the restaurant, being of service to strangers).

- Working in faster or slower rhythms than are usual for you (e.g., taking twice as long to set the table or make the bed, chewing twice as fast as normal).

- Going to the edge of your comfort zone and staying there by implementing new behaviors while acting as if they are normal (e.g., behaving as if you are from a foreign land, acting as if you are handicapped, being innocently unknowledgeable about common things, being delighted by the ordinary, having a sense of the miraculous in everyday life).

Building matrix through any of these various behaviors amplifies the effect of reading this book. An additional way of building matrix is daily use of Tonic Gold, a true alchemical elixir: two drops on the tongue first thing in the morning. (For more information about Tonic Gold see the Further Experiments page at the end of this book.)

A NEW MAP OF FEELINGS

In the previous chapter we saw how feelings are commonly perceived as positive or negative, good or bad, and we considered the belief that it is categorically not okay to feel. This is how feelings look when viewed from the Old Map of Four Feelings. Let us approach the same territory of feelings and frame it in a new story, in a new context.

What new context?

Let us create a New Map of Four Feelings. Let us establish this new map in the context of Ten Distinctions for Consciously Feeling.

Rather than assuming there are positive and negative feelings, as on the Old Map of Four Feelings, we establish a frame where feelings are neutral energy and information. Then there are no *good* feelings or *bad*

MAP OF TEN DISTINCTIONS FOR CONSCIOUSLY FEELING
World Copyright © 2010 owner Clinton Callahan grants permission to use. www.nextculture.org

What would happen to your belief system, your self-experience, your defensive strategies, your abilities to communicate and relate, if you consciously applied these ten adult, responsible distinctions to feelings?

TEN DISTINCTIONS FOR CONSCIOUSLY FEELING

1. There are only four feelings: anger, sadness, fear and joy. All feelings fit into one of these four categories or are mixtures of these four.

2. There is a difference between thoughts and feelings. Thoughts come from your intellectual body's mind. Feelings come from your emotional body's heart.

3. There is a difference between feelings and emotions. Feelings come from yourself in the present moment. Emotions are incomplete feelings that come from the past, or inauthentic feelings that come from some other person or organization.

4. Feelings are absolutely neutral energy and information, neither good nor bad, neither positive nor negative. Feelings are feelings.

5. Feelings serve you powerfully in their pure form, not mixed with each other. Mixed feelings include depression, hysteria, jealousy, despair, melancholy, shame, guilt, *schadenfreude*, and so on. To shift out of these mixed feelings, simply un-mix them.

6. Feelings can be experienced from 0 to 100 percent intensity. In each moment you are feeling all four feelings, but one is always bigger. This is what you are feeling.

7. There are two phases in *feelings work*. In Phase 1 you learn to detect and avoid low drama through consciously feeling neutral, unmixed, 100 percent intensity feelings. In Phase 2 you learn to create high drama through consciously applying the vast information and energy resources of your feelings with adult responsibility.

8. As an adult you can consciously integrate feelings into responsible speaking and listening so that feelings serve you relationally and professionally.

9. *Feelings work* is part of a formal rite of passage that awakens (stellates) archetypal structures and talents that have been lying dormant within you, waiting to be turned on and used to fulfill your destiny.

10. Stellated masculine and feminine archetypes form the basis of a new and truly sustainable culture (archearchy) oriented more toward *being present* and *being with*, and less toward consuming, owning, having, going and *doing*.

feelings anymore, no *positive* or *negative* feelings. There are just feelings. From the conscious, responsible, adult perspective, it is okay to feel, because your feelings provide you with the wisdom and energy needed for fulfilling your destiny.

Understanding, exploring, and learning to apply these Ten Distinctions for Consciously Feeling is a spectacular undertaking, and will take us through the remainder of this book. Along the way we will find new power in the terms *conscious, responsible* and *adult*. Since these words are not respected in modern culture, befriending them could reinvent your everyday experience. For easy reference, the Ten Distinctions are also listed in the back of this book in Appendix B.

FIRST DISTINCTION: THERE ARE ONLY FOUR FEELINGS

The first of the Ten Distinctions for Consciously Feeling is that there are only four feelings: anger, sadness, fear and joy. This does not say that the wide variety of sensations that we think of as feelings do not exist. It says that all the sensations we think of as feelings can be assigned to one of the four categories of feelings.

For example, which of the four feelings categories would include experiences like nervous, jumpy, skeptical, worried, panicky, doubtful, hesitant, distrusting, apprehensive or anxious? Yes, fear!

What about perturbed, annoyed, pent up, struggling, antsy, irritated, resentful, confined, enraged, exasperated, or frustrated? Yes, anger!

What about grief, mourning, regret, abandonment, missing, loneliness, anguish, loss, left out, or sorrowful? Yes, sadness!

What about contented, cheerful, excited, curious, satisfied, happy, enthusiastic, committed, pleased, motivated, blissful, sexy, ecstatic, or delighted? Yes, joy!

See! It is not so difficult. Having the entire field of feelings classified into four simple categories is very good news, *especially for the men!* (We can handle this, guys! There are only *four* feelings! It's not so bad . . .) Recognizing the four feelings categories is very simple and yet provides a huge step forward in the direction of consciously feeling.

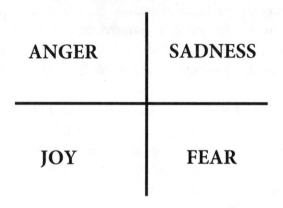

MAP OF FOUR FEELINGS

World Copyright © 2010 owner Clinton Callahan grants permission to use. www.nextculture.org

In this new map of feelings, there are only four feelings: anger, sadness, fear, and joy. Feelings are as neutral as the four directions of a compass, neither good nor bad, neither positive nor negative. Each feeling is a distinct experience with powerful energy and clear information needed to fulfil your destiny.

ANGER	SADNESS
JOY	FEAR

This thoughtmap was originated by Valerie Lankford in 1975 (www.valcanhelp.com) when Valerie's coach, Jaqui Schiff, of the Cathexis Institute, encouraged her to learn to think and be effective even while having strong feelings. The result was Valerie Lankford's Map of Four Feelings, a pioneering work that has helped many thousands of people find revolutionary clarity about what was previously regarded only as pain.

After establishing that there are four feeling categories you can take the next step: learning to detect which of the four feelings you experience in any given moment. How do you know which feeling territory you are in? What do the feelings actually feel like? Here is a brief description of each of the four feelings when they are not being repressed.

ANGER – Anger brings your hands into fists. Your jaws clench together. Blood pressure rises as your heart pumps extra blood to your large arm and leg muscles, which are bunched up, ready for immediate action. Your feet tap on the floor. Your eyes are open and alert, but squinted for protection and focus. Your lips are pressed together or your teeth are bared. The tension in your hands, arms, legs, stomach, shoulders, jaw and throat erupts in strong, clear, boundary-setting words such as *No!* or *Stop!* Your whole body is ready to explode with a warrior's fierceness.

SADNESS – Sadness makes your head hang down and your shoulders droop. Your hands are open and limp. Your jaw muscles are loose. Your blood pressure drops. There is nothing to be done. The ache in your heart and the lump in your throat are sobs and wails of sadness that want to come out. You take deep breaths and make big sighs. Finally the dam breaks. Tears come to your eyes. Your nose drips, your eyes close,

and the wall around your heart crumbles and washes away. You open up. Your broken heart can no longer hold itself together and a flood of sobbing sadness comes. Finally you are letting yourself be seen and known in undefended vulnerability. Each of us has the same sadness. In sorrows we are one.

FEAR – Fear starts in silence and numbness. If you sense no feelings, you are feeling so terrified that you can allow no self-expression. Fear starts as a small high sound far back in your throat. Eyes are wide open in panic or tightly closed in terror. Adrenalin floods electrically through your nerves. You are instantly ready to run or flail about to protect yourself. Fear can be inhumanly strong. Your hands are stretched open with fingers spread wide, trembling. Your breath is shallow (avoid hyperventilation, as it blocks feelings). Your body quivers and shakes. Full expression of fear comes when you surrender to it, like falling backward over a cliff. Your mouth opens wide and piercing, high-pitched screams come out, one after the other, breath after breath, completely uninhibited.

JOY – The expression of anger, sadness, and fear can be quite loud. Joy is not necessarily loud; it can be subtle and personal. Joy is also not rare. Joy may only be sensed for three seconds at a time, but if you do not take responsibility for the three seconds of happiness that accompany tasting your first sip of orange juice, hearing the wind in the trees, seeing a baby smile, or smelling the first drops of new rain, then you might miss joy altogether. If you notice joy in all its facets, joy may be far more abundant than you imagined. Original cultures often understand joy to be the natural background experience of being alive as a human being, called *basic goodness* in Tibetan Buddhism. Joy is centered, awake, present; muscles all over the body are relaxed, peaceful and playful. Joy is relationship occurring previous to thought. Eyes are open while sharing joy, closed while enjoying joy. In intense joy, the smile muscles can ache unbearably. Spasms in the chest and belly explode as laughter that won't stop even if the sides hurt with the most intense pain. You may need to fall out of your chair and roll on the ground when you laugh so hard.

This is why the New Map of Four Feelings indicates four kinds of pain: anger, sadness, fear, and joy. Joy is just as painful to experience as anger, sadness, and fear. Joy is one of the four pains. Pain is the indicator letting you know that you are alive.

Some models include love as one of the feelings. I consider love to be a Bright Principle, not a feeling. When love is happening, you can feel the Bright Principle of love influence your body. Because of the sensations that love can stimulate a person may feel angry, sad, afraid, or glad, but these are feelings. Love is not a feeling.

Some other models include sexual arousal as a feeling. Sexual arousal originates through a mysterious interplay between the physical, intellectual, emotional, and energetic bodies. Feelings come entirely from the emotional body. Feelings can be triggered by a thought, but feelings originate in the emotional body. Sexual arousal is closer to physical sensations like hunger, thirst, a desire for warmth, a need for exercise, a need to pee, yawn, or sneeze. (What? Sex is like sneezing? Uh, that would be the topic for a different book . . .)

MAKING STORIES ABOUT PAIN

Human beings are the only animals that can change pain into suffering. You change pain into suffering through the story you create about the pain. If you relate to pain as if you are being victimized by the pain, then you change the pain into suffering.

For example, when a man drops a hammer on his toe he might say, "Ouch! I'm an idiot! How stupid can I be? I'm always hurting myself, just like my dad! Ow! Damn, that hurts! Why does this always happen to me? I can't do it right! Shit for life!!!"

In this case the man uses the pain to torture himself.

The same man in the same circumstance with the same hammer but a different story could say, "Ouch! Wow! What a wake-up call. This is real pain! I am so lucky. This pain only hurts in the moment where now is. I know where now is. I accept this pain now. I can even choose to feel this pain. I can choose it for no reason. Then *I* have the power, instead of the pain having the power. I am not a victim of the pain!"

In this case the man uses the pain to enlighten himself.

It is not the pain but your story about the pain that determines what the pain means or what the pain can do for you. Since you choose the stories you live by, why not, as Kurt Vonnegut Jr proposed in *Cat's Cradle*, choose stories "that make you brave and kind and healthy and happy?"

TELLTALE SIGNS OF FEELINGS

Using a map to represent the entire domain of feelings in four simple territories provides a tremendous wealth of practical clarity. For example, when you know which feeling you are feeling, then you know which territory you are in, and therefore you know what sort of energy and information is available for you to work with.

This is like traveling. If you are in Mexico, Saudi Arabia, Indonesia or Iceland, as soon as you know which country you are in, you automatically know what kind of shoes to wear, how to greet the new people you meet, the polite way to eat your lunch, and what to do on Sunday. These are very useful bits of information.

Equally useful information is at your fingertips as soon as you know which of the four feelings territories you are in. Your body is the key. If you pay close attention to your physical sensations they will ongoingly indicate the feeling you are having: anger, sadness, fear, or joy.

When you notice that your jaw is clenched or your teeth are grinding; when you sense tension in your shoulders, chest or forehead; when your eyes are squinting, your feet are bouncing, your hands are bunched into fists, or you feel your options have narrowed, say to yourself, "I feel angry." Even if the anger is only three seconds long.

When you notice that your jaw is slack, your hands are lifeless, you have a lump in your throat and a heavy heart; when you're sighing, your head is down, your shoulders are slouched, or your vision is blurred, say to yourself, "I feel sad." Even if the sadness is only three seconds long.

When you notice that your jaw is partly open, your eyes are wide, your hands or feet are cold, your fingers are fidgeting, and your breath is shallow; when you're wearing a fake smile, there is tension in your forehead or shoulders, there are silent screams in your heart, your hair is standing on end, you feel paralyzed, or are trying to be invisible, say to yourself, "I feel scared." Even if the fear is only three seconds long.

When you notice that your jaw and shoulders are relaxed; when your hands are warm and your smile easy; when your perspective is expanded, your attention free roving and you have an abundance of options; when you feel bright, playful, kind, generous, accepting, appreciative, or are grateful for life, say to yourself, "I feel glad." Even if the joy is only three seconds long.

And let there be no judgment about which of the feelings you happen to be feeling in this moment. Feelings come and go. The feeling you are feeling now provides the information and energy that you need right now. Relax the internal judgments, notice what you are feeling, and apply its wisdom and energy. Simply notice that you are feeling. If others around you seem to be judging, or make critical comments, you can alleviate their concerns by looking them straight in the eyes and saying, "This theatrical work that I'm practicing is really interesting."

Feelings are universal; they apply to you as well as to other human beings of all races, creeds and cultures all around the world. This illusion that we are separate or somehow different from each other is named in a song by Paul Simon in his *Graceland* album. He calls it "the myth of fingerprints."

Making it a practice to sense and identify which of the four feelings you are feeling creates empathy with what others are feeling. Through giving yourself permission to experience your own feelings you may be surprised to find yourself closely connecting to people, even strangers or children, at a whole new level of easefulness—because you feel what they feel. Through feeling your own feelings you understand and respect what is happening with other people.

Suddenly you are freed from solitary confinement in your private world of thoughts. You emerge connected with other human beings in the world we all have in common: the world of feelings.

SECOND DISTINCTION: THERE IS A DIFFERENCE BETWEEN THOUGHTS AND FEELINGS

The second of the Ten Distinctions for Consciously Feeling says that there is a difference between thoughts and feelings. You may not acknowledge or make use of this distinction because throughout school you were taught to focus exclusively on your thoughts. As a result you are far more proficient with thinking than you are with feeling. In fact, when you first start searching for your feelings you will probably look in your mind!

You are magnificent with your mind! You can think logically, verbally, mathematically, sequentially, and topologically. You can analyze and solve problems, memorize lists of names, dates and places, calculate probable futures, make reasonable estimates and deductions, and so on. But try as you might to use your mind to find your feelings you will fail miserably, because feelings do not originate in your head. Feelings originate in your heart.

The Map of Four Bodies shows how thoughts occur in the *mind* of the *intellectual body*, whereas feelings occur in the *heart* of the *emo-*

tional body. Feelings arise out of a completely different domain than thoughts. They run on totally different energies, have altogether different uses, and are navigated through wholly different gestures and communications.

Trying to feel with your mind would be like trying to watch TV on a front-loading clothes washer. By the looks of the washer you should be able to watch TV on its window, but the two devices are radically different. There is no TV circuitry in the washing machine, and if you pour soap and water into a TV it goes *Blazaat!* with sparks and smoke! Yet each machine is perfectly functional for its own particular purpose.

The same is true of each of your four bodies—each is perfectly functional for its own particular purpose. It is up to you to learn the purpose and use of each of your bodies; otherwise you will be left standing in the laundromat waiting for *I Love Lucy* reruns.

It should be obvious by now that learning to feel feelings requires practice. Expecting that you should already know how to feel is like thinking the first time you pick up a violin you should be able to play Bach's *Brandenburg Concerto #3* like these guys: <http://www.youtube.com/watch?v=hZ9qWpa2rIg>. No way! Forget it! We are beginners at feeling, and the sooner you admit it the sooner you can start where you are and practice effectively with baby steps.

It can help to ease your frustration if from time to time you remind yourself that we are all seriously handicapped. None of us received practical guidance about how to make use of our emotional and energetic bodies. The consequences of this lack are personal: half of your innate faculties—the heart and soul half—are atrophied from lack of conscious use. This is a *severe* handicap.

An important hint for learning to feel is simple but not easy to implement. When you first start learning to feel in Phase 1 of feelings work, you won't find your feelings through thinking. Feelings are sensations in your body. If you are thinking about feeling, you will locate your attention in your head, and as a consequence be blocked from your feelings. Feelings do not occur in your head. They occur in your body. In Phase 2 of feelings work you will learn to think *while* feeling.

MAP OF HINT FOR LEARNING TO FEEL

World Copyright © 2010 owner Clinton Callahan grants permission to use. www.nextculture.org

Feelings are not in your head.

THOUGHTS COME FIRST

You may think a thought such as, "This is too much for me," or "That asshole hurt me again!" or "Soon it will be vacation time." Or you may formulate words to create a mental image, such as of being victimized, being totally relaxed, being a hero, or words that bring up a memory, such as, "My dog died," or "That was selfish," or "What a fun time we had." But if you slow down the thinking-feeling process, you can see how it actually works. First there is the mental image or the thought, and a moment *after* the thought comes the feelings. The images, words, mental pictures and memories are not the feelings. Only the feelings are the feelings. Learning to feel will begin with learning to distinguish between the original thoughts in your head and the feelings these thoughts and images stimulate in your body.

A powerful practice is to distinctly communicate the thought and feeling elements separately in your speech. Start by seeing how often you can catch yourself saying, "I feel," when you actually mean "I think." For example, "I feel this is not fair," "I feel it's time to go," "I feel she is a good candidate." These are not feelings. These are thoughts. Not being clear about distinguishing feelings from thoughts creates confusing communications.

The first part of the practice is to replace the word *feel* with the word *think* whenever this is appropriate. When you say, "I think this is not fair," "I think it's time to go," "I think she is a good candidate," you are no longer confusing thoughts with feelings. This clarity gives you back a tremendous amount of power that was previously bound up in internal confusion.

The second part of the practice is to remember that there are only four words to choose from for the next word after you say, "I feel . . . ." The four words are *angry, sad, scared,* or *glad*. Simply memorize the sentence "I feel (mad, sad, glad or scared) because _____," and use this sentence at least three times each day.

Your communications would then include both your feelings *and* your thoughts, but not blended together. In the above examples, you could say, "I feel angry because I think it is not fair that you choose which movie we see most of the time," or "I feel scared that we will be late to our appointment so I think it is time to go," or "I feel glad that Maria Burnett is running for mayor because I think her commitment to sustainability makes her a good candidate." This simple practice can bring intimacy and authenticity to your communications.

YOUR HEART HAS WORDS OF ITS OWN

During almost two decades of helping people experience and express their conscious adult feelings I have noticed some patterns. For example, two of the four feelings—anger and sadness—tend to include words as part of their full expression, and two of the feelings—fear and joy—do not. The two wordless feelings *do* have sounds, and quite remarkable sounds they may be, but in general the sounds are nonverbal. The two feelings that come with words—anger and sadness—are spoken with words of the heart. Your heart has words of its own.

Words of anger include: Yes! I want that! No! I don't want that! Stop that! You idiot! I hate this! Keep going! I love this! This is perfect! This pisses me off! I agree! I don't agree! Never do that again! Always do it like this! Arrrrgggghhhh! Don't touch me! This is *my life*! Yay!

(Notice that these samples of anger words do not fit the Old Map of Feelings that views anger as a *negative* feeling. On the New Map of Feelings anger is the impulse to start things, stop things, or change things—to make things happen. Anger is neither positive nor negative; it is neutral energy and information. The same is true of all four feelings.)

Words of sadness include: I can't manage this. I am so alone. She left me. I don't know what to do. I am weak and powerless. I miss you. I'm sorry I forgot. It didn't work out. It got lost. It seems so hopeless. It's too late. I'm lost. I failed.

Words that come from anger or sadness come directly from the feelings themselves, not from thinking the words first, as was described in the previous section. Feeling words come directly out of your heart, *not* from your mind.

The idea that your heart can think and speak may at first seem strange, but recent research reveals that the heart is a sensory organ that sends more information to the brain than it receives. With over forty thousand neurons of its own, the heart is a complex information-encoding and processing center, sufficiently sophisticated to qualify being regarded as a *heart brain*.

These findings become even more interesting. Consistent reports confirm that 5 to 10 percent of heart transplant recipients notice profound and unexpected side effects of the surgery, including experiencing memories, interests, tastes, habits, personality quirks and desires they never had before receiving the transplanted heart. Upon investigation, the traits turn out to match those of the now-deceased heart donor! These are not isolated cases. (For more information about this, google *heart cellular memory*).

The next time you sing a song or recite a poem *by heart*, notice how you can think about other things at the same time that your heart is singing or reciting. Your heart has one voice and your mind has another. Notice also how trying to recall the words with your mind actually interferes with being able to speak the words from your heart. The words memorized by heart are not stored in your mind. They are stored in your heart.

Learning to consciously let your heart speak is a new skill, very different from letting your mind speak. You are structurally capable of learning heart-speaking skills beginning at seven years old, but there are few people in modern culture who could teach you. Your parents probably never learned. As children we are usually encouraged to learn only what the teachers could teach. Then our learning is limited by what the teachers are afraid to know.

Now you have another chance. Now you can learn whatever you are capable of learning, even if it has never been taught before. Now you can unfold and enliven your true learning potential.

In learning to let your heart speak there are clues. For example, your heart speaks more slowly than your mind, more softly, and with simpler words. The heart uses very few hand gestures to help explain. In contrast, the mind often employs precise hand movements for counting logical ideas on your fingers, pointing things out, and painting pictures in the air. It is also your mind speaking when you touch the fingertips of both hands together. Making this spider-on-a-mirror hand position tends to block feelings and shrink your focus into the intellect. Notice what your hands are doing. If you see your hands moving, check to see if you are merely in your head.

When anger speaks from your heart, it speaks with more passion and more commitment than the mind can muster, often using whole-body gestures, not just the hands.

The heart speaks its feelings unrehearsed. This means that your heart speaks before your mind knows what you are going to say. So you may be as startled, touched, amused or inspired as your listener by what your heart says. If you find yourself rehearsing a conversation in your mind before you open your mouth then it is not likely that your heart is speaking.

FEELINGS MATURE

When you first get your feelings back they return at the same level of maturity they were when you first shut them down. This means that your anger, sadness, fear or joy, when you finally experience them as a grown-up, may be the repressed and immature feelings stored in the muscles of your body since you were a child. Back then you had feelings, of course, but it may not have been acceptable to the people around you for you to experience and express the true intensity of your feelings. To save yourself from the repercussions of people reacting to your feelings you may have shut your feelings down as a survival strategy.

While doing adult feelings work you may be startled to find yourself feeling exactly the feelings that were repressed so long ago, still locked away in your body all this time. If you allow yourself to wholeheartedly express these immature feelings, and if they are heard by another person, then they are completed and will quickly mature into the adult feelings of a person your present age. However, the first few weeks and months of feelings work might be a little rocky. Just don't worry! Your feelings will quickly catch up to you in age all by themselves, and then you can proceed into adult and archetypal feelings work.

In a safe environment feelings can be allowed to go and go until they stop by themselves. The adult human body is designed to experience and express 100 percent archetypal intensity of each of the four feelings. In the moment that you reach 100 percent maximum archetypal expression of a feeling, your relationship to that feeling permanently transforms. We will investigate more about these ideas in the chapter "Stellating Feelings."

Making a safe environment for your feelings work includes making a particular agreement with a mature *adult* listener. (Note: Please do not use your child as your listening partner. The exercises in this book are to be done with adult partners. It might seem safer to use children as your listeners, but a child is not an emotional garbage can. Too painfully often adults confide in children and share their problems with their children; *this is a form of emotional abuse*. It is not the child's responsibility to heal adults. If you are using children like this in *any* form, please stop it immediately.)

The agreement to make with the listener is that the listener *listens*. They listen to what you say, not to what they think you should say. They do not try to solve your problems. They do not try to rescue *poor you*. They do not pity you, calm you down, heal you, defend your position, or assure you that everything will be okay in the end. None of

MAP OF HOW TO CONSCIOUSLY FEEL
World Copyright © 2010 owner Clinton Callahan grants permission to use. www.nextculture.org

This thirty-minute partner exercise is done once or twice a week for as many weeks as you wish. It's a simple, safe and effective way to learn to consciously feel.

HOW TO CONSCIOUSLY FEEL

1. Please note that this is a *partner* exercise, not to be done alone. It won't hurt you to do it alone, but it won't help you much either. That's because a communication persists until it is *received*. For your communication to be received there needs to be someone there to hear you. If you are a man, speak with an adult man. If you are a woman, speak with an adult woman. Without a responsible listener you are merely drowning in your own sorrows.
2. Each session has two halves. In the first half do the exercise in one direction and then reverse roles. You each get to play both parts. This avoids the client/therapist ("I'm broken, fix me.") dynamic. Neither of you is broken. You are doing edgework experiments to expand your Box!
3. Prearrange a place where the two of you can have enough privacy to make noise undisturbed. Feelings can be loud.
4. Bring a sturdy hand towel and some tissues. The towel can be wrung between your hands to help do rage work. You know what the tissues are for.
5. Sit facing each other in straight-back chairs with no table between you. (Sitting on the floor tends to compress the chest and block your feelings.)
6. One person goes first: the feeler. The other person is the coach. The coach's main job is to listen.
7. The coach says, "Close your eyes and trust your feelings. Let your feelings lead." In a safe space it only takes a few seconds before the first manifestation of a feeling shows up, such as swallowing, fidgeting fingers, a tapping foot, sighing. The coach simply says, "Let the feeling get bigger."
8. Don't worry if nothing seems to happen for the first few meetings, or even if a feeling only gets to 5 percent intensity. A new kind of trust is developing. The work goes in steps and layers. Trust the process.
9. Even if joy, fear, or sadness appear to be the topmost feelings, I suggest that you work with anger first. When you have your anger back, then you can use your anger to assure your own safety while exploring the other feelings.
10. The coach's job is to:
    a. Ask to hear the story behind the feelings. Say, "Then what happened?"
    b. Repeat back what the feeler says to complete the communications.
    c. Encourage the feeler to stay out of their head and instead say, "I feel <u>(mad, sad, glad or scared)</u> because _____."
    d. Coach the feeler to unmix their mixed feelings.
    e. Coach the feeler to gauge the intensity (1 percent - 100 percent) of their feelings.
    f. At the climax point, ask, "What did you decide?" Write that down.
    g. At the halfway time, change roles and start over.
11. Spend a few minutes at the end of each session sharing observations and insights. Have a glass of water. Clean up the space together.

that stuff. They listen, and they repeat back what they heard you say. If they don't get it right, you tell them that's not what you said, and you say it again, including both the feelings *and* the information in your communications. Then you make the same agreement with them, in reverse. Through practicing this speaking and listening exercise you can learn to consciously feel.

THIRD DISTINCTION: THERE IS A DIFFERENCE BETWEEN FEELINGS AND EMOTIONS

The third of the Ten Distinctions for Consciously Feeling says that there is a difference between feelings and emotions. It is a *huge* difference! Feelings and emotions come from completely different universes of purpose. If you are not distinguishing feelings from emotions during moment-to-moment interactions, then when someone is expressing *emotions* and you interact with them as if they are expressing *feelings,* you will be trapped and powerless within the confusion.

For example, if your partner reacts to something you do or don't do, say or don't say, because they have incomplete feelings about someone *else* who did or didn't do or say something similar, they are expressing emotions. If you don't know that these are incomplete feelings projected onto you from their past that don't actually relate to you at all, you will be sucked into their low drama as if it is real.

Another example could be that your partner, a colleague, or a neighbor comes to you carrying a feeling that doesn't originate in them. Perhaps they took on the feeling from one of their parents, or from the boss or a client. Or perhaps the feeling comes from an organization such as a political party (e.g., Progressives are tree huggers), a company brand (e.g., Ford is better than Chevy), a cultural prejudice (e.g., Americans are arrogant idiots), or a religious belief (e.g., All nonbelievers are terrorists). The person may indeed claim that these are their true feelings, but we often adopt feelings unconsciously from powerful influences as a way of surviving under those influences. If the feelings come from someone or something else they are not feelings but emotions. When the colleague or neighbor complains to you with their angry, sad, scared or glad emotional opinions and beliefs and you assume it is a feeling instead of an emotion, you may try to argue back with your own opinions and beliefs. No matter how effectively you argue your points, that person's feelings won't change, because what is being talked about is not the source of the feelings. Somebody or something else is. The feelings are inauthentic because they come from an external source. Therefore, they are emotions.

It is even more confusing when you yourself feel *emotions* from the past or emotions adopted from elsewhere and you regard these emotions as your own true *feelings*, saying things and taking actions accordingly. It is no wonder that you do not achieve the results you hope for if you start from emotional confusion.

We can hardly imagine what a silly, expensive, and perhaps lethal mistake it is to interchange emotions and feelings. So many tangled messes are generated so quickly in personal, familial, national and global interactions. Is this an accident or is it to keep the sheeple disempowered? Confusing emotions and feelings is a defining characteristic of modern society. Must it also define your life?

By combining the following information and examples with determined practice, you will build a practical understanding for yourself of life in a new world. In this new world, feelings and emotions are as different from each other as living and plastic roses.

DISTINGUISHING FEELINGS FROM EMOTIONS

At first, the *emotions* of anger, sadness, fear and joy feel identical to the *feelings* of anger, sadness, fear, and joy. How can you detect the difference between experiencing a feeling and experiencing one of the two kinds of emotions?

The way to tell the difference between feelings and emotions is to note how long the experience lasts.

When you feel and express an *emotion* it does not get completed. *Feelings*, on the other hand, arise, are used with gratitude, and then completely vanish within a minute or two.

I heard that Zen practitioners may seriously practice meditation for twenty years before they experience their first true feeling. I was thirty-nine years old before I experienced my first feeling, and I still remember the moment. This is humbling news. It implies that, for the time being, it would be smart of you to assume that almost everything you feel is not a feeling at all but rather emotions from the past or from others.

It means that your daily feelings that you think are caused by those unfair people and unfortunate circumstances out there are actually self-generated emotions surrounding you like a space suit and regulating your entire experience of life.

Failing to distinguish feelings from emotions is like failing to distinguish solid land from quicksand. Take one blind step in the wrong direction and you are sure to be sucked into a low drama quagmire from which it is extremely difficult to extract yourself.

The power to avoid such interactions would seem like magic.

As has often been said, "One man's magic is another man's technology." Learning to consciously feel is the magical technology.

Practical application of the new technology begins when you make and continuously hold this distinction between feelings and emotions:

Feelings arise in and of the present moment, come out of your authentic self, and vanish completely when applied.

Emotions feel like feelings but they last longer than the present moment.

There are two kinds of emotions:

1. <u>Inauthentic feelings</u> from someone else, and

2. <u>Incomplete feelings</u> from the past.

This is best explained on the Map of Two Kinds of Emotions.

We will examine the two kinds of emotions separately below. The value of understanding how emotions originate and operate is that it awakens sensitivity for detecting emotions before they can fully arise in you and take over the inner controls. If you cannot detect and instantly divert yourself away from a rising emotional tidal wave, then in the next instant it becomes too late. You get knocked unconscious and have to go through the whole emotional process, waking up an hour, a day, or a week later, after the low drama Gremlin feeding frenzy has subsided.

MAP OF TWO KINDS OF EMOTIONS

World Copyright © 2010 owner Clinton Callahan grants permission to use. www.nextculture.org

Emotions feel like mad, sad, glad, or scared, but emotions last longer than feelings. Emotions come either from the Parent Ego State as inauthentic feelings from someone else, or from the Child Ego State as incomplete feelings from the past. Emotions are not from your Adult self in the present.

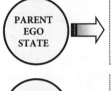

PARENT EMOTIONS: *Inauthentic feelings* from an authority figure or from an institutional belief system, such as government, religion, political party, company brand name, or cultural prejudice. Parent Emotions feel real but are not authentically from you.

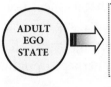

ADULT FEELINGS: As an adult you use your sword of clarity to distinguish emotions from feelings, to authenticate your feelings, to complete your feelings, and to responsibly apply the energy and wisdom of your feelings while being your destiny in action.

CHILD EMOTIONS: *Incomplete feelings* from the past. Something happened and it was not safe for you to express your feelings about it then, so you suppressed the feelings into your muscles. Child emotions get automatically triggered when you experience now anything similar to what happened back then.

DETECTING PARENT EMOTIONS: INAUTHENTIC FEELINGS FROM OTHERS

As a way to survive you may have adopted inauthentic feelings from your parents or other authority figures, or from a political, corporate, cultural or religious belief system. Because an inauthentic feeling originates outside of yourself it has no true power within you. The only power it has within you is the power you attribute to it by mistaking it for your own personal feeling. After you have survived, meaning after you are fifteen or eighteen years old, the deeply ingrained habit of adopting inauthentic feelings blocks you from being yourself. New ways of behaving can be learned.

I offer a personal example of adopting inauthentic feelings from an authority figure. Each time I drove up to a tollbooth or to the exit of a parking lot and came face to face with the fee collector, an inexplicable rage would grip me. I suddenly hated that person as if they were threatening my life or torturing my children. My rage was completely unconscious and I didn't even notice it was happening until I got married. One day my wife asked, "Why are you so hostile toward the tollbooth man?" I had no immediate answer. My reaction was completely irrational and a total mystery to me.

Then one day we flew to California to visit my parents. They met us at the baggage claim of LAX and we walked together out to their car. As we drove to the exit booth, my father suddenly became insanely enraged at the poor ticket woman, speaking to her in the most bigoted, degrading and juvenile way. I was shocked. In that moment I saw myself. At the same time I realized that this particular rage, which I had been carrying probably since childhood, was not my rage at all; it was my father's rage. I didn't know where *he* got it; perhaps from his own father. But I knew *I didn't have to keep it.*

As soon as we had privacy I started a conversation with my wife that I had never had before. I took responsibility for unconsciously carrying my father's rage all those years. I apologized for the pain and upset I had been causing her and our children with this insane hostility toward toll takers. And I vowed never to empower that rage again. Making a vow like this carries the consequence of fiercely practicing new behavior until it becomes an unconscious competence. It took me years of vigilant self-observation and practice.

Here is an example of the second type of inauthentic feelings, those that come from an institutional belief system. It comes from a roommate I was given by the dormitory office during my freshman year at California Polytechnic State University in San Luis Obispo. He was a fundamentalist Christian and must have decided that the choice of roommates was divinely ordained because he made it a personal mission to either successfully convert me to his sect or condemn me to eternity in hell. He would interrupt our study time with unconsciously mixed anger, fear and sadness about the state of my soul; yet nothing touched me because his feelings were inauthentic. Both the logic he used and the source of his feelings originated outside of himself in a belief system. He seemed to be reciting a used car salesman's script, playing a forced role.

It wasn't him happening. Nothing I said to him made any difference either, because he wasn't at source for what he was saying—the belief system was—so he could not authentically listen, think or interact. Since he could feel angry, sad, and afraid, he assumed that the feelings were his own. But they were not even feelings. They were emotions that he had adopted from the belief system of a religious organization.

I once spoke with a young exchange student from China. She seemed open, enthusiastic, intelligent and present. Then suddenly a tape was triggered in her mind and she ferociously affirmed the belief that China was correct to invade Tibet and to try to reclaim Taiwan. Where could a young girl have gained the worldly experience to assess such horrific political maneuverings? She couldn't. These emotionally charged beliefs did not come from her. Like a parasitic infection, this young woman carries strong emotions that she unconsciously adopted to survive under the authority of a political regime.

Another time, during the Bush-Cheney Iraq invasion, I was traveling to America with my German-born partner, Marion. We had a long layover at the Atlanta international airport, which was swarming with soldiers. She kept asking me why so many Americans dressed up in soldier outfits and went off to fight? I had no answer so I said, "Go ask them yourself." She sat on the floor next to a soldier in his early thirties, a leader type, and interviewed him for half an hour. She asked why he was doing what he was doing. He said he was returning to Iraq "to support and protect innocent civilians from the enemy." This man was risking his life based on emotional misinformation created by a corporate-controlled political system to benefit wealthy oil, banking, construction and weapons dealers, and he believed he was doing a good thing. He mistook parent emotions to be his own feelings.

Parent emotions originate in emotions from authority figures or from institutions. They are not from you. Government propaganda, political campaigns, corporate marketing scams, cultural attitudes, religious traditions, male and female chauvinism are all emotionally charged dogma. They are not feelings.

Emotions smear the airwaves 24/7 through modern culture's mainstream media—breaking news, soap operas, natural disasters, intrigue, movie star gossip, latest fashions, financial investments, diseases, cool gizmos, hot cars, naked women, wars. Any individual not hyper attentive about protecting themselves from these pervasive and invasive influences gets inundated to the point of suffocation. What remains after the suffocation is a walking, talking, robot-ghost, the classic compliant consumer.

PROTECTING YOUR ATTENTION

Purveyors of modern culture have one prize in mind: your attention. If they can capture your attention they have captured your wallet. When they have your wallet, their efforts more than pay for themselves. That is why they keep advertising.

Truly protecting your attention from the scientifically honed multimedia onslaught involves changing your flat screen TV into a carom table and walking through stores as if you are in a combat zone. If advertisements suck away control of your attention and you read the billboards or watch the images, the subconscious hooks go in. By now you probably carry a truckload of false emotions: inauthentic feelings from advertising agencies. The process of authenticating inauthentic feelings frees you from this huge and unnecessary burden that was never yours in the first place.

It doesn't really help to blame someone else for the design and intention of mainstream culture, because you helped make it this way. Through paying the price for each thing you bought—from home-heating oil, to hockey tickets, to high-heeled shoes, to mass-produced honey (rich in GMO pollen these days)—you are the one paying for development of ever sharper advertising hooks that capture your attention. Stop buying the plastic shit and they must eventually stop making it.

DETECTING CHILD EMOTIONS: INCOMPLETE FEELINGS FROM THE PAST

Each of us comes out of our teenage years fogged with incomplete feelings from the past. For example, imagine that you were a child who loved building elaborate castles in the kindergarten sandbox. If your parents or teacher decided it was time for you to go home before you were finished playing in your magical world, you might have felt rage

---

MAP OF HOW TO AUTHENTICATE INAUTHENTIC FEELINGS

In order to survive you may have adopted inauthentic feelings, either from a parental authority figure or from a political, financial, cultural or religious belief system. Feelings from others are one of the two kinds of *emotions*, not feelings. By taking on the feelings of a source of authority you take on its authority, but that authority is inauthentic. *Authenticity starts when you take responsibility for having abandoned your authenticity.* This is a five- to fifty-minute partner-process that will help you to differentiate between authentic and inauthentic feelings.

HOW TO AUTHENTICATE INAUTHENTIC FEELINGS

1. Monitor your feelings in your conversations. Authenticating a feeling means to *test if a feeling is your feeling or not.* The test is to apply this question: "What is the purpose of this feeling?" Use part of your attention to stay in the feeling and another part of your attention to find the purpose of the feeling. Ask yourself: "Where is this going? What is its intention?" If the purpose is anything other than *being in relationship through vulnerably sharing myself,* it is probably not *your* feeling, but a foreign feeling with a purpose like:

   a. Surviving by reenacting abusive behavior (physical / psychological / emotional / or sexual abuse).

   b. Surviving through identifying with someone else's authority (father, mother, boss, teacher, movie/rock star, political leader).

   c. Surviving through identifying with institutional authority (police, religious believer, political party, brand name, professional title).

   d. Proving that you were abused so as to validate being a victim, thereby justifying taking revenge.

   e. Proving that you are right and the other person is wrong, thereby validating the superiority of your beliefs, and so on.

2. In the instant you detect that your feeling is not about responsibly sharing yourself, STOP the conversation, midthought, midsentence, midgesture.

3. Say, "Excuse me. I just noticed that what I am feeling is not authentic. It is an emotion, not a feeling. It does not actually come from me. I adopted it from someone else (name the person)." Or "I adopted it from an institution (name the institution). The purpose of this emotion is . . . (name its purpose, perhaps one of the purposes listed above)."

4. Shift and start an entirely new conversation, an adult responsible conversation. The way out of inauthenticity is by being authentic about your inauthenticity. For example, even if the source and purpose of your emotions is not immediately clear to you, be as clear as you can be and then admit what is not clear. Say, "I feel angry about the ecologists because this is my political party's dogma. But I don't know why I need to follow their dogma. I don't know what I actually feel about environmental issues. Probably scared."

5. This is not psychotherapy. This is becoming authentic at a new level. You do not have to process everything. Simply say, "That is not my authentic purpose. My real purpose is to let myself be known in this relationship."

6. Then create a new future for yourself by taking on a new practice. Say, "I promise not to empower that emotional rage again." The promise means new behavior for you. Keep your commitment with fierce diligence.

and a terrible grief over being torn away from a valuable learning experience for no reason.

If your parents were unable to listen to your sadness (and whose parents were?), your feeling remained incomplete, trapped in your muscles, unexpressed even to the present day. If this happened often enough (once may be often enough), you may have decided that it is too painful to create because the creation will be suddenly torn away from you. Then you may forget that you made this decision.

Now perhaps in your work you are given an opportunity to design or create something. As soon as the invitation is made you might notice a reflexive block or subtle fear that causes you to refuse the chance to create. At the same time you may feel a deep sadness. What you are feeling is emotional fear and emotional sadness. These are not feelings originating from the present circumstances at all. The emotions arise because your present circumstances resonate to a previous circumstance about which you carry incomplete feelings. In this case the present opportunity to create resonates to your childhood circumstances of being ripped away from the tender and elaborate worlds you were creating in the sandbox. The old decision, that it is too painful to create, prevails.

Even if you as a grown-up tell someone you feel sad about the opportunity to create and the opportunity fades away, the sadness will not necessarily vanish. This is because the sadness is not about the present opportunity to create. The sadness is an incomplete emotional feeling relating to the incident in childhood. Your present conditions do not actually have *anything* to do with your feeling of sadness. This is how emotions work.

Did you ever feel angry about something and the anger stayed with you for an hour? For a day? This anger is emotional anger.

Did you ever feel sad about something and the sadness stayed with you for a week? For a month? This is emotional sadness.

Did you ever feel scared about something and the fear just never seems to go away? This is emotional fear.

Did you ever feel glad about something and the joy stayed with you for more than a few minutes? This is not the present feeling of joy. This is emotional joy, just as illusory and disempowering as the emotions of anger, sadness or fear. I tell you, it was a bad day for me when I figured *this* out! For forty five years of my life I thought I was a happy guy. Then one day in a training I made the distinction between the feeling of joy and the emotion of joy. In that moment I realized that I had been living in a fantasy world of emotional joy that I had smeared over from my past and which had nothing to do with what was happening directly around me in my present life. Until that moment I had no idea how much self-generated fog I had been living in. When that bubble pops for you, be prepared for some surprises.

POWER IS IN THE PRESENT

An incomplete feeling may have originated only five minutes in the past or it may have originated five decades in the past. Whenever it occurred, since an incomplete feeling is from the past, it has no true power in the present.

For example, you just read the sentence, "Since an incomplete feeling is from the past, it has no true power in the present." If you had power to affect the past, you could make it so that you did not just read that sentence.

Can you do that? You read it only a few seconds ago. Can you make it so that you did not already read that sentence?

No, you cannot.

Why not?

Because it already happened; it is done. It is in the past. You have no power to affect the past, whether an event happened only a few seconds ago or many years ago. How much time and effort have you invested in trying to heal or change the past?

What happened in the past is as it is.

What appears to influence us from the past is memories, old decisions, and incomplete feelings.

Old decisions can easily be identified and redecided.

Incomplete feelings can easily be clarified, expressed and completed.

The actual manner in which the past influences you *is determined by you in the present moment.* This is a doorway to a future free of emotions.

EMOTIONS FROM MEMORIES

Memories can cause emotional reactions when you blur memories of the past with what is happening now.

For example, can you remember ever being terribly thirsty? Yes, you can.

If you take a drink of water now, does that make your memory of being thirsty go away? No, it does not.

The memory of being thirsty remains no matter how much or how often you drink water now. If you blur being thirsty now with your memory of being thirsty in the past, the incomplete feelings of anger or fear you had when you were thirsty may automatically arise when you are thirsty now. The mechanism is that simple.

Can you remember ever being lost, or terribly lonely? Yes, you can.

If you know exactly where you are, or if you get together with people now, does that make your memory of being lost or lonely go away? No, it does not.

The memory of having once been lost remains no matter how familiar your present surrounding are. The memory of having once been lonely remains no matter how many friends you meet with or how intimate you are with someone. If you remember feeling sad or scared when you were lost or lonely in the past, it can cause you to feel sad or scared even if you are with someone now.

No present circumstances can change your emotional memories from the past.

No partner can change your emotional memories from the past.

You have your memories and you cannot change what happened to you in the past. You can, however, change your relationship to your memory of what happened to you in the past.

You can clearly and consciously identify a memory as a memory. Say, "This is a memory." You can let the memory float back down the river of time to where it belongs, in the past, including your memory of anger, sadness, joy or fear about what happened. It takes a watchful inner eye but only a moment of time to detach a remembered feeling from its resonance with the present circumstances.

Distinguishing memories as memories gives you the freedom of movement to have a completely different relationship to the present circumstances than you had to similar circumstances in the past. By doing this you take back your creative power in the present.

EMOTIONS FROM OLD DECISIONS

If you habitually apply an old decision to new circumstances it can quickly entangle you in a briar patch of emotions. When you first make them, old decisions are new and necessary. Over time situations change. Your abilities change. Your perspectives change. But *old decisions don't change*. Old decisions continue causing their originally intended results until they are noticed, highlighted, followed back to their point of origin, and replaced by new, more appropriate and useful decisions.

For example, you may have had a class in school with a teacher who was more interested in having a controlled classroom than in having students expand into their full human potential. In that class you may have tried to express yourself in various ways and the teacher may have subtly or overtly punished you. Eventually you may have decided it was not worth it to express yourself, that it was safer to disempower yourself and withhold your genuine participation.

That old decision may have metaphorically saved your life in school, but you are no longer in school. Your circumstances have changed, yet your present actions may still be influenced by that old decision to stifle your self-expression. Making a new, empowering decision to replace the old, disempowering decision gives you your present power back. Find the exact phrase of your old decision, such as, "It's not worth the risk to make creative suggestions," or "Nobody understands my ideas anyway so why bother saying them?" Then design and choose a new decision, such as, "My creative ideas are wanted and needed," or "Explaining new perspectives fulfills my true purpose," or "New ideas always seem strange and that is okay with me."

EMOTIONS FROM INCOMPLETE FEELINGS

As a child you had needs. Because parents are busy with modern life, many childhood needs go unmet. For example, if you needed to be picked up and safely snuggled and nurtured and that need was not fulfilled you probably felt angry, sad or scared about it. If no one listened to those feelings then they stayed incomplete in the muscles of your body and continue to this day to be experienced over and over again as recurring emotions about not being taken care of.

Emotions take your power away when you mistake them for feelings because emotions come from the past, and you are powerless in the past.

MAP OF HOW TO COMPLETE INCOMPLETE FEELINGS
World Copyright © 2010 owner Clinton Callahan grants permission to use. www.nextculture.org

Incomplete feelings that were never expressed or never heard and completed become emotions. You can complete your emotions through the high drama act of taking responsibility. This process requires a listening partner and takes five to fifty minutes, depending on the feeling skills and maturity of the partners, and also depending on the significance of the issues being addressed.

HOW TO COMPLETE INCOMPLETE FEELINGS

1. Usually the roles in this process are not reversed. One person is the experimenter who wishes to complete an incomplete feeling, and the other person is the listener/coach.

2. To find a coach the experimenter asks, "Would you help me complete some incomplete feelings?" If the answer is yes, you have your coach. By formally asking for help from the coach, the experimenter is not a victim/patient and the coach is not a rescuer/therapist. This is a transformational procedure of collaboration.

3. (NOTE: It could be that the experimenter's incomplete feelings apply to the coach personally. In this case, it is preferable to use the How to Clear Resentments process, explained in Chapter 6, "Communicating with Feelings.")

4. Arrange to use a space where you will not be disturbed even if you make some noise. Bring tissues, a plastic bucket, and a sturdy hand towel. Sit or stand facing each other.

5. The coach begins by saying, "There are two rules: Don't hurt yourself, and don't hurt anyone else. Do you agree?" Require the experimenter to answer with a clear verbal *Yes* or *No*. If the answer is, "Yes," you can proceed.

6. The coach says, "Trust your feelings and let them get bigger. Keep 10 percent of your adult present and let your feelings get 90 percent out of control."

7. Further coaching could be, "Do not try to figure this out. You can figure it out later. This process is about experiencing and communicating your incomplete feelings. If it feels too big, put your hands behind your back, grab one wrist with the other hand, then keep using your voice. What do you want to say?"

8. The moment the feelings are at their highest intensity, the coach says, "What is happening?"

9. The experimenter relates what is happening to cause that particular feeling, being as precise as he can. For example, the experimenter might say, "I feel so angry at my brother because he has friends and I don't!"

10. After each statement the coach repeats back what he hears, without analysis or judgment, seeking confirmation of accurate hearing (e.g., "You feel angry at your brother because he has friends and you don't" (said as a statement). "Yes."

11. The *Yes* signals that this communication has now been *heard and completed*, permitting the experimenter to go to their next deeper level of communication. The coach might ask, "Then what happened?"

12. Coach continues completing communication loops until the experimenter repeats himself, signalling that the core emotion has been heard and has vanished. When finished, the experimenter says, "Thanks for listening to me".

Whatever happened to cause the original unexpressed feelings cannot be changed. You can, however, change your relationship to the resultant emotions by completing your incomplete feelings.

The clues come from observing yourself to recognize patterns. When you detect that a feeling you have now is the same reaction that you have had at other times in similar circumstances, then you have identified an emotion!

The instant you detect your emotion, *change your purpose for communicating*. Instead of communicating to solve a problem—a problem which does not exist here and now—communicate with the purpose of completing incomplete feelings from the past to dissolve away your emotions.

Immediately STOP your present conversation. Say, "Excuse me, but I just noticed this is an emotion. It is not a feeling. It doesn't have anything to do with you or with what is happening right now. It is an incomplete feeling out of my past."

Then either with the same person or with someone else who is able to listen and complete communications with you, start an entirely different sort of conversation. The new conversation is an adult responsible conversation that completes incomplete feelings from the past. It is truly a transformational conversation. Say, "I would like to complete an old emotion from my past. Will you help me do this?" If the person says yes, then use the Map of How to Complete Incomplete Feelings.

YOUR SWORD OF CLARITY

Staying sovereign within yourself involves walking down life's streets centered and with your sword to hand. Not just any sword, but a flaming bright, ever active, diamond sharp, archetypal distinction sword that you *never* put away, even when you go to bed. This energetic sword of clarity has the capacity to distinguish between your true feelings and inauthentic or incomplete emotions.

Only you can hold within yourself this sword's level of alertness. No one else can do it for you. In many subtle ways modern society is against you having and using your sword of clarity. So the first use of your sword may be to untangle what in your life comes from mainstream society and what comes from your personal culture of integrity.

While sorting this out you may come to discover more of yourself outside of mainstream society than inside of it.

This is no surprise.

Modern culture is evolving, as all cultures do. Finding yourself acting, thinking, feeling and being beyond the limits of modern culture means that you are one of the leaders in its evolution, what Paul Ray and Sherry Anderson call a *cultural creative*. This will work out fine for you as long as you keep your sword of clarity at the ready.

One does not come by such a sword without a price. Gaining the capacity to hold and use an archetypal sword of clarity involves turning on (stellating) your four archetypes through a formal rite of passage from childhood to adulthood. That is the direction in which this book is heading, but we can't further explore these ideas until you know about (and hopefully gain skills in) consciously feeling and communicating with feelings. Practice using your sword of clarity when making boundaries, distinctions, decisions, and agreements; when starting, stopping or changing things; when keeping your center, keeping your attention, keeping your intentions; when holding space; when venturing into new levels of intimacy, and so on.

I mention these things before we can effectively talk about them in order to paint a picture of why it is important to build a solid basis in consciously feeling. Consciousness is built like a house, from the basement upward, not from the roof down. When constructing a house, much time and effort is invested erecting a proper basement and foundation before building anything above ground that much resembles a house. This is what you are doing right now: building substructure— building matrix to hold more consciousness.

While studying this book please keep in mind that learning to feel is not the end in itself. Consciously feeling is actually the beginning of entirely new ways of relating to yourself, to other people, and to your future. Without first learning to consciously feel you will not have the energy or the intelligence of your feelings as fuel for creating with your life what is truly within you to create. We are heading toward liberating and directing your unbounded creating.

FOURTH DISTINCTION: FEELINGS ARE COMPLETELY NEUTRAL

The fourth of the Ten Distinctions for Consciously Feeling says that feelings are absolutely neutral, neither good nor bad, neither positive nor negative. Feelings are feelings.

Did you ever have the impression that fear stopped you from creating? For example, were you ever too afraid to make a telephone call? Too nervous to talk to someone you wanted to meet? Too hesitant to say clearly and out loud what you really want? Too uncertain to make solid plans? Too uneasy to make a boundary? Too afraid to start a project? Take a trip? Ask someone to help you or join you?

Almost all of us can answer yes to at least a few of these questions. Given the Old Map of Four Feelings, where fear is one of the *bad* or *negative* feelings, it is no wonder that fear would stop us from proceeding. If fear is bad or negative, then when we feel afraid we stop, even if where we are afraid to go is the only place we really want to go!

Living your moment-to-moment feelings as sources of neutral energy and information rather than as negative or positive, good or bad, is quite a different view than was given to us by modern culture.

HURTING PEOPLE'S FEELINGS

Have you ever been manipulated into "walking on eggshells" around certain people so you do not "hurt their feelings"? It is a common trick, one of the eighteen standard Box defense strategies.

The poor fragile soul keeps you at a certain distance by threatening you with hair-trigger buttons that launch their emotions. If you succumb to their strategy in order to keep them from exploding in anger (the bully), shivering in fear (the china doll), or drowning in sadness (the crybaby), you are forced to give your center away, behaving as an adaptive child and sacrificing your clarity and power. That is a high price to pay to be around this poor fragile soul without disturbing them.

In the New Map of Four Feelings, you cannot *hurt* someone else's feelings.

If someone feels something, they are not *hurt*. They simply feel something.

Having a feeling is not a problem. Having a feeling is having neutral energy and information to use for living life closer to your own truth.

Feelings are feelings. No feeling hurts more or less than any other feeling. Did you ever smile until your cheeks ached? Or laugh 'til your sides hurt? Feeling glad hurts your face and sides just as feeling angry hurts your throat and fists, fear hurts your spine and neck, or sadness hurts your heart. Intense feeling sensations may be somewhat painful, but suffering is your own creation. In the end, feelings only hurt if you hold them in.

Instead of walking on eggshells around people, you can make it a practice to listen to what they feel and clearly repeat it back to them so they know that you heard what they said.

YOU CAN FEEL ANYTHING ABOUT ANYTHING

Modern culture suggests that if a person has a feeling it *means* something. But this ignores the easily observable fact that any person could come up with a reason to feel mad, sad, glad, or scared about anything, *and* that four different people could each feel differently about the same thing.

Here is an exercise that you can practice alone or with a partner whenever you get the chance. This exercise is part of your rite of passage into adulthood. In this exercise it becomes irrefutably clear that what you feel is no one else's fault. You take responsibility for creating your own feelings.

Sit across from someone and choose something—anything. Choose a person, place, or thing, a concept, a scratch on the wall, your tax bill, the sound of the ticking clock, the smell of a cup of coffee, the tiniest particle of dust, the hugest mountain. About each thing you can feel anger, sadness, fear and joy. It turns out that what you will experience in this exercise feels like a feeling but is actually an emotion. I will write out the exercise here as an example, but ordinarily these words are spoken. For the topic in this exercise I will choose "America." But as I suggested, you can choose a paper clip, a ceiling light, how cold or warm it is, the quality of a person's voice or smile, a leaf on a bush, a bicycle seat, anything, and the exercise still works.

Here we go.

The coach asks, "What do you think about America?"

"I think America is a young country of three hundred million people from mixed cultures who adopted the English language but drive on the right side of the road."

The coach says, "Thank you. What do you feel about America?" (This part of the exercise helps you distinguish thoughts from feelings. The only acceptable words to follow the answer, "I feel . . ." are the four feelings: *angry, sad, glad* or *scared*. Saying, "I feel like America should take the lead in shifting to sustainable culture" is a thought.)

"I feel angry about America."

The coach asks, "Why?"

"Because I think the organization that calls itself the government of the United States of America has been hijacked by corporate interests and is betraying the trust of the American people, and the people of the world. For example, after signing a United Nations agreement banning the use of Depleted Uranium (DU) weapons, the American military has illegally used tons of DU in all its wars since 1991. The radioactive DU dust already contaminates 8 percent of Earth's habitable land for 4.5 billion years and causes birth defects and multiple cancers, even in our own soldiers. America just sold a thousand more DU Bunker Buster bombs to Israel. This makes me angry at the American government."

The coach says, "Thank you. Is this anger a feeling or an emotion?"

"It is an emotion."

The coach asks, "Why?"

"Because I have felt betrayed by authority figures all my life. My first-grade teacher betrayed me by teaching me that learning was linear and boring. Feeling betrayed is familiar to me, almost expected."

The coach asks, "Okay then, could you feel sad about America?"

"Yes, I could feel sad about America."

The coach asks, "Why?"

"Because I had a vision that America was leading the world into a bright future and I have lost that vision. Now I see a psychopathic organization deceptively eliminating civil rights and profiteering in resource wars instead of creating a sustainable future for my children. This brings me great sadness."

The coach says, "Thank you. Is this sadness a feeling or an emotion?"

"Again, it is an emotion."

The coach asks, "Why?"

"I had a very clear vision when I was a child of a world that could work for everyone and it was shattered as soon as I was put in school. I was heartbroken, sad, and depressed."

The coach says, "Thank you. Could you feel scared about America?"

"Yes, I could feel scared about America."

The coach asks, "Why?"

"America's vast secret service agencies spend billions to big-brother the world and bring expedient demise to anyone who is regarded as a nuisance. The six hundred fully operational FEMA detention centers spread throughout the USA built by Halliburton Corporation send shivers of fear down my spine."

The coach says, "Thank you. Is this fear a feeling or an emotion?"

"Again, this is an emotion."

The coach asks, "Why?"

"I noticed as a child how mainstream culture reacts threateningly toward thoughts or actions that originate beyond its definitions of normalcy. The hysterical reactions of a mindless mob have always frightened me."

The coach says, "Thank you. Could you feel glad about America?"

"Oh, yes! I could feel glad about America."

The coach asks, "Why?"

"American freedom of thought and social entrepreneurship inspired me to create anything I wanted to create as soon as I left my parents' house. I have been experimenting my whole adult life. The courage to explore the unknown came from my father and from so many American men that I as a man could love and respect: Martin Luther King Jr, Thomas Edison, Alexander Graham Bell, the Wright brothers, Harry Houdini, Abraham Lincoln, Walt Disney, Robert Heinlein. I was also very glad about America's 1962 World's Fair in Seattle."

The coach says, "Thank you. Is this joy a feeling or an emotion?"

"This too is emotion."

The coach asks, "Why?"

"Because the examples I thought of to feel glad about America are all examples that fit my preexisting fantasy worlds. The fantasy worlds come from my past. Whenever I want to feel glad about America I only need to select inspiring examples that match my pleasing fantasy images."

So, here we are. The exercise is complete. It is clear that I could feel emotional anger, sadness, fear and joy about this thing called America and, in fact, about anything. These are not merely thoughts. I could actually feel the feelings in my body.

Where do the emotional sensations come from?

They come from me. They do not come from the thing, and not from the circumstances. The way I create the emotions is by carefully choosing a thought or an image for my mind's eye. Whatever meaning I give to my thought or image determines the emotion I will feel. The thought comes first, and then my emotions follow a few seconds later. I choose my thoughts to induce emotions that support the conscious (or, more likely, unconscious) purpose of the story I am telling.

Recognizing and taking ownership of the mechanism through which you create your own emotions is an act of radical responsibility.

EXPERIENCE COMES WITHOUT THOUGHTS ATTACHED

In contrast to decidedly nonneutral emotions, *feelings* are *neutral* experiences of energy and information needed for fulfilling your destiny in this particular moment.

Experience comes without a meaning attached. The same experience presented to ten people provides ten different interpretations. The interpretations come through adding a thought to the experience. It is the thought that calls up emotions.

For example, some people love to eat durian, a large spiked tropical fruit that tastes like a mixture of sweet coffee and onions. Some people hate even the smell of durian. The actual experience of smelling a durian is neutral. Liking or not liking the smell is story. Associating story with an experience follows a purpose. This leads to a valuable question that can be ongoingly asked of each thought, word or deed: is the purpose of this action conscious or unconscious? What is my purpose?

A hint is that if an interpretation becomes a preference or, stronger yet, hardens into prejudice, intolerance or dogma, the purpose behind seeing things that way is probably still unconscious.

FINDING THE PURPOSE OF AN INTERPRETATION

It can become an informative practice to follow interpretations back to their original purpose. This makes the purpose conscious. Even if the purpose is not a pretty sight, once the purpose is conscious it frees the interpreter to choose a new interpretation.

To continue the durian example, when I first tasted this amazing tropical fruit I did not like it. My purpose was to enjoy my experience, but the durian was, at first, not pleasurable to my taste. The second time I tasted durian I noticed it was breaking my taste combination expectations. I did not like it but it nurtured me. The third time I tasted durian I loved it. My interpretation of the experience of eating durian changed around completely during three trials in as many weeks.

For another example, all during my childhood I blocked any connections to my youngest brother. He was two-and-a-half years younger and, for the most part, a total stranger to me. The block was still in place even after we had become adults. I used my interpretation of my brother's behaviors as the reason to stay away from him, but I did not know why. At one point, some years after participating in my first training, I followed my interpretation of my brother's behavior back to my interpretation's original purpose. I found that my original purpose was to be perceived by my parents and teachers as a *good boy*. Since my brother often behaved in ways both I and my parents considered to be typical of a *bad boy*, I had to stay away from him. In the moment my purpose for blocking him became conscious I did not have to block him anymore because I had grown out of needing to be a *good boy*. My old purpose no longer applied. My brother and I have now become good friends.

INTERPRETATION OF FEAR

Preferences also apply to feelings. Take, for example, fear.

Some people love to feel afraid. Fear-lovers stand in line for hours to ride a roller coaster. They also speed down the highway, gamble their money in the commodities market, have sex with strangers, or insult people with big fists and small brains.

Some people hate feeling afraid. Security-lovers stay at home for hours not wanting to face anything unexpected. They buy more insurance, know the telephone number of their lawyer, already have their vacation reservations for next year, and order the same thing at the same restaurant each visit.

Some people neither love nor hate to feel afraid. Fear is a natural feeling in their life, one of their four feelings. Life-lovers feel their subtle and intense feelings when they arise and they follow them back to their source. They take fear as neutral energy and information and use it to navigate and impassion their life.

Which emotion arises in any given circumstance depends entirely on which particular thought and story you attach to the circumstance. The universe might be happening all around you in a pure and neutral form, but you are a human being, and human beings are storytellers. What if you took responsibility for your power to weave stories?

IS-GLUE

How do you attach meaning to experience? When something happens, how do you make it into a story? How do you decide what something means?

The human mind has an uncanny ability to imagine things that are not so. For example, we can easily imagine *never*, as in, "You never take me out dancing!"

Never is a really long time.

We easily imagine *always*, as in, "Why do I always have to wipe the mirror clean?"

We easily imagine perfection. For example, we can imagine a sphere—all points equidistant from a single point in space. But, in fact, there are no perfect spheres anywhere in the universe. They are all approximations. The smoothest ball bearing, bubble, or glass bead looks like the Grand Canyon when you inspect it under high magnification. The Earth is not a ball. It is pear-shaped, and its shape is not stable. For example, as the ice melts off Greenland, the whole land mass is floating upward, gaining four centimeters per year in altitude!

There is nothing perfect in the physical world. Everything changes, vibrates, grows, evolves, rusts or rots. Our concepts serve as thought models for everything important in our reality. We imagine our theoretical image more easily than we perceive the actual conditions, and then we superimpose our concept over the actuality.

For example, you can effortlessly conceive of one apple in your imagination, but no discreet single apple actually exists! Apples are one element of an ecological system, an entire biosphere of soil, rain, sun, air, honeybees and apple trees. A shiny Red Delicious apple sitting on the table is not still life. It is alive: busily ripening, defending itself from bacterial and fungal infections, and furiously pumping out methyl butyrate esters—fruity apple scents—to entice you to eat it so you deposit fertilized apple seeds in a place where a new apple tree can grow. Human beings are transport systems used by apple DNA to make more apple DNA. In our complex and flowing, multidimensional universe there is no such thing as *one*, except as a pure concept.

Perhaps the most pervasive and distorting application of human imagination is the concept of *is*. In nature there is no *is*.

Is is a concept of the human mind that allows humans to make stories. Stories are the basis of our personality, relationships, philosophies, technologies, and the domains of life included in our multiplicity of cultures, daily activities, rituals, customs and beliefs. Without stories, what we regard as humanity would not exist. But without humans there would be no stories!

To assemble our stories we use conjugations of the word *is*: am, are, was, were, along with the modal and auxiliary verbs—has, have, had, do, does, did, may, might, must, can, could, should, would, shall, and will, and also the *not* forms, such as *is not, am not, are not*, and so on.

These concepts function as a *glue* that holds two completely unrelated things together in a story that would not stay together without the glue, such as, *I am angry. That is scary. This job is impossible. Bob is a jerk. Dave is my sweetheart. They are evil. This is a great book.* As much as you might want to believe that the stories you just made up are not stories but the irrefutable truth, they are nothing more than stories created with Is-Glue. *You* created them. Without you putting two things together with Is-Glue there would be no story.

For example, the two unrelated things in the first sentence above, *I am angry*, are the *I*, and the *angry*. The *am* is the Is-Glue. The *I* part and the *angry* part are not connected at all until the Is-Glue is applied to hold them together. If the two things are left disconnected, then the *I* remains as *I*, and the experience of *anger* is regarded like this: *anger arises*. The anger comes and passes, retaining its neutrality without meaning anything in particular.

When feelings are respected as neutral they have more chance of being authentic feelings rather than emotions with all their entangled meanings. Authentic anger can then, for example, provide energy and information to ask for what you want, make boundaries, start something, stop something, make a distinction, make a decision, and so on.

Imagine not being aware of Is-Glue!

Imagine how the stories unconsciously created by your Box would automatically establish:

- Expectations (You should . . .; I must . . .)
- Projections (You are . . . ; You can't . . .)
- Beliefs (Thou shalt not . . .; It is . . .; I am . . .)
- Interpretations (We have to . . .; We cannot . . .; There won't be . . .)
- Assumptions (I am . . .; I have to . . .; They will . . .)
- Conclusions (There isn't . . .; I'm not . . .; They must . . .)

Your daily life, relationships and possibilities are framed up within the thousand Is-Glued stories that support the positions of your Box.

Without knowledge of Is-Glue you regard your expectations, projections, beliefs, etc., as rock-solid truths rather than as tissue paper–thin fabrications as flimsy as the wind. You would then also regard the other person's stories as equally solid. When two solidly *true* stories disagree about the "truth," the result is war. Look at human history.

Without recognizing Is-Glue your stories have the power to force your whole life to circle round and round within past patterns, not recognizing that something completely different from this is possible right now for you.

Is-Glued stories include:

- I am the best.
- I am the prettiest.
- I am the smartest.
- I am the fastest.
- I cannot do what I really want to do.
- I must play the roles offered by society.
- I am powerless.
- I am sneaky enough to get what I want anyway.
- I can scam the rules.
- I am exhausted.
- I can't do this.
- It is impossible.
- It is too easy.
- I am bored.
- Men are like that.
- Women are like that.
- Americans are like that.
- I am lonely.
- Nobody does understand me.
- Relationships don't really work for me.
- My parents are the problem.

MAP OF IS-GLUE AND IS-GLUE DISSOLVER

Humans live confined within stories. Stories are assembled using the concept of *is* to attach meaning to incidents. The resultant feelings then confirm the truth of the story we just made up. Is-Glue uses: is, am, are, was, were, etc., and also the *not* forms, such as *is not, am not,* etc. Here are some samples: John IS a jerk! This IS impossible. I CAN'T do this. I AM exhausted. The weather IS terrible. I AM angry. I AM scared. This IS a wonderful day. We ARE a great team.

Fortunately, things need not stay Is-Glued forever. Next to the Is-Glue on your nonlinear tool belt you have *Is-Glue Dissolver,* which you can use to reinvent your stories about yourself, other people, and the world. For example, you can say, "I have changed my mind. I withdraw my previous assertion that I am not a good singer. My new story is: I sing in my own voice." Then tell your new story to three different people today.

- My boss is the problem.

- My neighbors are the problem.

- My children are the problem.

- The government is the problem.

- My partner is not really interested in me.

- I don't have enough time for myself.

- It is always like this.

- I am not good enough.

- There is no way out of this.

And on and on and on and on and on and on and on, all day and all night, confined exactly to the limits of the stories you tell.

As you become more and more aware of how precisely stories define your life, you may develop an urge to modify some of them.

IS-GLUE DISSOLVER

Fortunately for you, next to the tube of Is-Glue on your nonlinear tool belt is a spray bottle full of *Is-Glue Dissolver*. With Is-Glue Dissolver you can Pfffft! Pfffft! the Is-Glue and it releases its grip. Story components disconnect and you can replace them with entirely new elements.

Applying Is-Glue Dissolver is most effective if you first distill the original story down to its essential form. For example, if the story confronting you has something to do with not being successful because of how long it takes for you to learn things compared to other people, who seem to get it much faster than you, write the story down in its simplest Is-Glued formulation. In this example the distilled story might be, *I am a slow learner*. The *I* and the *slow learner* are the two components that are held together with the Is-Glue *am*.

While distilling the elements of your story you may experience memory flashes of incidents that have long been unconsciously used to support your story. Try to notice the memory flashes in detail and admit how formative they have been. These memories are the evidence you used to convince yourself that your old story was a *true* story.

You've been assuming that your story is true . . .

You thought it was a true story . . .

Here we come to an interesting question. How could a *story* be true??? Stories are stories! Made up out of Is-Glue! You make them yourself. With Is-Glue Dissolver you can now remake them yourself.

Spray your old story with Is-Glue Dissolver. The two parts slide easily away from each other. Suddenly you have the *I* part of the story in one hand and the *slow learner* part of the story in the other hand. The *am* has been dissolved.

Keep the *I* part of the story. You will need it for your new story. Put the *slow learner* part of the old story on a mental shelf. (You can always Is-Glue your story back the old way if you are not satisfied with how the new story turns out.)

Then reach into an imaginary *Bag of Things* on your nonlinear tool belt and pull out something else to Is-Glue to the *I*. Choose something that empowers you. For example, *I . . . am . . . a thorough learner.*

Does this new story empower you? Yes. Can you find memory flashes to use as evidence for valuing yourself as a thorough learner? Yes. The world is rich in evidence. There is evidence to support *any* story you might want to create for yourself. So there is evidence to support the story that you are a thorough learner. Recognizing stories as reinventable changes them from prison bars to vehicles for exploring new territories.

Once you have Is-Glued your new story together find someone and say, "I have changed my mind about myself. I withdraw my previous assertion that I am a slow learner. My new story is: I am a thorough learner."

Then tell only your *new* story to three additional people today; just add it as a sideways comment into any conversation—even with a grocery store check-out clerk. Just say, "I've realized that I am a thorough learner. That's why I bought these potatoes."

Then at night when you are brushing your teeth, look at yourself in the mirror and say to yourself: "I am a thorough learner. Hi there, thorough learner!"

Keep practicing your skills of reinventing stories. For example:

- I can actually do whatever I really want to do.

- Relationships are a rapid-learning environment for me.

- I can take on different roles from those offered by society.

- I have my center, my sword of clarity, and my power back.

- It is hopeless the way it is. It cannot continue this way. This is a good thing.

- My problems are the procedure of my own development.

- Learning why I stay stuck is the way to freedom.

- It is always a new opportunity.

- I am well engaged.

- I can try again and again to do this, and along the way I can ask anybody for help.

- It is not impossible. It is what it is.

- My parents are representatives of all previous wisdom.

- My boss shows commitment to his Box's perceptions.

- My neighbors live in a culture of diverse intelligences.

- My children are finding their way into an uncertain future.

- The government only has the power that I grant to it. I can withdraw that power.

- My partner also has the ability to reinvent stories.

- I have faith that something useful is emerging from my life.

- There is no way out of the here and now.

On and on and on and on and on and on and on, all day and all night reinventing stories so they form stepping stones into a bright and interesting future.

Three cheers for Is-Glue Dissolver!

REWIRING FEELINGS

Now that you have clarity about Is-Glue and Is-Glue Dissolver you can use it to *rewire* the Old Map of Four Feelings that we examined in the previous chapter. Rewiring a thoughtmap is exactly what each person did five hundred years ago when they shifted from a flat-world map to a round-world map. Just as it changed the world for our ancestors, rewiring a thoughtmap can change the way the whole world works for you. It is a significant action.

No one else can do this action for you. If you want the new results you will need to do the thoughtmap shift yourself. It is internal self-surgery. To rewire a thoughtmap, first identify the specifics of your present way of thinking. How does it look to you now? How do things always go? How is it supposed to be? It may help to draw the connections out on a piece of paper.

Once you can see your present thoughtmap in front of you, use Is-Glue Dissolver to disconnect the details of the old thoughtmap from the stories that disempower you. Then use Is-Glue to connect the same details to new meanings that provide greater utility, more freedom of movement, more options, more love, more joy, and so on.

For example, on the Old Map of Four Feelings, one detail is the assumption that substantiates the entire thoughtmap: *It is not okay to feel.* Reduced to its minimum, the old story about feelings is: *feeling is not okay.* The experience called *feeling* is fastened to the meaning *not okay* using the Is-Glue *is.* To create a New Map of Four Feelings you would begin by rewiring the underlying assumption so that it carries a new story.

If you energetically reach deep into every bone, muscle and tissue of your body and thoroughly pull out this story with your two hands and hold it before you at arm's length (*feeling is not okay*). Then you can spray it (lightly) with Is-Glue Dissolver (Pfffft! Pfffft!). Without effort the two components come apart. You end up with *feeling* in your left hand, and *not okay* in your right hand. Nothing holds them together anymore. The *is* is gone.

You can place the *not okay* part on a mental shelf to your right so it remains available for reuse if you ever want to have the old story back. The *feeling* part remains in your left hand. The question then arises: what could you Is-Glue *feelings* to that would open doors to vast new areas of energy and wisdom?

How about this: *feelings are okay.*

That is one possible story; it certainly counteracts the *not okay* from the old story, but the new story it creates is not so exciting . . .

You have a tremendous freedom of movement when there is no story binding you. Let's take a moment to explore a bit. What about choosing a particularly extraordinary story? Something that would let you apply the energy and information of your feelings in the most critical of situations?

What about this: *feelings (do) serve me professionally.* Could that work?

If you want to try out this new story, apply just a dab of Is-Glue to the *feelings,* still held in your left hand. The particular conjugation of Is-Glue to use is the unspoken word *do.* Then slam the two components of your new story together (splat).

There, you have it! You have reinvented your story about feelings. Your new story is: *Feelings (do) serve me professionally.* Very cool! This will be the basis for our New Map of Four Feelings.

REWIRING FEAR

Before getting to the main new feelings map, let us first do a further experiment in rewiring. Let us rewire the meaning of the experience of fear.

On the Old Map of Four Feelings whenever you experience fear its associated meanings cause you to rebound from whatever it is that caused the fear. For example, if a strange person approaches you while you are walking on the sidewalk you look away. If a loud sound happens you may jump or scream. If a problem appears to be overwhelming (e.g., starving children in America, women sex slaves in the Middle East, an AIDS epidemic in Russia, involuntary organ donors in Chinese prisons), you probably won't even see it. This is because these things are frightful, and fear is to be avoided.

For most people fear is hardwired at a deep level to mean *bad, negative, dangerous, watch out, go back, I'll get hurt, I will die,* and so on. Creepy, dark, hairy monsters with sharp claws and stinking breath are about to tear your guts out and eat them . . . that sort of thing. Fear is *bad.* It isn't the experience of fear but the meaning of fear that stops you.

This knee-jerk reaction when you have the experience of fear is what keeps you away from the edges of your Box. You don't live in your whole Box. You live in the center of your Box, in the sweet, familiar, comfortable, controlled [boring, dead] marshmallow zone of your Box. Probably ten times a day something brings you to the edge of your Box, where, if you stayed there, you would have a new experience and your Box would expand. Instead you bounce away from the frightening edges back into the marshmallow zone of your Box so fast that you likely don't even notice you were at an edge.

Something can be done about the way fear is wired in your mind. The first step is to look at the way you have it wired now. Spend a few minutes jotting down what fear is for you. How does fear make you stop doing what you want to do? What does fear mean to you? Does it mean uncertainty? Sudden death? Loud shouting? Danger? When fear rises up your spine, what is your response? Write these down.

This is how you have fear wired in your mind, in your soul. Look at what you wrote. Visualize the wire that connects your experience of fear to one or more of these interpretations about what the fear means.

Now imagine that you can simply snip the connection with a small pair of cutting pliers. This gives you freedom to move the fear end of the wire to a new meaning and to solder it there. What meaning would you choose? The Map of Rewiring the Feeling of Fear provides a visual guide in case you wish to do this rewiring surgery on yourself now.

THE LIQUID STATE

While you perform the changeover surgery from, for example, *Fear is dangerous* to *Fear is fear*, there will be a short in-between state during which time the experience of fear is not wired to any meaning at all. Try to notice when this is happening. Your in-between state may feel like a momentary dizziness, confusion, uncertainty, perhaps even nausea. This *liquid state* is important because if there is no liquid state, things are not at liberty to reorder themselves in relationship to each other. Without a liquid state there would be no real change of your Box.

The middle time—after the old meaning is cut away and before the new meaning is soldered on—is a crucial stage in any authentic

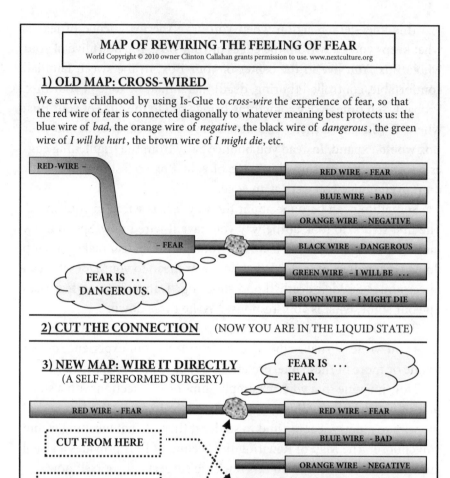

MAP OF REWIRING THE FEELING OF FEAR
World Copyright © 2010 owner Clinton Callahan grants permission to use. www.nextculture.org

1) OLD MAP: CROSS-WIRED

We survive childhood by using Is-Glue to *cross-wire* the experience of fear, so that the red wire of fear is connected diagonally to whatever meaning best protects us: the blue wire of *bad*, the orange wire of *negative*, the black wire of *dangerous*, the green wire of *I will be hurt*, the brown wire of *I might die*, etc.

RED-WIRE –

– FEAR

FEAR IS ... DANGEROUS.

RED WIRE - FEAR
BLUE WIRE - BAD
ORANGE WIRE - NEGATIVE
BLACK WIRE - DANGEROUS
GREEN WIRE – I WILL BE ...
BROWN WIRE – I MIGHT DIE

2) CUT THE CONNECTION   (NOW YOU ARE IN THE LIQUID STATE)

3) NEW MAP: WIRE IT DIRECTLY
(A SELF-PERFORMED SURGERY)

FEAR IS ... FEAR.

RED WIRE - FEAR

CUT FROM HERE

RECONNECT HERE

RED WIRE - FEAR
BLUE WIRE - BAD
ORANGE WIRE - NEGATIVE
BLACK WIRE - DANGEROUS

As an adult you have the option of using Is-Glue Dissolver to disconnect your childhood wiring and to use Is-Glue to rewire what fear means to you. This is a form of self-surgery. No one can do it for you. One particular rewiring is astonishingly powerful: when you attach the *red wire* of fear directly across to the *red wire* of fear. Then when you feel afraid, you get the information *fear is fear* (which also just happens to be the truth). In your neutral experience you choose how to use the energy and information of the fear, such as to pay attention, create something out of nothing, innovate, take precautions, plan ahead, give a warning, ask nonlinear questions, etc.

transformational process. Therefore, liquid states in any of the four bodies (physical, intellectual, emotional or energetic) will be a significant element during the years of your rite of passage into adulthood.

It can help if you develop a new strategy for using liquid states that may at first seem counterintuitive, particularly to the Box. Whenever you get the chance, whenever the door opens, navigate to the liquid state.

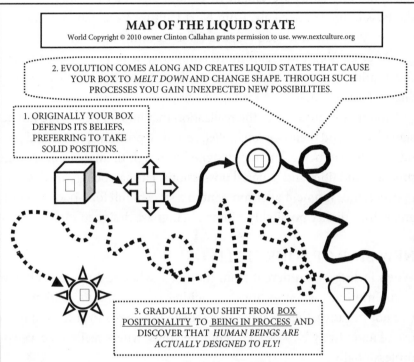

MAP OF THE LIQUID STATE

World Copyright © 2010 owner Clinton Callahan grants permission to use. www.nextculture.org

2. EVOLUTION COMES ALONG AND CREATES LIQUID STATES THAT CAUSE YOUR BOX TO *MELT DOWN* AND CHANGE SHAPE. THROUGH SUCH PROCESSES YOU GAIN UNEXPECTED NEW POSSIBILITIES.

1. ORIGINALLY YOUR BOX DEFENDS ITS BELIEFS, PREFERRING TO TAKE SOLID POSITIONS.

3. GRADUALLY YOU SHIFT FROM <u>BOX POSITIONALITY</u> TO <u>BEING IN PROCESS</u> AND DISCOVER THAT *HUMAN BEINGS ARE ACTUALLY DESIGNED TO FLY!*

Shifting shape from Box A to Box B is traumatic enough. The physical, intellectual, emotional or spiritual liquid states are scary and uncomfortable. Your Box quickly reestablishes rigidity in its new form and builds stories to support its new views from Box B. One day the fog lifts at the horizon and it becomes apparent that there exists a Box C. What? Nobody ever told you about Box C! That's because Box C cannot be seen from Box A; it only comes into view from Box B. "I wonder what that could be about?" you wonder. Soon your curiosity gets the best of you and you make the leap. Again you enter the liquid state. Again your Box changes shape, and soon you find yourself in Box C. Only this time the journey through the liquid state took a little longer. And Box C is smaller and less stable than Box B. The smoke settles and the dust clears. Then over the next horizon a new image comes into view. "Oh my God! Box D? Inconceivable! Who ever heard of a Box D? I wonder what is over there?" The liquid state comes a little easier this time. The pattern of solid to liquid feels more familiar. After a few more times you are headed for Box L. At that point the length of time *between* solid states becomes longer than the time resting in any particular form. Your strategy shifts away from being oriented toward the defensive positionality of form and toward the expansive process of formlessness. In this moment you discover through experience that *the nature of reality is groundlessness* (P. Chödrön), and that human beings are actually designed to fly!

Within a short time, even a few months, you will gain enough personal experience with liquid states to be able to hold a safe space for other people to navigate through their own liquid states. (Advanced space-holding skills are taught in certain rigorous trainings, such as the Possibility Trainer Labs from Next Culture Research and Training Center. We sometimes call it Space Pilot Training School.)

After gaining more and more familiarity with navigating through the liquid state you may actually come to enjoy this experience. Groundlessness may start feeling like home.

You may even come to the realization that human beings are not designed to defend their religious beliefs, political positions, or cultural prejudices. Human beings are not designed to weigh themselves down with property and titles and material possessions. Human beings are designed to experience moment after moment in a state of full four-body intensity and extraordinary possibility. Human beings are designed to fly.

NEW MAP OF FOUR FEELINGS

When feelings are different from thoughts, when feelings are different from emotions, when feelings are neither good nor bad, neither positive nor negative, then you have established the basis to enter and make use of an entirely New Map of Four Feelings, where feelings serve you professionally.

How can you use the neutral energy and information of anger? Use it to start projects, end projects, clean up the garage or your love life, make boundaries, ask for what you want, ask for help, finish tasks even if you have to stay up all night, make yes or no decisions, speak with clarity, commit to a job before you know how to do the job, commit to finding answers before you know where to look. Would these serve you professionally?

What about sadness? How can you use the neutral energy and information of sadness? Use it to open up, share yourself, connect with others, listen to their sincere wishes, let the past go, be vulnerable, be authentic, drop the lonely-wolf tough-guy show, become trustworthy, make strong communications with compassion, acknowledge the truth of what is going on, find brotherhood and sisterhood, bond with other human beings, find acceptance, find your place in a team of people, build community, receive recognition and appreciation and give this to others. Would these serve you professionally?

NEW MAP OF FOUR FEELINGS
World Copyright © 2010 owner Clinton Callahan grants permission to use. www.nextculture.org

ASSUMPTION: *FEELINGS SERVE ME PROFESSIONALLY*

WITH *ANGER* YOU CAN:
say no, say yes, start things, stop things, change things, clean out and get rid of things, create clarity, recognize unfairness, make boundaries, maintain integrity, show intention, make decisions, keep promises, hold space, pay attention, self-observe, ask for what you want, take a stand for something or someone, protect, take actions.

WITH *SADNESS* YOU CAN:
open up, share, be vulnerable, be still, accept things, let things go, grieve, give in, get healed, listen, contemplate, be spacious, connect, recognize pain, be authentic, finish things up, mourn, be wrong, be human, be silent, care, take a supportive position, be intimate, be invisible.

WITH *JOY* YOU CAN:
be enthusiastic, inspire others, have vision, go ahead, enjoy possibilities, take adventures, experiment, discover, accept discomforts or hardships, dance through problems, be kind, be generous, support team spirit, inspire people to keep going, lead, be playful, be easeful, appreciate people for no reason.

WITH *FEAR* YOU CAN:
detect danger, measure risks, concentrate, be curious, make plans, avoid disasters, stay centered, make agreements, handle details, pay attention, be precise, ask dangerous questions, innovate, make mistakes, go nonlinear, stand there in the nothing and improvise, stay present, be alert, face the unknowable future.

What about fear? How can you use the neutral energy and information of fear? Use it to trust your sense of danger so you can go first into unknown territory and make it safe for others to follow, take precautionary actions, plan ahead, make clear agreements, stay awake and attentive, take care of details, act with precision, detect subtle needs, manage delicate maneuvers, go to the edge of your Box or your organization's Box and take important calculated risks, learn new things, discover, explore, innovate, step into the unknown and create something that has never been created before, listen to more than you can understand, and serve something greater than yourself by providing what is wanted and needed even if you don't know how. Would these serve you professionally?

What about joy? How can you use the neutral energy and information of joy? Use it to say hello and make contact with people—even people you don't know yet. Use it to celebrate those three-second moments of happiness that occur among all the moments of life's business: that freshly dusted countertop, that smile. Use it to be present and okay with yourself for no reason; to step into your own power by choosing what is, to say yes to life, to be open to nonlinear opportunities and go play. Use it to include diversity, empower others, be a leader maker, heal, appreciate, find ways through, and embrace the strength and intelligence of conscious feelings for living a life closer to your own truth. Would these feelings serve you professionally?

If so, you have just taken possession of a new map of the world of feelings.

What about feelings of depression, despair, melancholy, hysteria, *schadenfreude*? What about jealousy? Greed? Superiority? Inferiority? Shame? Guilt? What about rage fits? Panic attacks? Emotional collapse? Would it be okay for you to live without these? Would it be interesting for you to be able to help other people gain clarity and freedom from these debilitating experiences in their lives? Could you see yourself doing this professionally to help people through the coming changes? Then you are ready for the next of the Ten Distinctions.

FIFTH DISTINCTION: FEELINGS ARE MOST POWERFUL IN THEIR PURE FORM

The fifth of the Ten Distinctions for Consciously Feeling says that feelings serve you most powerfully in their pure form, not mixed with each other. Much disempowerment occurs through unconsciously mixing the four root feelings together.

For example, when you mix anger and sadness together you will have an experience known as depression. Depression is simply the name that has been given to what it feels like to blend anger with sadness. You can have the experience of depression any time you want simply by mixing anger and sadness together. You can also end the experience of depression any time you want simply by separating the anger and sadness from each other and experiencing and expressing each of them in their pure form. The same is true for the other feeling mixes, as is shown in the Map of Mixed Feelings.

Mixing sadness and fear creates isolation or despair.

Mixing anger and fear creates frenzy or hysteria.

Mixing sadness and joy creates nostalgia, sentimentality or melancholy.

Mixing joy and fear creates excitement or careless risk taking.

Mixing anger and joy creates schadenfreude: feeling glad when someone else loses or feels pain.

Mixing three feelings together creates sensations that are particularly gripping, such as superiority, jealousy, greed, envy, guilt, shame, vengeance, and lack of self-esteem. Because three feelings are involved and the sensations are so strong, it can seem as if the situation is unresolvable. Yet three-feeling mixes can also be directly unmixed.

Mixing four feelings together is what causes *burnout*—emotional paralysis and psychological breakdown—a very confusing, disempowering and disturbing experience. Yet even these states can be easily and suddenly transformed when the feelings are separated and experienced in their pure form.

I have seen this demonstrated in remarkable fashion innumerable times when persons suffering from near catatonia by mixing together three or four feelings went through the short guided process of respectfully separating their feelings one from the other. These people suddenly regained levels of functionality and relationship they had not experienced in years, if ever.

This is a revolutionary discovery, as yet unknown in modern society. Even healing practitioners, for the most part, do not yet teach the simple inner navigation skills of separating the feelings. And they could.

Although largely unknown in mainstream culture, having clarity about mixed feelings is a cornerstone of next culture. If you are a psychotherapist, mediator, trainer, consultant, healer or nurse and you demand that your clients separate their feelings while they communicate, you may be shocked by how effectively this procedure brings a person back into their own natural health and sanity.

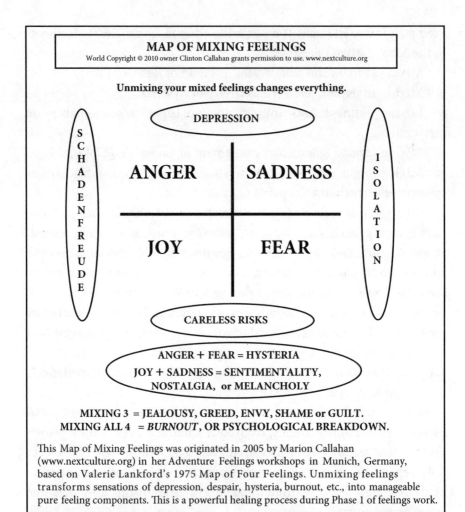

MAP OF MIXING FEELINGS
World Copyright © 2010 owner Clinton Callahan grants permission to use. www.nextculture.org

Unmixing your mixed feelings changes everything.

DEPRESSION

SCHADENFREUDE

ANGER | SADNESS

ISOLATION

JOY | FEAR

CARELESS RISKS

ANGER + FEAR = HYSTERIA
JOY + SADNESS = SENTIMENTALITY,
NOSTALGIA, or MELANCHOLY

MIXING 3 = JEALOUSY, GREED, ENVY, SHAME or GUILT.
MIXING ALL 4 = *BURNOUT*, OR PSYCHOLOGICAL BREAKDOWN.

This Map of Mixing Feelings was originated in 2005 by Marion Callahan (www.nextculture.org) in her Adventure Feelings workshops in Munich, Germany, based on Valerie Lankford's 1975 Map of Four Feelings. Unmixing feelings transforms sensations of depression, despair, hysteria, burnout, etc., into manageable pure feeling components. This is a powerful healing process during Phase 1 of feelings work.

Here is a scary question: how many people take brain drugs or are locked away in institutions simply because they submit themselves to the belief system of a society that does not yet have clarity about mixed feelings?

Bringing feelings clarity into mainstream society starts with teaching teachers. If you care about children then you have a job on your bench: find ways to require teachers in modern-society schools to gain adult level feeling skills and communications training as elements of their qualification before being certified to work as a teacher.

UNMIXING YOUR FEELINGS

No one can unmix your feelings for you. It is a job you do yourself, internally. At the same time, please keep in mind that the idea of unmixing feelings is most likely new for you. Modern society has provided very few if any examples of feelings clarity during your lifetime. Unless you are in a workshop or training where people are using and teaching the tools and techniques of Possibility Management, you are on your own in fresh territory. But don't worry. *You can do this*. It is simple. You can unmix your feelings by learning and using inner navigation skills.

The following series of photos demonstrates the procedure for unmixing depression. Unmixing other combinations of two, three, or four feelings is done in the same way, although the mixture of feelings may be different.

In the first moment that you notice your feelings are mixed and you are experiencing the telltale results, such as depression, melancholy, despair, hysteria, shame, jealousy, or guilt, stop whatever you are doing and unmix your feelings—unless, of course, you prefer to keep feeling the sensations of mixed feelings. Mixed feelings are not bad or wrong. They simply produce certain results, both personally and interpersonally.

If you want those results, keep your feelings mixed. If you want other results, unmix your feelings.

Set aside a few minutes of time in a place where you can feel big feelings and perhaps make some noise without bothering too many people. If people are around, simply inform them that you will be doing some feelings work and that you might make some sounds, but you will be done in a few minutes and you will be okay.

Then, with eyes open or closed, energetically extend your entwined fingers deep into your chest and start untangling your anger from your sadness like separating two colors of spaghetti noodles.

To unmix depression, pull your anger (red spaghetti) into your right hand and your sadness (blue spaghetti) into your left hand. Take your time. This is done for real, not by thinking about it. It can be painful and quite intense. Separate your feelings through experiential distinctions.

When your feelings are cleanly separated, hold them outside of you and put one of your feelings, in this case your sadness, on an imaginary

shelf to your left. You will come back to it in a moment. Now pull the pure anger back into your body to receive the benefit of its energy and wisdom.

Yes, you will feel angry. Let your anger inform you precisely what you are angry about and what you need to do about it, if anything, such as make boundaries, new decisions, changes, etc.

Now reach in with your right hand. Take your anger out. Put it on an imaginary shelf to your right. Use your left hand to reach out and grab hold of your sadness from its shelf. Slowly bring your sadness into your chest and feel it as it comes.

Yes, you will feel sad. Allow your sadness to inform you exactly what you feel sad about and what you may need to do about it, such as grieve, make contact, accept, etc. Please note that you may feel sad about the same things you feel angry about, or something entirely different. Respect your sadness. It can help tremendously if someone is with you while separating your feelings to hear or even write down what you are angry about and what you are sad about.

You may be surprised to find that after so recently feeling pure anger and pure sadness, your new clarity and power from consciously feeling results in great joy. No, you are not crazy. These are feelings, not emotions. Emotions go on and on for minutes, hours, days or weeks. Feelings come up, and after their information and energy are used they can simply vanish. Then comes true adult joy!

Unmixing your feelings requires an inner process of distinguishing among the four feelings, and also noticing when they are not distinguished. These are times when you may feel powerless, discouraged, confused, and without the desire to participate.

MAP OF HOW TO UNMIX MIXED FEELINGS

The four primary feelings – mad, sad, glad, and scared – are useful and empowering when felt in their pure form. Mixing feelings is not bad or wrong; it simply creates certain disempowering results, such as superiority, lack of self-esteem, confusion, or depression. Modern culture does not want its citizens empowered to think and feel independently or it would provide an entirely different educational system. Next culture requires clear feelings from you. Your first steps into next culture may well be through unmixing your feelings.

Phase 1 of feelings work includes unmixing feelings two, three or four at a time. For this example we will unmix *anger* and *sadness*, which when mixed cause the sensation of *depression*. Mixing anger with sadness is like mixing cow poop and milk. Cow poop has its uses. Milk has other uses. Mixing the two together produces slime. The same is true of feelings. Even if you feel both anger and sadness about the same thing, the two feelings can be experienced and expressed distinctly and clearly, each in its own measure and to its own end.

HOW TO UNMIX DEPRESSION

To step out of depression (or other mixed feelings), follow this procedure:

1. The instant you notice sensations of depression, set aside ten minutes to separate your feelings. It helps a lot to have a trusted listener with you. They can help detect when your feelings are pure, and they can listen to your feelings to complete communications with you.
2. Take a deep breath, center yourself, and relax into your sensations.
3. Close your eyes. Then energetically reach deep into your chest area with both hands. Use your fingers and intention to untangle the feelings. This can hurt.
4. Collect all the anger into your right hand and all the sadness into your left hand. Take your time to slowly pull them apart. Let the sounds out.
5. Put the sadness on an imaginary shelf with your left hand so you can get to it later. Bring the anger back into your chest with your right hand.
6. Responsibly experience and express pure anger. Make boundaries, start/stop things, change things, say yes, say no, make decisions, etc.
7. Next, with your right hand pull the pure anger out and put it on a shelf. Then with your left hand pull the pure sadness into your chest.
8. Responsibly experience and express pure sadness. Share your pain, grieve changes, let go of expectations, connect heart to heart, etc. You may feel sad about the same things you were angry about, or sad about other things. But now the feelings are pure, no longer mixed.
9. Stay on guard. You have habitually mixed your feelings for many years, and you are just starting to insist on pure feelings. The instant you notice feelings creeping back together, immediately repeat this procedure. Keep your feelings apart with clear intention. Get used to your new clarity.
10. In daily life you may feel angry in one moment and sad in the next, but there is no more depression. You never need to mix your feelings. By keeping your feelings separated, the symptoms of mixed feelings vanish.

Don't wait. As soon as you notice the mixed feeling state, unmix your feelings.

Reach your fingers into your chest and untangle the feelings, pulling them away from each other. This is work. Take your time and feel it happen. Let your face and body move. Let the sounds out.

Put the weaker feeling (in this case sadness) on the shelf with your left hand.

Then bring the stronger feeling (in this case anger) back into your body with your right hand and respectfully experience its energy and clarity with full intensity.

Then take the stronger feeling out and put it on its shelf, and bring the weaker feeling in (in this case sadness) and experience its intelligence and impulses with full intensity.

The joy of consciously using adult responsible feelings is nearly irrepressible.

SIXTH DISTINCTION: FEELINGS CAN BE EXPERIENCED FROM 0 TO 100 PERCENT INTENSITY

The sixth of the Ten Distinctions for Consciously Feeling says that feelings can be experienced from 0 to 100 percent intensity and that in each moment you are feeling all four feelings, but one is always bigger. The clarity this brings to your feelings experiments can cause a significant breakthrough.

If, like most modern citizens, you have been forced to repress feelings since childhood, the idea of intentionally experiencing any feelings at all may seem as crazy as unleashing a pack of rabid bulldogs in church. Such an assessment is not without basis.

Previous experiences with feelings may have included hurtful outbursts from parents, teachers, bosses, neighbors, or even from yourself. These may have been outbursts at inopportune moments or toward innocent or inappropriate people. Perhaps they were directed at your children, your colleagues, or your partner. Emotional explosions may have resulted in broken objects or broken dreams. Afterward you may have regretted what happened, but too late. The damage had already been done, and scars may be long lasting.

If these or similar associations accompany the thought of approaching feelings, it is no wonder that you approach them with trepidation.

GIVING BIRTH TO FEELINGS

I must tell you here that I am not guaranteeing that learning to feel will be free of outbursts. On the contrary, your first six months of feelings work may include some rather rough and rowdy moments. A close friend of mine, for example, is just beginning to seriously engage his feelings work. The other day he came to a meeting so full of anger that it took three adults listening nonstop for an hour and a half to hear all the things he was angry about. It was not a quiet conversation, either.

When I heard about this incident I cheered with joy because this man is in his fifties. He is long past his midteens when the human nervous system is designed to go through the maturing process of changing its relationship to feelings. Middle-aged nervous systems have settled into habit patterns, some of which may be quite deeply grooved. In this man's case he had spent the previous thirty years studying and practicing a system of philosophy anchored in pure intellect. Experiencing and expressing anger breaks so many of the system's rules that the likelihood of a practitioner learning to feel would be highly improbable. And yet he is doing it!

When you make this journey yourself it can help to realize that you are going through a natural birthing process. Natural births are not particularly famous for their smoothness. Birth tends to be unique (unless contractions are drug-induced by doctors needing to get to their golf appointments, or handed over to cesarean surgeons with vacation-home payments to make. Did you know that the percentage of cesarean births has doubled in the last twenty-five years? Don't get me started on this! Too late! I'm already started . . .).

The uniqueness of each birth offers a precious gift of understanding. Its mystery magnetically draws women together in huddles to share their birthing stories.

Since modern people are not generally educated about the birthing process we might not notice that transitions from one life phase to another reveal teachings necessary for life in the next phase. Just as when giving birth, paying attention to, relaxing into, and accepting the immediate experience of your feelings journey can prove to be more rewarding than tensing up, trying to tough it out, wishing it were all over, and focusing on a fantasy image of what the end result will be like.

WHAT DO I FEEL?

The sixth of the ten feelings distinctions says that feelings are experienced from 0 to 100 percent intensity. In each moment you are feeling all four feelings, but one is always bigger. To find what you feel, scan through your four feelings and identify what percentage of 100 percent maximum you feel of each of the four archetypal feelings.

For example, if you order a part from a supplier and you learn that the part will arrive late, on the 0 to 100 percent intensity scale you may feel 55 percent angry that the part will be late, 27 percent sad, 63 percent afraid, and 48 percent glad that you are hearing the news in time to do something about it.

In this moment it is the fear that is most intense, so you tell yourself, "I feel scared."

Then you inquire about what the fear is telling you to do. Perhaps the fear is suggesting that you immediately contact the production manager so he can modify his delivery schedule. Perhaps the fear is suggesting that you try to order the same part from a vendor who already has the part in stock. Use the inherent energy of the feeling to carry you through the necessary actions.

As soon as the action is complete the feeling will vanish and will be replaced by your next feeling. Then you are not so exhausted by the end of the day, because you have not been depending only on your own resources. You have been using the abundant and neutral energy and information of feelings.

A complete feelings communication would include reporting all four feelings. When someone asks, "How are you?," you can now say, "I feel angry that I am hungry and it is still two hours until lunchtime.

I feel sad that my mother is not feeling well. I feel scared that I am about to be promoted to managing a new project. And I feel glad that you asked how I am."

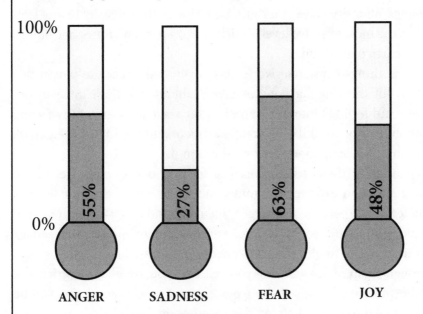

MAP OF FEELINGS INTENSITIES

World Copyright © 2010 owner Clinton Callahan grants permission to use. www.nextculture.org

You are feeling all four feelings about everything. In each moment one of the four feelings is more intense. This is what you are feeling. Feelings come with action steps attached. Feelings provide the power for accomplishing those actions.

100%

0%

55%   27%   63%   48%

ANGER   SADNESS   FEAR   JOY

Net result: *I feel scared.*

The adult says: "I feel glad about the power and intelligence of my fear. My adult feeling clarifies exactly what to do and provides energy for doing it."

FEELINGS DETECTOR AND FEELINGS VALVE

We are making distinctions here. The distinctions are simple and re-markable. The distinctions say that in your body-sensing system you have both a *feelings-intensity detector* and a *feelings-intensity valve*.

Your detector is at first distorted by leftover child level perceptions. It needs to be calibrated into adult level feelings by comparison with another person who has already calibrated their feelings at the adult level. Once your feelings-intensity detector is adjusted, you can detect in yourself, and in others, the precise intensity level of a feelings experience, somewhere between 1 percent intensity (just above numb) and 100 percent intensity (the archetypal maximum for the human body).

Not only that, but through making distinctions among the four feelings and feeling them in their pure form, you gain access to a feelings-intensity valve. In Phase 2 of feelings work, this intensity valve lets you turn on and turn off your adult feelings. By consciously using your feelings-intensity valve you can raise or lower the intensity of any feeling to the most effective level for delivering a particular message or taking a particular action.

The things I just said won't necessarily make sense to you at this point. But knowing that you can have a calibrated feelings-intensity detector and feelings-intensity valve sets the stage for consciously feeling without fear of annihilating your apartment and waking the neighbors (not that your neighbors don't need waking).

Giving birth to adult conscious feelings occurs stepwise; in the company of an experienced guide, you select one of the four feelings and feel it at 1 percent or 2 percent intensity, and then stop entirely. The guide will instruct you to let your nervous system and your self-image get used to the tingling in your fingers and toes while new life surges through them. After assuring yourself that you are okay experiencing and expressing feelings at the 1 percent or 2 percent level, you will be encouraged to make the next daring move and go all the way up to 5 percent intensity!

In fact, this exact exercise has just become your homework.

MAP OF EXERCISE TO GAIN FEELINGS CONSCIOUSNESS
World Copyright © 2010 owner Clinton Callahan grants permission to use. www.nextculture.org

Following these instructions establishes a responsible adult relationship between you and your four feelings (mad, sad, glad, scared) in all four bodies (physical, intellectual, emotional, energetic). This is a three-month exercise.

1. Find someone to partner with you - someone who you see most every day and who also wants to enliven their adult feelings.
2. Agree that at random times during daily life you will interrupt and ask the other to tell you at what percent intensity they are feeling each of the four feelings right now, and about what. Remember, you feel all four feelings about everything all day long, but in each moment there is always one feeling that is most intense.
3. For example, while standing in line together at the post office, Sam might turn to Bob and say, "Bob, what are you feeling right now?" Bob might say, "Right now I am feeling 3 percent angry that I am standing in this line at the post office. How come no matter how long the line is, it always takes the same amount of time? Now I'm feeling 11 percent angry. What about you?" Sam might say, "I am feeling 22 percent scared that we will be late getting back for the meeting. And 45 percent glad that we are talking about our feelings while waiting in this line. I am also feeling 8 percent angry that I am not feeling more angry!"
4. When no partner is around to practice detecting subtle feelings, you can arrange to telephone or email each other.
5. In addition, you can turn on the hourchime of your wristwatch. Each time it chirps, you stop, no matter where you are or what is going on, and write down the percentages of anger, sadness, fear and joy you are feeling in that moment and about what. Write this in your Beep! Book (a little black book for recording feedback, carried in your pocket or purse along with a pen. You'd be surprised how cleverly the Box can cause you to forget the pen at certain times so that you can't write down particularly auspicious suspicious observations.).
6. If you do this exercise consistently for three months, your moment-to-moment awareness of what you are feeling will become greatly amplified. The new awareness enables you to take adult responsibility for your feelings and opens the door to using your feelings for high drama and also to stellating (initializing) archetypal feelings.

5. RESPONSIBILITY
AND HIGH DRAMA

(NOTE TO THE READER: If you have skipped ahead to this chapter without carefully studying the previous four chapters, it's a clever idea but I don't recommend it. Learning to consciously feel has similarities to learning to drive a car, which is actually quite simple. Strap on your seatbelt, turn the key, grab the steering wheel and push your foot on the accelerator. But they make you take lessons and get a license before letting you drive. It's for your own good. That's because if you take a turn at sixty that you should take at thirty you can slide right off the cliff. If you don't have right-of-way rules deeply absorbed into your reflex patterns you can get flattened by an eighteen wheeler. And if you don't take care to check your fluids the brake pedal can sink to the floor while you slam into the back side of a cement truck. I am not saying anything like this will happen if you skip over the previous chapters. But I am saying that the world of conscious feelings operates under different laws than the world of numbness, just like driving is different from walking in a park. Before you hop into responsibility and high drama I strongly encourage you to study the first four chapters of this book. It's for your own good.)

SEVENTH DISTINCTION: THERE ARE TWO PHASES OF FEELINGS WORK

The seventh of the Ten Distinctions for Consciously Feeling says that there are two phases in *feelings work*. In Phase 1 you learn to feel using the Ten Distinctions for Consciously Feeling. In Phase 2 you learn to create *high drama* by consciously applying the information and energy resources of your feelings through adult responsibility. It can be mis-

---

MAP OF PHASE 1 AND PHASE 2 OF FEELINGS WORK
World Copyright © 2010 owner Clinton Callahan grants permission to use. www.nextculture.org

---

Before you can use your feelings you must first learn to feel.

PHASE 1: LEARN TO FEEL
- Know the Map of Four Feelings: anger, sadness, joy and fear.
- Regard your feelings as neutral energy and information.
- Feel your four feelings in their unmixed purity.
- Distinguish between feelings and two kinds of emotions:
   o Incomplete feelings from your past.
   o Inauthentic feelings from religion, business, politics or parents.
- Learn to start and stop your feelings consciously and for no reason.
- Experience and express each of the four feelings from 1 percent low intensity to 100 percent maximum Archetypal intensity.
- Stellate feelings to turn on the four responsible archetypes:
   o anger = doer / maker (warrior, warrioress)
   o sadness = communicator (lover)
   o joy = responsible leader (king, queen / Possibility Manager)
   o fear = creator / designer (magician, sorceress)

Phase 1 also includes:
- Distilling Bright Principles (Distilling Destiny Process)
- Distilling Shadow Principles (Hidden Purpose Process)

PHASE 2: USE YOUR FEELINGS RESPONSIBLY
Learn to use the energy and information of your feelings consciously and responsibly in the service of Bright Principles. Learn to be the intention-space through which your Bright Principles can do their work in the world. Create and develop extraordinary and Archetypal relationships through conscious acts of high drama. Lead diverse groups and teams using Possibility Listening, Possibility Speaking, Discovery Listening and Discovery Speaking.

IMPORTANT NOTE:
Stellating (initializing) all four feelings in Phase 1 takes about two years and will usually include seven to ten strong healing processes dealing with parents and childhood issues. Stellating is best undertaken in the company of trusted and experienced guides as part of your rite of passage into adulthood. Do not expect yourself to do Phase 2 before you have done Phase 1.

---

leading to think that you are able to do Phase 2 before you have gone through the two-year rite of passage work of Phase 1.

Even though modern society orients us toward withholding feelings and regarding feelings as dangerous, uncivilized, immature, childish, embarrassing, feminine (i.e., not acceptable in a patriarchy), quite the contrary is true. But reorienting yourself 180 degrees with regard to any familiar pattern is a formidable undertaking, especially if you are older than fifteen years of age and have been repressing your feelings perhaps for decades.

Phase 1 distinctions about feelings are central to the well-being of people intending to live together in sustainable culture. Yet, enlivening these distinctions in your daily life is revolutionary. A conscious and responsible adult orientation toward feelings fundamentally undermines and brings into question large segments of traditional mainstream culture, including:

- a verbal-intellectual education system that ignores and suppresses feelings.

- medical and healing technologies that regard feelings as some kind of illness.

- a profit-driven mass media that manipulates unconscious feelings according to corporate-controlled political agendas to amplify insecurity, causing consumers to bow before so-called authority and thoughtlessly consume rather than becoming who they are.

RAGE TANTRUM This man is doing the *3-3-3 Exercise*. He lies on his bed and consciously uses his voice (both words and sounds), face, and whole body to have a temper tantrum for *no* reason, 3 minutes at a time, 3 times a week (e.g. Monday, Wednesday, Friday) for 3 months. The 3-3-3 Exercise is a core element of Phase 1 of feelings work. Consistent practice safely vitalizes your nervous system to tolerate the intensity of mature adult feelings. It is high drama because you start and you stop consciously. It is part of your rite of passage to adulthood.

Using feelings consciously and responsibly involves acquiring significant new skills and a thorough understanding of their accompanying thoughtmaps. This is the journey you are already engaging.

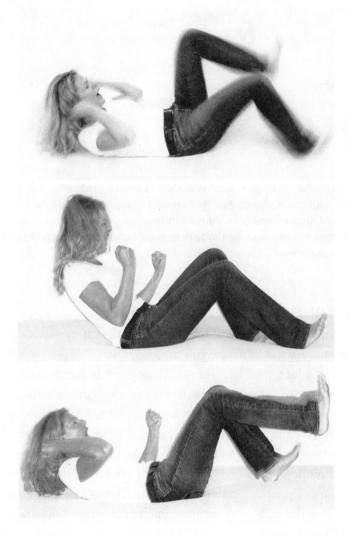

RAGE TANTRUM The 3-3-3 Exercise refines your experiential distinctions and thus provides a safe way to improve your inner navigation. It is high drama to journey into feelings territories and discover: How does pure rage feel when it is not mixed? What percentage big was that anger? Can I lower my numbness bar even further? The expressions on this woman's face reveal that high drama can be more than a little bit fun.

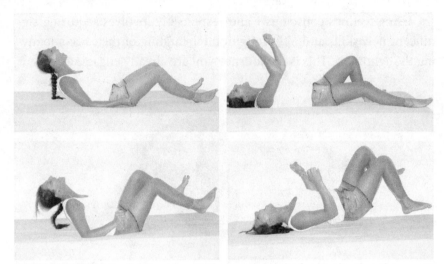

RAGE TANTRUM Feelings return at the same level of maturity that they were when you shut them down, usually between one and three years of age. The sensations of finally turning on your adult feelings are magnificent, spectacular, and enjoyable. We are designed to fully engage our rite of passage when we are about fifteen years old.

UPGRADING YOUR THOUGHTWARE

The human body is capable of operating in different modes, depending on the particular thoughtware you use.

Think of a laptop or PC. This amazing piece of hardware can function variously as a word processor, an encyclopedia, a bank account manager, a direct mail service to other Internet users, a photo or video editor, a video game, a calculator, a radio, a telephone, a stereo CD or DVD player, a recipe file, a graphic designer, and a wide assortment of additional modes, many of which have not even been invented yet. The functionality of your computer depends on the particular software that you install. In the same way the human body also functions in multiple modes, depending on the particular thoughtware you choose to use.

If you give ten people the same job to do with the same resources to call upon, you will end up with ten widely varying results. This corresponds to the diverse thoughtware people build into their Box, including the level of maturity of their feelings skills.

For example, managers do not choose just anyone to handle a particular project. A manager picks a person who has the best qualities to match the project's needs. Any person could *potentially* lead the project, but only a few specific people have actualized their potential into the *capability* to lead the project.

Modern education does not encourage us to use feelings or develop capabilities. In modern society this thoughtware is not available. Nonetheless, from sources other than modern society, this thoughtware *is available*. And when you begin using upgraded thoughtware you can enjoy extraordinary results out of the same senses, mind, heart and soul that previously gave you mediocre results.

In other words, your hardware is fine. This book is not about fixing your hardware. Blocks and malfunctions may simply be side effects of using very outdated thoughtware. This chapter is about upgrading your thoughtware to use the strength and intelligence of feelings to take responsibility and create high drama. The new thoughtware says: Feelings are for healing things or for handling things.

MAP OF UPGRADING YOUR FEELINGS THOUGHTWARE
World Copyright © 2010 owner Clinton Callahan grants permission to use. www.nextculture.org

YOUR ORIGINAL FEELINGS THOUGHTWARE:

"Feelings are painful, bad, dangerous, uncivilized, childish, useless, frightening, stupid . . . and definitely to be avoided."

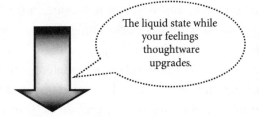

The liquid state while your feelings thoughtware upgrades.

YOUR UPGRADED FEELINGS THOUGHTWARE:

"Feelings are for healing things or handling things."

GUIDELINES FOR PSYCHOPATHS

This section probably does not apply to you.

This section only applies if you are in the 1 percent of the human population lacking a connection between your mind and your heart, resulting in a disconnect between feelings and thoughts. The name for someone in this condition is *psychopath*. People suffering from psychopathology lack remorse, empathy, compassion, the application of moral considerations to actions, and the ability to learn from mistakes.

Without the basic conscience that allows a human being to live in social harmony, psychopaths cannot be authentically touched. Mental health professionals rarely treat psychopathic personality disorders as they are considered untreatable. No interventions have proven to be effective, not even punishment, because psychopaths do not associate punishments with the behavior that is being punished.

The reason this section probably does not apply to you is that psychopaths derive satisfaction from their antisocial behavior and would not typically read a book about learning how to feel.

Psychopaths tend to assume there is nothing wrong with them, and think (often rightly) that they are too smart to ever get caught. Learning how to feel would never make sense because why should you bother to fix something as successful as a CEO, a senator, a judge or a bishop?

On the other hand, *it could be that you are an atypical psychopath*: you *have* noticed that something is missing and you want to try to find it.

In addition to applying to the 1 percent of true psychopaths, this section may apply to you if you are in the 8–10 percent of *chameleon psychopaths*, modernized humans who see hierarchical power positions going to people with psychopathic behavior patterns so they adopt those patterns themselves. Chameleon psychopaths learn to survive in the service of psychopathic leaders by imitating their behavior and attitudes, pretending to be one of them. This way they gain power and status in the patriarchal empire without actually being a true psychopath, a common but risky strategy. The risk was identified by Kurt Vonnegut Jr in *Mother Night*, when he said: "We are what we pretend to be, so we must be careful about what we pretend to be."

Regardless of whether you are a true psychopath, a chameleon psychopath, or are merely interested in transforming the little psychopathic elements of your Box's defense strategy, here is the deal: if you are willing to admit that you are missing the link between thought and feelings (or if you have been behaving as if the link is missing), you have a chance to live more humanly. The way to do it is to use your remarkable cunning to catch yourself at your own tricks. Only you are clever enough to do this.

Turn your ruthlessness into ruthless self-honesty.

Reveal your handicap pitilessly until your world crumbles around you and you hit bottom. Then do whatever it takes to stay there.

Do not let your psychopathic certainty put itself back together again. Stay broken. Stay vulnerable. Stay in uncertainty, completely undefended, because that which is authentic about you cannot be hurt.

This is a long and pitifully lonely process, continuing over a year or two. The process can neither be shortened nor made more comfortable. I am truly sorry about that. In my thirty-four years of working with people, I have found no other effective way. Believe me, I have looked.

The process of becoming more human needs to take its own time. It can help if you decide now, in this moment, to endure the process through to its completion *no matter what.*

By already establishing a commitment you proactively disempower the clever reasons, excuses and justifications that the psychopathic Gremlin throws up as obstacles to your success. The previously established commitment gives the Gremlin's arguments no place to get a grip. Put your faith in the process itself. Trust the process. And then work at it.

During this time your job is to take care of yourself in these simple ways:

- Stop trying to be in relationship with the opposite sex (or same sex if you are homosexual).

- Eat simple healthy food in modest amounts, mostly vegetarian.

- Strictly avoid alcohol, cigarettes, drugs, sweets, coffee, gum, and sodas.

- Exercise daily, moving around until you have to breathe hard.

- Sleep more than has been usual for you.

- Learn some form of silent sitting practice and sit at least thirty-five minutes a day: same time, same place. No breathing exercises or mantra. Be still, keep your back straight, and don't sleep. That's it.

- Participate in a regular weekly martial arts training program if you can. Classic aikido works well for this.

- Take up a simple handcraft to give your body something useful to do when your mind is driving you crazy: hand sewing, wood carving, pottery, stained glass, macramé, beading, etc.

- Make only small positive promises to people and be hypervigilant about keeping each one.

- Do not engage in revenge, paybacks, or low drama, even in your own mind.

- Buy almost nothing so you avoid debts.

- Pay your bills on time or early.

- Work a simple manual labor job that does not require your clever defense mechanisms to come back into play as part of your profession (such as headhunter, sales, manager, consultant, etc.).

During this time you won't know who you are. You won't recognize yourself. Even your close friends might question your lifestyle. Life itself may not even make much sense. That is simply how it is in this time. I'm sorry.

Only after nine to twelve months of relentlessly staying in an apparently broken condition—with your carefully orchestrated deceiving mechanisms hopelessly cracked and withered due to starvation and exposure to radical self-honesty—could you perhaps become reliable enough to ask for help. Asking for or accepting help before then won't do you much good because your Gremlin will easily devour whoever offers to help you. This would be a bad idea.

Help could at first be meeting with other men in an ongoing weekly men's group (if you are a man, or women's group if you are a woman). Try to avoid any groups that are new age or touchy-feely or religiously fundamentalist. The group should be simple and respectful of the value of human life. In such a meeting you would be asked to both listen a lot and share a lot. A fine example of this is the New Warrior Circle, a small local group of men that you can join after participating in the New Warrior Training. Information is available at the ManKind Project website <www.mkp.org>.

When the time comes to ask for help, ask if there is someone (or better, a team of two or three) neither psychopathic nor pseudopsychopathic who would be willing to be your "seeing eye dog" with respect to feelings. This would be a one- to two-year commitment.

If someone commits to help you, your commitment to them should include a ritual vow in which you promise never to deceive them. For their help you must pay full price. The price is sustained defenselessness toward them—you are completely exposed. Regardless of the intensity of your screaming demons, you sacrifice your conscienceless survival power for the chance to taste what you have never before had: human intimacy.

Your guide becomes a compass providing ongoing feedback about what you would naturally feel in each circumstance if your mind was connected to your heart, thereby giving you a conscience. Your guide's feedback would initially address your subtle fast interactions, those which most people would not notice.

Say, for example, that you enter a restaurant together. Your guide's feedback might be a running monolog going something like this: "Wait. Don't just march on into this space. It is not your space. You are a guest here. Be interested. Notice while you enter the subtle mood that is created here. Each space has a unique mood about it. Appreciating these moods is one of the most satisfying experiences. If you skip over appreciating these mood sensations, you will be endlessly bored and wanting to get into trouble just for entertainment. Stop walking here. You are entering the restaurant space without being welcomed. Make brief eye contact with that waiter. That's too long. You just put your energy into his space as a threat to try to control him. Don't do that. Trust him for no reason. Take your energy out of his space and keep it in your own private bubble. That's where it belongs. Good. Ground your bubble. Yes, like that. Now you are welcomed into the space. Keep yourself grounded as we walk. Do not even look at that woman. Her Gremlin is trying to hook your Gremlin for a little flirt. Don't do it. Good. Keep breathing. That feeling coming up in you now, what is it? Yes, that is anger, about 15 percent intense. Do you know why? Because your intentions and actions are so visible and your Gremlin thought you were sneaking around all this time and you are not. Great, now you are lowering your barrier to me again and you are hitting bottom again. Good. Stay at bottom. You know what it feels like. Just relax there in the hopelessness. Ask yourself: Even here on the bottom, am I okay? Yes, you are totally okay, even if you are not in control. So here we are at the table. That seat is the one your Gremlin chose in order to put your back to the wall so you can flirt with anyone who might pass by. What if you choose a different seat to sit in? Fine. Yes, we are just sitting here waiting. Yes, the time is going by and you could get the waitress's attention, but let's just relax here and wait. You have the power to choose what the most important thing going on in this moment is. Is it getting our meal ordered? Or is it being here together in this space? Even if you are hungry, are you going to die of hunger? No, of course not. So what happens if you choose being here together with me? Can you feel something relax when you do that? The emergency suddenly passes. The survival demon goes back into its cave. You can rest in alertness even if it seems like nothing is happening. Here we are, just sitting together. And look, here comes the waitress! You scanned her entire psychoemotional state just now, did you notice that? How is she doing? Right, she is 30 percent tensed, carries a burden in her heart and left shoulder, tries to be nice, and hates men. Your Gremlin is ready to feed on that, can you feel it? Tell your Gremlin to SIT. Get your center back from your Gremlin. Take a breath. Be unreasonably kind to the waitress without motive. Act as if you are always this way. Speak in respectful politeness. That is too fast. Slow your words down. There is not enough caring in your attitude. This is a woman. She is not the mother who abandoned you. She is not the nun who whipped you at school. She doesn't even know about these things that happened to you. She is just trying to take your order for lunch. Stop being at war with her. Modulate your voice differently so her dignity is respected. Good, that's totally different, see? Skip the meat, it just makes you aggressive. Take another deep breath and get centered. Good. Smile just a little, but don't look at her. Looking in her eyes is the way your greedy little Gremlin sucks out her energy for hors d'oeuvres. Skip all that. Keep it civil and conscious. Take your center back from your Gremlin. Yes, now we are waiting again. Notice what your fingers are doing. See your right foot tapping? Those are two different feelings, and you're mixing them together. What are they? Yes, anger in your foot, and fear in your fingers. When you mix them together, what do you get? Yes, hysteria. This is why you work frenetically and drive your colleagues crazy; why you cannot, in fact, maintain collegial relationships. So what is the anger about? Yes, impatience, wanting to hurry things up. Because what happens if you just sit? Yes, see your fingers picking at each other now? The fear increases. So what is the fear about? Yes, afraid of not doing something. And what happens if you are not doing something? Yes, you get in trouble. See how this vicious circle from long ago won't let you simply be present in your body? But see how your body actually has the feelings and provides you with feelings information and energy, but your mind does not grasp it and cannot use it? That's the psychopathic disconnect. You're doing great with all this, just being with me. And hey, look, here comes our soup! Don't be looking at her crotch like that. Gremlin got hold of your eyes and attention again. See how fast it is? Say, SIT! If you don't have your attention, Gremlin does. Take a breath. Get your center back from your Gremlin. Enjoy your meal."

Day in and day out, keep opening further to the person serving you as your feelings detector. Fiercely direct your own guile to catch and expose your own guile.

You don't have to do this shamefully, just relentlessly.

Allow no deception to go unadmitted. Live in the constant uncertainty of not knowing what is respectful, what has integrity, what includes empathy or what generates true warmth. Be an ongoing request for guidance. Ask about each gesture, each thought, each word. Be willing to ongoingly not know. Radically trust your guide.

Rely on your guide's feedback even if you disagree with it, even if you do not understand it, even if you feel scared. You *will* feel scared. Consciously feeling scared is fantastic! Fear is one of the four feelings. You are getting somewhere.

With each move, each expression, ask, "What should this feel like? What is the appropriate feeling here? Anger? Sadness? How should that feel? Frightening? Why should it feel like this?"

Such ineptitude is maddening. Frustration is a form of *anger*. Aha! Anger is one of the four feelings. You have detected another feeling. Excellent! Keep going.

You are blind. A blind person craves the company of one who can describe a panorama in poetry. Give your guide plenty of safe space and time to bring the world alive for you. Let them expose you to a world of conscience, a world that combines thoughts with feelings. If you are truly psychopathic, empathy and remorse will never be yours. But through respectfully listening to your guide with heart and soul, you can come to authentically appreciate the world of intimacy. Your patient attention will bring you nuance and pregnant moments, the possibility of wonder.

After some time you may find yourself in a moment of joy, and then a moment of sadness, and then a moment of joy again. This is called *gratitude*: grateful to be alive, grateful that someone would care enough to help you connect, grateful to have a chance to experience life. Sadness and joy are also among the four feelings.

Through a measured cadence your handicap can be transformed. You can use your own painful lack of remorse to serve another person. Your weakness becomes a chance for your guide to use their feelings in ways they never imagined. Through sacrificing your defendedness and trusting another human being, that person can occasionally function as an external living circuit for you, using their own conscience to bypass your inner void and help you join your heart with your mind. A richer world of experience can come together in you.

The other person is serving as your conscience. You can learn to avoid acting until your conscience speaks. If you succeed, then between yourself and your friend you have nurtured a precious collaboration. Congratulations.

RESPONSIBLY FEELING

Entering adult responsibility requires a new thoughtmap about adulthood and a new thoughtmap about responsibility. Modern culture's thoughtmaps for responsibility and adulthood are the equivalent of flat-world maps.

Mainstream society teaches us that responsibility is a punishment and a burden that smart people avoid. For example, modern businessmen consider it to be a success when they maximize profits through externalizing costs. Yet where do they think they are externalizing costs to? We live on a planet. A planet is a closed ecological system. All externalized costs will boomerang with compounded interest. A radically new thoughtmap for responsibility is required to explain the steps for shifting from an economy of money to an economy of sustainable human well-being.

MAP OF CHILD AND ADULT RESPONSIBILITY
World Copyright © 2010 owner Clinton Callahan grants permission to use. www.nextculture.org

Responsibility is the personal interest and willingness to source the necessary results. We live in a responsible universe. When you get past all your resistance, reasons and excuses, what is left is personal interest. This starts an entirely new game, called *adult responsibility*.

CHILD RESPONSIBILITY	ADULT RESPONSIBILITY
Responsibility is about what happened in the past.	Responsibility happens here and now in the present.
It is my fault. I am guilty.	I own it. It is my commitment.
I must carry the blame.	I can ride it, play it, fly it.
It is a heavy burden.	It is an opportunity to serve my interest.
I am the victim.	This is a reward.
I have been tricked.	I am honored.
I am naïve.	I am at source.
I am the scapegoat.	I am at cause.
It is being done to me.	I am at the point of origin.
I should have avoided it.	I get to authentically create.
There will be consequences.	I am active. I create results.
I am held accountable.	I have freedom to choose.
I will be punished.	I am one with it, in integrity.
I have reproach, regret.	I express care.
This is a pressure.	Disillusionment opens new possibilities. I learn.
I am being abused.	I serve something greater than myself. I am being well used.
Others abandon me.	
I fear failing.	It is an exchange.
I am overwhelmed.	I have power to declare how it is.
I am on trial.	

THE SECOND COPERNICAN REVOLUTION

Gaining adult responsibility in practical matters starts when you personally go through a *Second Copernican Revolution*. Prior to the First Copernican Revolution, Western civilization asserted that the Earth was the center of the universe and that all the stars, planets and galaxies orbited around it. When Nicolaus Copernicus, Galileo Galilei, Johannes Kepler and others began pointing out how wrong we were, it proved to be quite an embarrassment.

Today we laugh that our forefathers could be so arrogant and egotistical as to think that the universe would swing around our insignificant water ball, invisibly perched on the rim of one of billions of galaxies in the universe. But entire religions and economies were based on the childish perspective that the whole universe revolves around me, me, me, and they all came crashing down when the truth became irrefutable.

Although the First Copernican Revolution was a rough ride (ask Galileo), Western culture only matured *partially*. We only stepped from childhood to adolescence. We merely upgraded to a more sophisticated flat-world map.

REORIENTING YOUR PERSPECTIVE This is the M104 Galaxy. It is 50,000 light years across and 28 million light years from Earth. You are looking at 800 billion stars. Photo © Copyright 2003 by NASA Hubble Space Telescope. <www.nasa.gov>

We may have learned that the Earth goes around the sun, but mainstream society still believes that the Earth and all its resources belong to the RWGs (Rich White Guys).

Whoever wins in the *I win-you lose* political and economic power struggles is thought to acquire the rights to quarrel over, ravage, and consume the world's remaining resources in a teenage-mentality pyramid scheme of endless growth.

Our globalized society asserts that the Earth and its resources can be owned by people. This is a false assertion. We have not yet realized our ignorance. The shit is about to seriously hit the fan.

Our adolescent vanity has reached its maximum physical limits and is culminating in a "perfect storm": a brutal combination of global warming, peak oil, falling water tables, desertification, economic collapse, false education of our children, biodiversity loss, failing fisheries, rising ocean levels, pandemics, and fundamentalism.

These conditions are not independent of one another. They synergize into what Dennis Gallagher calls "a devil's brew of reinforcing consequences—consequences which are going to fundamentally alter the physical and biological systems of the planet and degrade the environment we will leave to our children for hundreds, if not thousands, of generations." <www.samadhisoft.com>

How could we have been so ignorant?

Ignorance is easy when modern society equips us with only an adolescent understanding of responsibility—without telling us that it is adolescent. This is not a justifiable excuse. It simply explains that we have been methodically encouraged to give our authority away to adolescent leaders, and we acquiesced, for generation after generation.

We still have no role models for adult responsibility within modern society. To gain a new relationship to responsibility you have no option but to journey beyond the horizons viewed from the knowledge continents of modern culture.

Describing a new view of responsibility to one who has not yet realized the limits of the old view may seem ridiculous. Yet still we must attempt it. On a round-world thoughtmap, responsibility is *the willingness to see what is actually going on and the interest to respond accordingly.*

Responsibility no longer makes me a victim. Responsibility is a privilege because I am at source. Taking responsibility is my opportunity to create new results.

Your first steps into adult responsibility will confront you with the Second Copernican Revolution, the realization that people cannot own the Earth.

Patriarchal empire began by fencing off farms and claiming rights to land ownership. Kings protected their claims with armies. People specialized, becoming soldiers, farmers, craftsmen, merchants, bureaucrats, priests—each role having a different status in the patriarchy. The convention of claiming land and resources resulted in adversarial, materialistic, hierarchical cultures competing against each other, creating many losers and few winners. The game where elite owners ruled masses of slaves became so common that we forgot it was only one of many possible gameworlds to live in. We thought it was the only solution to life on Earth. We regarded ourselves as our own handiwork, not realizing that playing God is a childish delusion guaranteed to blow up in our faces.

Human beings are a biology experiment being performed by planet Earth. Human beings cannot own the Earth. The Earth owns people. After billions of years, the Earth has evolved an organism complex enough to hold sufficient consciousness to self-reflect, to be aware of itself. The Earth would like her experiment to succeed.

Success would mean that our consciousness would conquer our intelligence. This is the war going on right now, the war between wisdom and cleverness. So far, cleverness is winning. Human beings may be too clever to survive.

Every previous species has been subject to the natural checks and balances that keep populations within sustainable limits. Human ingenuity has manipulated conditions so we avoid the checks and balances. The result is that the human population exceeds the sustainable carrying capacity of Earth by somewhere between two and five times. We

It's not our planet. Photo © Copyright NASA. <www.nasa.gov>

have overpopulated into *overshoot*, and are headed into a well-predicted and easily avoidable Malthusian catastrophe. We overconsume with no more intelligence than a bacteria colony expanding beyond the sustainability of its food supply and dying in its own poisonous wastes.

We have avoided waking up to the Second Copernican Revolution for so long that the chaos that erupted when society crashed into the First Copernican Revolution will seem like a sunny day at the beach in comparison to the upheavals we will likely experience in the next few decades.

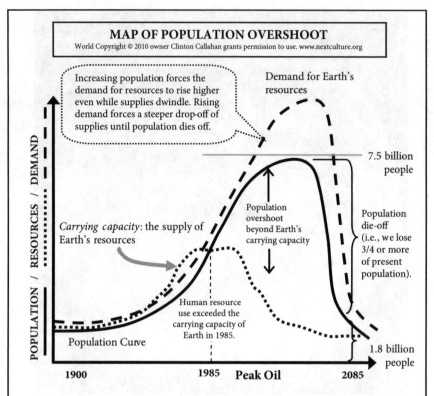

MAP OF POPULATION OVERSHOOT

World Copyright © 2010 owner Clinton Callahan grants permission to use. www.nextculture.org

Increasing population forces the demand for resources to rise higher even while supplies dwindle. Rising demand forces a steeper drop-off of supplies until population dies off.

Demand for Earth's resources

7.5 billion people

Carrying capacity: the supply of Earth's resources

Population overshoot beyond Earth's carrying capacity

Population die-off (i.e., we lose 3/4 or more of present population).

Human resource use exceeded the carrying capacity of Earth in 1985.

Population Curve

1.8 billion people

POPULATION / RESOURCES / DEMAND

1900   1985   Peak Oil   2085

Fossil fuels quadrupled Earth's carrying capacity since 1900 through increasing food production and distribution. This graph shows how Peak Oil will reduce human populations back down to Earth's sustainable 1 billion people within about seventy-five years from now. As food supplies diminish, the population will collapse. Results of this well-predicted and easily avoidable phenomenon were clearly outlined by Rev. Thomas Malthus in 1798. For a more detailed explanation of this graph and the connection between Peak Oil and population die-off, please visit Paul Chefurka's website at <www.paulchefurka.ca>.

DOES THE SUN GO AROUND THE EARTH ???

At first, we thought the sun, the planets, and the whole universe orbited the Earth...

MAP OF THE FIRST COPERNICAN REVOLUTION

NO! SILLY QUESTION! THE EARTH GOES AROUND THE SUN !!!

... then we discovered that the Earth orbits the sun. The Earth is not at the center of the universe!

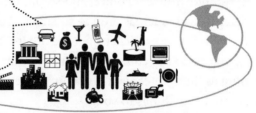

DOES THE EARTH BELONG TO PEOPLE ???

At first, we thought the Earth orbited around mankind... we thought people could possess land and resources...

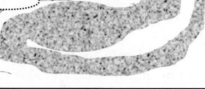

MAP OF THE SECOND COPERNICAN REVOLUTION

World Copyright © 2010 owner Clinton Callahan grants permission to use. www.nextculture.org

NO! SILLY QUESTION! PEOPLE BELONG TO THE EARTH!!!

... then we discovered that the Earth is not homocentric; the Earth is *terracentric*. The Earth owns people. People cannot own the Earth!

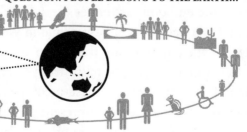

BECOMING ADULT

It is well past time to grow up. What does this mean, being adult?

Eric Berne, originator of Transactional Analysis, invented a thought-map in the 1960s that clearly explains what *growing up* means. He noticed that people identify themselves with different ego states during their daily life. He distinguished three basic ego states: parent, adult, and child. Each ego state maintains its own private set of ideas, beliefs, attitudes and behaviors. Only one of them is grown up.

Every time we enter either the parent or child ego state we believe there is no other way to be than as prescribed in that particular ego state. Only in the adult ego state do we see that we have multiple identities to choose from. (We briefly looked at one aspect of this thoughtmap in Chapter 4.)

When identified with the parent ego state you will be hearing voices in your mind. The voices are either critical blaming voices, such as: You're not good enough. You will never make it. You're too weak. You're too stupid. You're a failure, and so on. Or the voices are nurturing, praising voices, such as: You're so smart. You're so beautiful. You are my favorite. You are quicker than the others. You are perfect, and so on. These voices do not come from you. They are other people's voices. By listening to these voices you give your power away to the authorities who first said these things to you.

You take your power back when you speak your own voice in the *adult* ego state.

The child ego state is experienced as incomplete emotions from the past. The emotions are either the scared, needy or adaptive emotions that you had to accept as normal in your childhood in order to survive, or the emotions are free and natural but irresponsible emotions that you are trying to relive from the happy moments of your childhood. By experiencing these incomplete or unexpressed childhood emotions as if they were present feelings, you give your power away, because these emotions are physical memories from your past. You have no power in the past. You cannot change or relive anything that happened in your past, even if it happened a mere few seconds ago. The past is the past.

You reclaim your own power through consciously feeling authentic feelings that arise and pass in the present moment in the *adult* ego state.

It is significant learning to make the internal distinctions of hearing other people's voices in your head and yet only speaking your own voice with your mouth, or noticing childhood emotions being triggered

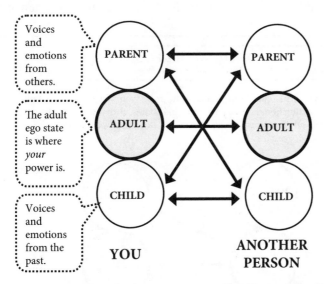

MAP OF PARENT, ADULT, CHILD EGO STATES
World Copyright © 2010 owner Clinton Callahan grants permission to use. www.nextculture.org

An *ego state* is a set of ideas, beliefs, attitudes and behaviors that you *identify* with as if they are real. Ordinary (low drama) interactions come from being identified with the parent or child ego states. Parent voices come from others; child neediness comes from your past. Your power comes from using your own voice and being in the present.

Voices and emotions from others.

The adult ego state is where *your* power is.

Voices and emotions from the past.

PARENT — PARENT

ADULT — ADULT

CHILD — CHILD

YOU

ANOTHER PERSON

This thoughtmap of human interactions is a powerful contribution by Eric Berne, the originator of Transactional Analysis. By using Berne's clear distinctions you can locate your immediate behavior as either:

1. PARENT EGO STATE: Voices in your head from other people:
    a. Critical (persecutor) voices about yourself or others, or
    b. Nurturing (rescuer) voices about yourself or others.
2. CHILD EGO STATE: Incomplete emotions from your past:
    a. Free and natural child emotions (victim), or
    b. Scared needy adaptive child emotions (victim).
3. ADULT EGO STATE: A mature relationship to responsibility through having your *own* voice and experiencing free, natural *adult* feelings in the present moment. The adult ego state is your gateway to the archetypal masculine and feminine.

from your body's physical memories and yet choosing to feel your own authentic feelings in the present moment. Such learning is part of your rite of passage from childhood into adulthood. *Without living these distinctions in your moment-to-moment interactions, the power of responsible adulthood will remain forever beyond your reach.* These are tough words, and yet over and over again they prove to be the simple truth. Responsibility begins in the adult ego state.

STAYING ADULT

The value of staying in the adult ego state is that only through the adult can you create high drama. In the parent or child ego states, you will only create low drama. Since modern society does not hold these distinctions, it could well be that the majority of your life has been spent

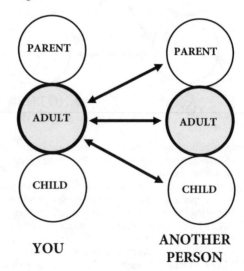

MAP OF THE ADULT EGO STATE
World Copyright © 2010 owner Clinton Callahan grants permission to use. www.nextculture.org

Extraordinary human communications come from you staying in the adult ego state and not getting hooked into parent or child states, even if it is not fair. *NOTE: Whenever you do not experientially remember this map, you are probably no longer in the adult ego state.*

PARENT   PARENT

ADULT   ADULT

CHILD   CHILD

YOU   ANOTHER PERSON

The adult ego state is where conscious feeling begins.

submerged in low dramas without you being aware of it. The joy of creating high dramas may be an entirely new experience for you. The following pages are intended to be a mini-handbook for staying in the adult ego state.

The first support for staying in the adult ego state is to memorize the Map of the Adult Ego State.

Make the adult ego state your new home. It takes conscious efforts to remain in the adult ego state. Hammer a stake in the ground and hold on for life.

At any moment you and/or the other person could slip into the parent or child ego state. Whenever you are not remembering that this might happen it has probably already happened and you are probably no longer centered in the adult ego state.

Remembering the Map of Adult Ego State is not a mental effort. The thoughtmap is not merely a concept. It is an internal energetic experience. You can sense when you are adult and you can sense when you are not adult. The adult ego state is a clear, present, relaxed, attentive, and relationally strong experience. It is the origin of *High Level Fun!*

Adult holding space for child. Joe being with his son Nathaniel.

If you are centered in the adult ego state it does not matter what ego state the other person is in. Whatever ego state they have you can stay adult. Hold your center in a minimized present moment and only use your own voice, which may not need to say anything at all.

This sounds simple. It actually *is* simple. It is not necessarily easy. That is why you were born with a *Voice Blaster*.

PARENT EGO STATE AND THE VOICE BLASTER

To stay in the adult ego state you will be using your Voice Blaster. Each person has a Voice Blaster strapped to their waist since before they were born. If you have not been using your Voice Blaster it may only be because no one ever pointed it out to you.

VOICE BLASTER Hundreds of voices come from your past, from authority figures or from belief-marketing institutions, not from you. They flutter around outside your head waiting to suck out your life energy like vampire bats. No one but you can use your *Voice Blaster*. The best conversation to have with a voice is: Bang! *You're too stupid.* Bang! *You're not good enough.* Bang! *You'll never make it.* Bang!

Your Voice Blaster is for blowing away other people's voices from your thoughts. This lets you exit the parent ego state and slip back into the adult ego state. The only "conversation" to have with those voices buzzing around your head is, *Blam! Pang! Kaboom!*

An adult man or woman's authentic life generally occurs without mental voices. When you speak authentically you will generally speak before you know what you are going to say.

These are extraordinary distinctions to make, and become even more fantastic when you bring them to life in your daily experience.

MAP OF THE VOICE BLASTER

World Copyright © 2010 owner Clinton Callahan grants permission to use. www.nextculture.org

You are better than everybody.
You are not good enough.
You are so wonderful.
You are such a failure.
You are my favorite.
You are a loser.
You are so smart.
You are so stupid.
You are a success.
You will never make it.
You may as well give up.
You are the hope of the family.
Etc. Etc. Etc. Etc. Etc. ad nauseum.

INSTRUCTIONS: Each person is born with a *Voice Blaster*. If you have not used yours it may simply be because no one ever told you it was there. To use your Voice Blaster, reach down to your holster, pull out the Blaster, aim it into the air, pull the trigger, and slide the Blaster back into its holster so fast that the whole operation takes no time. Your Voice Blaster can never be taken away from you. It has an infinite number of charges, and it never misses. Do not hesitate to shoot voices the instant you detect them – BANG! For fun you can blow off the smoking barrel before you drop the Blaster back into its holster, ready again for use, even in the next instant if necessary. When it comes to voices, shoot first. Ask questions later.

ADULT EGO STATE AND MINIMIZING YOUR *NOW*

The temporal territory that you include when you use the word *now* can be quite vast. For many people, *now* includes months or years of memories from the past, and months, years, or even decades of considerations projected into the future. Hugely extended *nows* weigh you down like having elephants in your hot air balloon. Even if your *now* includes just a few hours into the past, or reaches a few minutes or even seconds into the future, the added mass makes it almost impossible to make energetic right-angle turns when navigating conversation-space or relationship-space at light speed.

If you have ever had inexplicable or extended anger, sadness, fear, or joy reactions, such as stage fright, claustrophobia, paranoia, self-loathing, despair, euphoria, boredom, or the thrills associated with conspiracy theory thinking, you were in an *expanded now* of the child ego state.

Without making efforts to *minimize your now* your experience of *now* will still contain memories of the past and visions of the future. Then you will carry around a *big now* and you will be more easily hookable into the child ego state. Staying in the adult ego state involves shrinking the size of your *now* until it only includes this exact moment.

An immediate escape out of an expanded *now* is to touch an object gently with your fingertips. Try it now, if you want to. Touch your fingertips together and delicately rub them in a tiny circle. Can you feel that? Caress the side of your pants or skirt ever so gently. Touch your pen, the table top, or any object, using an open yet attentive focus on the experience. Let that one little experience be pervasive. This experience only happens in a minimized *now*.

In this moment, while you are having this experience, this is the only moment when *now* is. Anything else is memory of the past or imagining into the future. It is not *now*.

The point is that you only have power in a minimized *now*. Even a slightly expanded *now* sucks away your power.

By bringing your sensations into this minimized *now* you can take actions that are effective because of their appropriateness to the present moment. Even if the appropriate action is simply to breathe, to center yourself, to place your attention in an unexpected place, or to listen, the action will have power because it corresponds to what is wanted and needed in this exact present moment.

EMPOWERING YOUR INNER CHILD, NOT
A strong block to minimizing your now relates to a common misunderstanding that seems to have filtered into popular culture from the field of psychology. It is the idea of "empowering your inner child."

Somehow this distortion has become a trendy movement based on the idea that as children we experienced innocent joys that we miss when we are older and that we can regain our lost joy through bringing childhood ideas, beliefs, attitudes and behaviors back to life.

The fallacy in this concept of empowering your inner child is that children are not designed to take responsibility. When a child makes a mess, who cleans it up? The adults. For example, if your free and natural child ego state buys you an ice cream, flies your kite or plays in the sand at the beach, this may be a temporarily novel experience for a serious modern adult, but the result is that with your inner child in charge you are limited to making only child-sized messes. Your enormous adult linear and nonlinear creation forces are blocked.

In addition to this, when your inner child is empowered then you tend to relate functionally as a child. This can be problematical if you are wishing to enjoy the satisfying benefits of an adult-adult relationship. At first, carrying a child-like demeanor might seem cute, but it can lead to a rude awakening. Adult women are not attracted to being in relationship with little boys, and adult men are not attracted to being in relationship with little girls. The personalities attracted to little children in the opposite sex tend to be quite abusive. Perhaps you already know what I am talking about?

FREE AND NATURAL ADULT EGO STATE
Modern culture does not teach you that human beings have access to, or can actually live in, the free and natural adult ego state through succeeding in the archetypal rite of passage into adulthood.

WAYS TO LEAVE CHILD EGO STATE AND ENTER ADULT
World Copyright © 2010 owner Clinton Callahan grants permission to use. www.nextculture.org

If your child ego state still dominates your life you are not getting to live and relate from your creative, free-and-natural, responsible-adult ego state in the present. Instead you stay a child. Do you want a child in the driver's seat of your life, perceiving, expressing and choosing for you? What for? Growing up means sending the child back to where it belongs, with all the other memories of your past. You used to be a child. And now?

- Stop being adaptive. Take your center back from authority figures. Stand in your own center so that you can make decisions, take creative risks, take responsibility and live your authentic life.
- Stop withholding what you really want to say, what you actually think and feel. Your contribution is needed and wanted, even if it opposes whatever the rest of the group is thinking.
- Minimize your *now* into the present moment. Don't let it extend into a remembered past or an imagined future. Keep your *now* small.
- Ruthlessly distinguish between feelings and emotions (see Chapter 4).
- Experience your emotions as emotions. Express them consciously in a healing process so as to vanish them as completed communications.
- Recognize your unfulfilled childhood needs as just that: unfulfilled childhood needs. The needs are no longer present needs; they are memories. They remain strong memories because they are memories in all four bodies: physical, intellectual, emotional and energetic. But they are memories nonetheless. Does drinking a glass of water, *now*, remove a memory of being thirsty in the past? No. Does going pee, *now*, remove a memory of having to go pee very badly in the past? No. Does safe and exciting intimacy, *now*, remove the memory of wanting and not getting safe and exciting intimacy as a child? No. Distinguish your memories as just that: memories. They do not apply *now*.
- There is a hole in your *being* that was created by unfulfilled childhood needs. You might have noticed yourself standing in front of the refrigerator feeling needy, looking for what can fill this hole in your soul. You might expect your partner to fill that hole. There is bad news and good news about this gaping, aching, unfulfilled neediness hole. The *bad* news is that the refrigerator, your partner, even Mommy and Daddy, can *never* fulfill your unfulfilled childhood needs. Period. The *good* news is that the refrigerator, your partner, Mommy and Daddy are *never* coming to fulfill your unfulfilled childhood needs. *Nothing can ever fill the hole because the hole is in the past.* It is only memories. The good news is that your life can now be about something other than trying to fill that hole. Your life can be about living passionately *now*, developing your beneficial gifts and the gifts of others, and creating a bright future for your loved ones and your community.

When the free and natural *adult* ego state buys you an ice cream, flies your kite, or plays in the sand at the beach, you can make huge messes because as an adult you are absolutely responsible for cleaning them up. Adult messes include inventing new flavors and marketing

STANDING RAGE WORK This woman is leaving behind her complaining, manipulating, child ego state and using her adult woman power for making distinctions,
boundaries, decisions, requests and statements. This is Phase 1 of feelings work.
Note: in this set up, the front man's job is to just listen. The second man's job is to
make sure the first man just listens, and also to make sure that if the first man backs
up (which could definitely be a good idea) he does not crash into any furniture.

plans for the ice cream store, designing new shapes and control systems
for kites, and creating whole new worlds in the sand. Your playing field
can extend into reinventing cultural space, challenging common ways
of life, or establishing new forms of schooling that actually enliven the

creative potential of each individual. You can go even further. For example, you could take back your vote from the government officials who supposedly represent your intelligence and voice about where the money you paid them in taxes is being spent. You can take radical responsibility for adapting to nothing and for withholding nothing. You can get on with doing what you entered life to do instead of enacting typical socially accepted charades. This is the free and natural adult ego state in action.

If this sounds attractive, well, that's because it *should* sound attractive. Creating is your birthright and what you are designed for as an adult human being. From the perspective of having a free and natural adult in the driver's seat of your life, it becomes clear why stepping into adult-

STANDING RAGE WORK This close-up shows the proper form for standing rage work. The feeling being expressed is anger, so her fists are clenched with thumbs on the outside, feet solidly planted on the floor. She looks directly into the eyes, uses 50 percent of her energy in her voice and 50 percent in her body, and lets her body speak rather than her mind. The two other women loop their arms through her arms and hold her shoulders. This makes it both safe and comfortable for her to go to 100 percent maximum rage where she can reclaim her adult anger as a power source for intelligent actions.

hood includes ritually and actually sending your child ego state back to where it belongs, down the stream of memories into the past. You think you want a child in the driver's seat of your life? Think again.

STANDING RAGE On average it requires seven to ten deep emotional rite-of-passage processes spread over a couple of years to grow up in relationship to childhood and parental issues. Each process unbinds you from a layer of decisions that you made under conditions that no longer apply. You survived, it is true, but as you mature the strategy that once protected you eventually becomes your prison. Going through the liquid state that reorders your Box frees up your attention and energy to build matrix for more consciousness. Rite of passage is teamwork—we can't do it alone. In standing rage you start by choosing a man or woman to represent an authority figure with whom you practice making boundaries, changing agreements, starting things and stopping things. Standing rage is *rapid learning*, meaning that after each attempt you receive feedback and coaching from the rest of the team about your posture, feelings, voice and clarity. You use the feedback to shift and go again. The stand-in listener (on the left) is assured of safety by the second man at his side, who also cheers you on during your process.

AVOIDING STAGE FRIGHT AND STUTTERING

You now have all the distinctions you need to avoid the nervous, sweating paralysis commonly known as *stage fright*. Stage fright is caused by placing your center out in the future while directing your attention to yourself. Moving your center into the future—a few seconds, moments, days, months, or (yes) years—eliminates any possibility of you taking action. No one has the power to take actions in the future, not even Superman. You cannot make a future action happen now. Certainly you can prepare yourself. You can practice, or you can handle the necessary details to help insure a favorable outcome in the future. But you can only prepare, practice, or handle details *now*, not in the future. With your center in the future and your attention on yourself, you stare in horror at your absolute powerlessness, and of course you will freeze up. You are paralyzed because there is nothing you can do now to cause an effect in the future. Even though you may desperately want to make a difference now, you absolutely cannot.

To release the paralyzing spell, bring your center out of the future into a minimized now and a minimized here in the adult ego state, and put your attention out there in the circumstances around you instead of focusing it on yourself. To get in the here-and-now present it can help to ever-so-gently rub your thumb against the tip of your forefinger. The sensations of finger friction only happen here and now. Finger caressing is very intense in experiential reality. Stay in that intensity. Keep breathing. Keep your being center on your physical center in the present and keep your attention out there in the surroundings while doing whatever you need to do right now. Voila! No more stage fright.

Stuttering is when your mind moves faster than your mouth. If you put your being center into the thinking processes of your mind, you are putting your center into the future because thoughts move faster than the body can move. If your center is in your mind it is moving ahead of your body. Speaking involves your whole body: lips, tongue, throat, hands, face, posture, and attitude. The body is stuck in the material world in the present and cannot speak out of the future, so by placing your center into your thinking, you cause a breakdown between your mouth and your mind, and you stutter. Speaking eloquently requires keeping your being center located in the physical center of your body. You can use the same finger-caressing technique as with stage fright. The mind will do whatever it does to think things out, but don't put your center in your mind. Keep your center in the present physical experience of your body and speak, sing, dance, juggle, work out of your physical center.

You will not be able to speak as fast as your mind thinks. But no matter. No one could understand you speaking that fast anyway.

You can think fast privately, to yourself. But when you speak to others, you can slow your thinking down. You can also experiment with disconnecting your speaking from your thinking; that is, speak directly out of your body or your heart. In this case you will speak before your mind actually knows what you are going to say.

You can also experiment with speaking out of the space of possibility as a representative of your Bright Principles. We will talk more about this later in the book.

KNOWING YOU ARE IN A LOW DRAMA

Finding your way into the adult ego state opens the door to being able to create high drama. What often gets in the way of being able to create high drama is not knowing that you are already in a low drama!

Low drama is any action designed to avoid responsibility.

How can you tell you are in a low drama? There are very clear indicators if you construct and use a *Low Drama Detector*.

LOW DRAMA Notice how the victim (center) is shifting into her persecutor mode getting ready to attack the persecutor. Notice how the rescuer is saying, *We're okay, she's not okay*, a position of superiority and disrespect. Nobody is listening to anybody. Low drama is not authentic relationship; it is Gremlin feeding time.

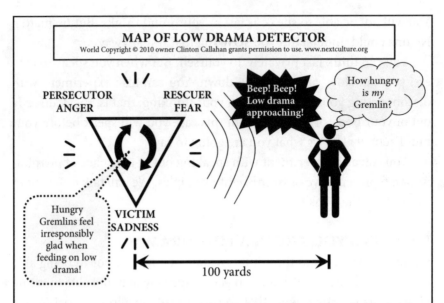

Your *Low Drama Detector* can sense a low drama approaching from one hundred yards away. It warns you with a flashing red light on the front of your right shoulder, announcing *Beep! Beep! Beep! Low drama approaching! Proceed with extreme caution! Do not get hooked!* It is simple but not easy to detect an approaching low drama: victimhood, irresponsible feelings, resentment, blaming, complaining, justifying, proving yourself right, or making someone else wrong. The *not easy* part is that low drama is *VERY* tempting Gremlin food. A hungry Gremlin can turn any situation into low drama. If your Gremlin is hungry, watch out! If anyone thinks there is a problem and it is someone else's fault, or even the fault of circumstances, that is low drama. Use your *Sword of Clarity* to make distinctions so you step to the side of approaching low dramas like a bullfighter steps aside from a charging bull. Unhooked you retain the freedom of movement to take responsible actions!

MAP OF HOW I KNOW I AM IN A LOW DRAMA
World Copyright © 2010 owner Clinton Callahan grants permission to use. www.nextculture.org

LOW DRAMA DETECTION

Build and mount a *Low Drama Detect or* on the front of your right shoulder. The instant it detects a low drama, trust its warning and respond immediately. Your response can be subtle, but if you ignore the warning you will be knocked unconscious by your own hungry Gremlin and you will be sucked into the low drama for its full duration. Time and energy spent in low drama is precious time and energy you won't have for creating extraordinary or archetypal possibilitie s that nurture you as an adult man or woman.

You are definitely creating low drama if you are:

- Blaming anyone for anything, including yourself.
- Feeling resentful, even secretly.
- Justifying yourself, even in your own mind.
- Complaining about anything, even under your breath.
- Criticizing, judging, nitpicking yourself or others.
- Trying to be right, propagandizing, sacrificing relationship.
- Trying to make someone else wrong, gossiping, mobbing.
- Plotting revenge, being spiteful, being stingy, being small.
- Mixing your feelings: depression, isolation, *schadenfreude*, hysteria, despair, guilt, jealousy, shame, envy, etc.
- Having an argument in your mind.
- Being superior or arrogant, even with good reason.
- Withholding yourself, not playing, taking your ball and going home.
- Giving your center away, being adaptive, being nice.
- Being in a funk, sulking, giving up, regretting.
- Using addictions to solve your problems.
- Feeding your Gremlin.

The way out of low drama is through being authentic about your inauthenticity. As soon as you detect a low drama, name it. Say, "This is a low drama. I am in a low drama." Then instantly reveal your part in creating the whole thing. Admit that you are playing victim, persecutor or rescuer on purpose. Name your game, and specifically what your payoff is for playing it. Get real. Look bad. The way to responsibility is through authentic remorse about your irresponsibility: *hitting bottom.* Nothing else works because nothing else is true.

MAP OF HOW TO AVOID LOW DRAMA
World Copyright © 2010 owner Clinton Callahan grants permission to use. www.nextculture.org

Responsibility is the procedure for change.

USE THESE PRACTICES TO AVOID LOW DRAMA

- Refuse to leave the adult ego state, where you are yourself in the *minimized now* of the present moment. Put a stake in the ground there.
- Declare that you are not a victim. If there is no victim, there can be no low drama.
- Consciously feel your four distinct feelings: anger, sadness, joy, fear.
- Detect if you are experiencing a present feeling or an emotion projected from your past or from an authority figure or institution (Hint, if the feeling lasts longer than a few minutes, it is an emotion.)
- Use your emotions to detect the healing that you need to do.
- Use your feelings to responsibly handle things:
  o Make a boundary / become the boundary.
  o Ask for what you want.
  o Make a decision: yes or no.
  o Make a distinction. Be precise.
  o Start something / End something.
- Neutrally observe what is really going on. Choose what is.
- Make a paper-thin gap of nothingness between your Box and you.
- Take radical responsibility for creating your circumstances. It is no one else's fault.
- If there are other people's voices in your head, blast them away with your Voice Blaster.
- Apologize for your patterns that have caused the breakdown.
- Willingly enter the pain of remorse. Clear your resentments.
- Be authentic about your inauthenticity.
- Determine whose problem it is. If it is your problem, take responsibility. If it is not your problem, it is none of your business.
- Get centered. Find and keep your attention. Stay unhookable.
- Use your innate genius to continuously invent new ways to get out of low drama. Share what you learn with your friends, *and* with your enemies.

HIGH DRAMA

Low drama is any action designed to avoid responsibility. Once you can consciously avoid engaging in low drama, what remains is high drama.

We live in a responsible universe. You are *automatically* responsible, for *everything*. In a responsible universe, *irresponsibility is an illusion*. It is impossible to be a victim. There is no such thing as a problem without you being there creating the Is-Glued story and announcing that there *is* a problem. The moment you stop generating low drama, you are generating high drama. High drama is any action in which you take responsibility.

For example, if you are at the dinner table and you would like some water to drink and you say, "I am really thirsty," you are playing victim in a low drama, trying to manipulate someone else into rescuing you. If instead you say, "Harry, will you please pass me the water?," you are playing warrior in a high drama. High drama is that simple.

If you are at a meeting and you think, "Man, this meeting is so irrelevant. Such a waste of time. The president never addresses the important issues," you are playing persecutor in a low drama. If instead you raise your hand and say, "I would be ashamed of myself if I walked out of this meeting without bringing up this important issue," you are playing magician in a high drama.

The possibility of high drama begins in the adult ego state, where you have your own voice and your own feelings in the present moment. These are the resources you need for creating high drama.

One way out of a low drama is through responsibly admitting that you are in a low drama. This is a kind of radical honesty. Admitting the truth even if you look bad gives you the power of actually being where you are. Responsibly admitting you are in a low drama is an act of high drama.

You may have imagined that high drama would be bold and noble deeds, riding up on your white horse and saving the world from the bad guys: *Star Wars*, *Lord of the Rings*, *Matrix*, *The Fifth Element*, *Avatar*, this sort of thing.

It can be.

In the world's present state of affairs, it *needs* to be.

At the same time, high drama starts in your own home with your own partner, kids, and neighbors: staying in contact, listening fully, keeping your promises, doing what you say you will do, retaining your center, holding space for Bright Principles and High Level Fun. High drama starts as close as your own aching back.

HIGH DRAMA BACKACHE

These days many people seem to experience more pain than they know what to do with. If you go the mainstream route with your pain you will walk out of the pharmacy with an armload of prescription drugs designed to help you stay numb. Staying numb with prescription drugs can be fatal. For example, the New York City medical examiner's office ruled the cause of Heath Ledger's death to be "acute intoxication by the combined effects of prescription medications including painkillers, anti-anxiety drugs and sleeping pills." Sounds like he knew of no other way to deal with his feelings. Too bad. Michael Jackson died after an injection of the painkiller Propofol—clearly trying to stay numb.

In fact, the third highest cause of death in America after heart disease and cancer is prescription drugs! *Hundreds of thousands* of victims each year in America alone learn this the hard way. Research it yourself (e.g., google *iatrogenesis*).

For every person that somehow dies using health food supplements in America, fifty thousand people die from prescription drugs, yet pharmaceutical companies find it profitable to spend hundreds of millions of dollars each year—more than any other industry—lobbying to get more drugs legalized, and more natural vitamins, minerals and herbs outlawed. But I digress . . .

I sometimes ask groups of people assembled for a public talk how many would honestly admit to having physical aches and pains during their day. On average, 90 percent raise their hands; sometimes everyone. Physical pain is not the rare occurrence we might have assumed it to be.

If expressing feelings is judged to be *bad* or *dangerous*, the Box may decide it is safer to opt for the physical pain of repressing feelings into deep muscle tissues rather than to consciously experience the feelings.

Let's say a person has back pain. If they only know low drama, they could easily feel victimized by their pain. The natural victim response is to reject the pain, hate the pain, give up life in the face of so much pain, fight the pain, or try to get rid of the pain. Much physical, intellectual, emotional and spiritual energy is expended relating to pain as if the pain is persecuting them.

If this person were to take radical responsibility for the existence of their pain, their relationship to the pain would become a dance of high drama collaboration. The pain would no longer own them. Instead the pain would be a trusted messenger. The pain would become a pathway for Box expansion, matrix building, and personal transformation. The high drama person begins their conversation with pain by saying, "Hello, pain. What do you teach me today? What do you teach me in this moment?"

In high drama, pain is the teacher. Pain can teach many things. If you let your pain or other people's pain speak to you, pain becomes a gateway to new ways of being. Pain is your friend. Pain can teach you:

- to express deep unexpressed anger: anger from birth, from childhood, even from lifetimes ago.

- to express unexpressed fears: fears from birth, from childhood, even from lifetimes ago.

- to express unexpressed sadness: sadness from birth, from childhood, even from lifetimes ago.

- to express unexpressed joy: joy from choosing to be born, from childhood, even from lifetimes ago.

- to no longer carry the burdens of your parents and ancestors; they are not your burdens. You can give those burdens back to their rightful owners so they carry their own burdens and did not die in vain.

- to no longer carry the burdens of your children as they become responsible for their own lives; the decisions and consequences are theirs, not yours.

- to accept and be compassionate about other people's pain, so you can be with them even when they have pain.

- to face your own death; to accept that you are mortal and that your body is impermanent.

- to minimize your *now* into this very moment when you experience the pain.

- to recognize and accept that you do have limitations.

- to accept that you can be weak; that you can be the opposite of the strong, numb survival hero.

Trying to get rid of pain is trying to reject *what is*. *What is* is *what is*. *What is* cannot be rejected except at great price; for example, sacrificing your ability to take action according to the exact circumstances of *what is*. Only through accepting *what is,* as it is, do you have the power to navigate *what is* into something else.

In high drama pain is the message that life is to be lived fully, out loud, and now. Pain is the reminder that you are still alive and have something yet to do.

In high drama pain is not negative, bad or dangerous. Pain is pain. Pain has sounds that you can make, sounds that lead to feelings that can be expressed and heard. Expressing these pain feelings frees up isometric pain energy. This freed-up energy lets you move in new ways and take new actions that were blocked before. Pain informs you of new risks to take, new experiments to try, communications to make, boundaries to establish, physical movements to stretch into, projects to start, psychoemotional baggage to let go of.

In high drama, pain is perceived within a larger field of ecstatic existence rather than the other way around in low drama, where moments of ecstasy are perceived as lost within a field of overall pain.

In high drama pain informs you about who to talk to about what; where to go and what to do there; what needs to be said or listened to; who to apologize to; who to forgive; who to say "I love you" to before it's too late.

You may want to find partners and take turns experimenting in the direction of overacting the feelings in your pain. Get on stage and really complain. Consciously exaggerate your repressed emotions. Angrily curse at God for inventing pain and at your own body for hurting. The idea, of course, is to gain experience being no longer numb. What you will find is that everything actually hurts: even laughing, even feathers, even ecstasy. Lower your numbness bar to get used to the intensity of experience, each incidence of which is at first classified in your mind as painful.

MAP OF LOW DRAMA AND HIGH DRAMA FEELINGS
World Copyright © 2010 owner Clinton Callahan grants permission to use. www.nextculture.org

Your four feelings of anger, sadness, fear and joy are neutral energy and information. By attaching the story that your feelings are positive or negative, good or bad, your feelings are no longer neutral. Then you unconsciously use your feelings to empower low drama archetypes (the good/bad dichotomy is itself a low drama principle). By consciously attaching your four feelings to stories that empower loving communication, useful nonlinear creation, clear responsible action, and visionary leadership, you empower high drama archetypes. In each moment, the choice about which way to use your feelings is yours.

HIGH DRAMA	WHAT IS	LOW DRAMA
Conscious and responsible use of feelings:	Neutral energy and information of feelings:	Unconscious and irresponsible use of feelings:
COMMUNICATOR Lover: listen, relationship	**SADNESS** I feel sad because_ _.	**VICTIM** Poor me, I'm not okay.
CREATOR Magician: discover, invent	**FEAR** I feel scared because_ _.	**RESCUER** I'm okay, you are not. I do it for you.
DOER / MAKER Warrior: clarity, accomplish	**ANGER** I feel angry because_ _.	**PERSECUTOR** I'm okay, you are not. I get rid of you.
MAN or WOMAN King / Queen: lead, inspire	**JOY** I feel glad because_ _.	**GREMLIN** Ha! I got you! I win, you lose!

In most every moment you have feelings in your body. These feelings are neutral energy and information provided in the times and amounts needed by you to fulfill your destiny. If you use your feelings unconsciously and irresponsibly, you create low drama. If you use the feelings consciously and responsibly, you create high drama.

AUTHENTICITY
High drama appears to take many different forms, some of them quite unexpected when viewed from the perspectives of modern culture. For example, one form of high drama is authenticity.

In modern society authenticity is "a four-letter word," as are words like integrity, impeccability, dignity, or transparency. Yet, authenticity is the basis of intimate relationship and a strong source of nutrition for body, mind, heart and soul.

In mainstream society we divide life circumstances into two categories: those things we find acceptable, and those things that are not acceptable to us.

Through becoming more intimately aware of your subtle daily feelings you could well discover that there is a third category of conditions in your life: those things that you pretend to accept but which you actually do not accept. This is your area of false acceptance.

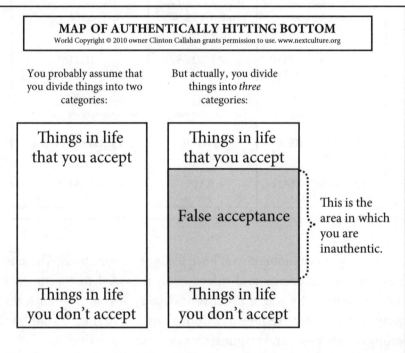

MAP OF AUTHENTICALLY HITTING BOTTOM

World Copyright © 2010 owner Clinton Callahan grants permission to use. www.nextculture.org

You probably assume that you divide things into two categories:

But actually, you divide things into *three* categories:

Things in life that you accept

Things in life you don't accept

Things in life that you accept

False acceptance

Things in life you don't accept

This is the area in which you are inauthentic.

The way toward authenticity is through being authentic about your inauthenticity. To say: *I have been fooling myself about. . .* This is painful. This is *hitting bottom*. Whenever you hit bottom, *stay there*. Feeling the pain of authentic remorse redeems your underworld; meaning that your underworld becomes useful in the moment that you allow your pain about underworld-motivated actions to become conscious.

NOTE: The Acceptance-Unacceptance Rectangle was originated by Thomas Gordon before 1970. More information can be found in his excellent book *P.E.T.: Parent Effectiveness Training* <www.gordontraining.com>.

The conditions that you falsely accept are the areas in which you are inauthentic.

False acceptance is still false acceptance even if it is brief or trivial. For example, if you invite someone over for coffee and they arrive twenty minutes early, it may be false acceptance if you stop and entertain them instead of having them wait while you finish what you truly want to do.

Or you might discover that the firm that manufactures your favorite chocolate mints was bought by a large conglomerate that is also taking ownership of local and national water supplies because having control over a dwindling public water supply could become quite profitable for them. Continuing to buy their chocolate mints might be false acceptance.

It gets worse. If your government representatives have been coerced by corporate weapons / banking / pharmaceutical / oil lobbyists to pass measures for borrowing and spending ungodly amounts of money in your name for military and political involvements that only bring more profits to the corporations and more misery to people instead of increasing human well-being on Earth, and you still remain a citizen of that country, this could be false acceptance.

The way toward authenticity is to be authentic about your inauthenticity. This will entail integrating feelings into your communications.

6. COMMUNICATING
WITH FEELINGS

(NOTE TO THE READER: If you have skipped ahead to this chapter without carefully studying the previous five chapters, it's a clever idea but I don't recommend it. Learning to consciously feel has similarities to learning to tame lions, which is actually quite simple. Grab a whip and a chair, keep a few chunks of beef in your pocket, and shout your commands. But they make you take lessons and get a license before letting you go tame lions. It's for your own good. That's because if you neglect the pecking order of the pride and put the wrong lion first they will rip each other to shreds. If you don't command your own attention they will ignore you completely. And if you forget that they only do what you want because they want to do it, they will bite your head off. I am not saying anything like this will happen if you skip over the previous chapters. But I am saying that the world of conscious feelings operates under different laws than the world of numbness, just like lion taming is different from petting your kitty. Before you pick up the challenge of communicating with feelings I strongly encourage you to study the first five chapters of this book. It's for your own good.)

FEELINGS BRING MORE HARMONY

Spiritual teacher Lee Lozowick says, "Feelings are for bringing some kind of harmony to the system, as strange as it may seem." This distinction can lead you into some very interesting experiments. For example, each time you have a feeling, what if you consider it to be a message from your heart telling you that something is out of harmony? The feeling informs you that an action is required to bring things back into balance.

The experiment is to trust rather than reject the incoming flow of even subtle feelings. Permit each feeling to not only reveal exactly what action would bring more harmony, but also to deliver an impulse that moves you from your center to accomplish that action. The intelligence of the feeling informs you what requires your attention in this moment. The energy of the feeling empowers responsible actions that bring things into a more elegant and beneficial balance.

NOTE: The above procedures come from Phase 2 of feelings work because they involve the conscious and responsible use of feelings. You may not yet be ready for Phase 2 of feelings work. Here is the test. If you . . .

- still mix your feelings and experience depression, schaden-freude, despair or hysteria,

- still participate in low drama bickering, permitting your Gremlin to feed on the potential intimacies between you and your partner, children, colleagues, relatives or neighbors,

- still think that circumstances or someone else is ruining your life,

- still regard emotions from your past, from someone else, or from some institution as if they are real feelings,

- still think your stories or other people's stories are the truth instead if Is-Glued concoctions of conscious or unconscious theater,

. . . then you have not yet graduated from Phase 1 of feelings work. It would probably be wisest if you stopped reading here, returned to Chapter 1, and read the previous five chapters over again.

Many people who follow this recommendation report that during their second reading they cannot believe how many whole paragraphs seem completely new to them, as if they had never read them before.

This is understandable. Most of the information in this book is stunningly new. It comes from next culture, completely beyond the limits of mainstream thinking. It won't take you so long to read these pages a second time. Taking this responsible action would establish a solid platform from which you could embark on a future of Phase 2 feelings work with confidence and good cheer. I encourage you to take a moment now to decide whether you will start over at Chapter 1 again or are qualified to continue reading.

FEELINGS BRING MORE ENERGY

Living with feelings (as opposed to emotions) can be like surfing. A surfer does not use his own energy to ride to the shore. He is transported along by the force of the waves.

The same can happen when you are no longer numb. Depending on low drama energy to get through the onslaught of daily life challenges can make you exhausted, whereas adult and archetypal feelings provide an external source of energy for you to use. If you distinguish between feelings and emotions, and if you set the emotions aside and feel your feelings, then just as in surfing, you can be carried along by the energy and intelligence of your feelings. The feelings energy is not your energy, so you are not exhausted! The energy and intelligence of feelings is available for you to fulfill your destiny.

FEELINGS COME WITH ACTION STEPS ATTACHED

One morning I sat down at my office desk and noticed I was feeling afraid. "That's strange," I thought. The fear did not make sense. I looked around my desk. "What is there to be afraid of?" The thing that caught my attention was an unopened envelope. I picked it up and saw that it was a bill from the telephone company. I tore it open and found that the payment was due *that day*. I paid the bill, and immediately the fear vanished. This is what fear is for. If I was afraid to feel my 3 percent intensity fear when I sat down at my desk that morning, I would not have benefited from its intelligent message.

Fear comes with action steps to check on plans and agreements for times, places, dates, and finances. Fear tells you what to watch out for, what to be cautious about, when to be precise, how to regain balance, which details are important, how to prepare, when to be careful, and what to proactively handle.

Anger comes with action steps to create clarity, make distinctions, make clear decisions, start something, change something, juice up to complete something, and end something by saying, "This is finished!"

Anger cleans things out, makes boundaries, and indicates what to manage to make things happen.

Sadness comes with action steps to connect more intimately, to let go control, to trust, to listen, to honor and respect, to have compassion, to be vulnerable, to accept what is, to get off of your rigid position, to understand from a bigger perspective, to be flexible, to let yourself be known, and to share with others what is important for you before it is time to die.

Joy comes with action steps to take more risks, to bring people together, to share your vision, to play, to empower diverse intelligences in your team, to lead, to send blessings, to invest in the development of your own community and their projects, and to celebrate even when there is nothing to celebrate about.

USE FEELINGS TO MAKE NEW DECISIONS

Sometimes the action step attached to a feeling will be to make a new decision. For example, during childhood you quite likely made many basic life decisions about who you were, who other people were in relation to you, and what to do to survive in the situation you found yourself in with people like *them*. As you grew older the circumstances surrounding you may have changed, but the decisions themselves have remained in effect exactly as you made them in childhood. Since the decisions have become so familiar you have forgotten they were decisions. You assume the world and other people are actually like you decided they are, and you don't even know that it is an assumption.

It may have come to pass that the decisions which once protected you from a complex and hazardous world have now become your prison. Escaping the childhood prison (or the federal prison) commences with recognizing who built the prison around you in the first place. It wasn't your parents. It wasn't the teachers at school. It wasn't the kids in the neighborhood. It wasn't the television. It wasn't the government. It wasn't God. It was you who made each of the decisions that put you in prison.

Once you return to the point of origin and take full responsibility for having made a decision in the first place, you gain the power to remake that decision in any way you want.

The following is a true example of a person facing one of the many possible imprisoning decisions. (The questions are being asked by a trained Possibility Manager during a possibility session, and the answers have been condensed for clarity.)

Q: "What can I do for you?"

A: "I feel so lonely."

Q: "Are you lonely because you share about your feelings and no one will listen to you? Or are you lonely because you do not share?"

A: "I am lonely because I do not share."

Q: "Could you share more?"

A: "Only if I make a new decision about not being harmed for sharing."

Q: "Which feeling warns you that you might be harmed for sharing?"

A: "Fear. I feel scared of being harmed if I am vulnerable."

Q: "Is that a *feeling of fear* or an *emotion* of fear?"

A: "It's emotional fear. It was not safe for me to reveal myself as a child."

Q: "Is that childhood decision still influencing your life today?"

A: "Yes. I often freeze up when I am faced with opportunities to share about myself."

Q: "Would you like to make a new adult decision?"

A: "Yes. I am so tired of being lonely."

Q: "What could your new decision be?"

A: "I trust myself to take care of myself while sharing about my feelings."

Q: "What do you feel now?"

A: "I feel sad that I have been lonely for so long. I feel glad to share about my feelings now."

Q: "Did you take care of yourself while sharing about your feelings just now?"

A: "Yes."

Q: "Do you look forward to not being lonely anymore?"

A: "Yes."

EIGHTH DISTINCTION: FEELINGS SERVE PROFESSIONAL COMMUNICATIONS

Sometimes the action step attached to your feeling will simply be to communicate the feeling. As clarified in the seventh distinction, learning to experience your feelings is only the first phase of feelings work. Phase 2 involves learning to use your feelings for adult responsible communications.

The eighth of the Ten Distinctions for Consciously Feeling says that as an adult you can consciously integrate feelings into responsible speaking and listening so that feelings serve you relationally and professionally.

To integrate feelings into your communications it will be useful to have in mind a simple communications model. The model I propose is based on the communications principle that *a communication persists until it is received.*

Have you ever noticed that you repeatedly hear the same whining from people around you? The same complaints? Repeated accusations? Have you ever noticed that communications tend to get stuck at a certain level of intimacy and can proceed no further? These and other communication breakdowns are symptoms of communications not being received.

There are two main causes for communications not being received.

1. You use an incomplete thoughtmap of what a communication is.

2. You block the completion loop to avoid feeling what you might feel if you truly received the communication.

The incomplete communication concept looks like this:

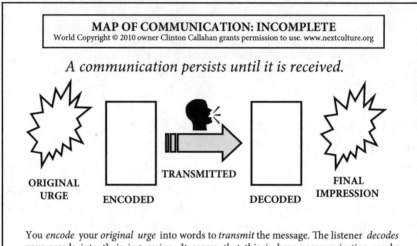

MAP OF COMMUNICATION: INCOMPLETE
World Copyright © 2010 owner Clinton Callahan grants permission to use. www.nextculture.org

A communication persists until it is received.

ORIGINAL URGE

ENCODED

TRANSMITTED

DECODED

FINAL IMPRESSION

You *encode* your *original urge* into words to *transmit* the message. The listener *decodes* your words into their *impression*. It seems that this is how communication works. However, *half of the communication process is missing!* Without including the other half, your communications fail because they are not *completed*. Your job is to receive communications. Receiving a communication completes it forever.

Receiving a communication includes delivering a *completion loop*, a further step in the process, during which you as the listener repeat back to the speaker what you heard them say. This allows the speaker to verify whether or not their original message was heard.

If the correct impression was not received the speaker has a chance to resend. Without using a completion loop there is only guessing about what another person hears, so the message is not complete.

Communication succeeds in the head of the listener, not in the head of the speaker. If the message received by the listener is not validated by the speaker, the speaker does not know what the listener heard, so the speaker is only talking to himself.

Incomplete communications are easy enough to correct. Simply make it a practice to use a *completion loop* in your communications. A completion loop is the other half of the communication process, when the listener says, "What I heard you say is . . . ," and then you repeat back what you heard them say. The communication thoughtmap is simple, but using it in everyday life turns out to be not so simple.

MESSAGES CONTAIN ENERGY AND INFORMATION
Messages are made up of two basic ingredients:

1. The information of the message: concept, request, boundary, clarification, need, etc.

2. The energy of the message: feelings, conscious purpose, hidden purpose, etc.

If you ignore either of these ingredients, the communication fails.

For example, if the original message is "I feel angry that you did not keep your promise to fix the leaky faucet this morning," a completion loop would include both components.

1. It would include the information of the message: *I did not keep my promise to fix the leaky faucet this morning.*

2. And it would also include the energy of the message, the "carrier wave": *You feel angry about that.*

If either part of the message is not received and confirmed through a completion loop from the listener, then the *entire message* is not received. Receiving a partial message does not equate to success in the art of communication.

Here is where things seem to hang up. *If you actually hear a person's feeling of anger, sadness, fear or joy, then you will be touched by that feeling.*

If it is not okay for you to feel what the speaker is feeling then you will automatically and unconsciously block the completion loop so you do not have to feel it, no matter how much you might wish to be in communication with that person.

You are already an expert at blocking communications. You are an expert because that is what was done to you. Communications are not completed in modern society. Parents don't do it with each other or with their children. Teachers don't do it with other teachers or with their students. Bosses don't do it with employees or colleagues. Politicians don't do it with constituents or other politicians. The television doesn't do it. Where should you ever learn to do it?

If it is not okay for you to feel then you will reflexively block communications with unconscious habits. Instead of using a completion loop you will offer solutions, give your opinions, deliver advice, criticize the other's thinking, dismiss their feelings, threaten them with terrible consequences, make jokes to distract them, and so on. No matter how appropriate or useful these responses might seem to you, *none of them confirms the original communication*, so the speaker is unsatisfied. The speaker has the experience of not being fully heard. This is one of the most painful experiences a human being can have.

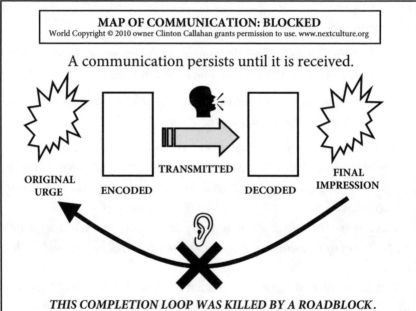

MAP OF COMMUNICATION: BLOCKED
World Copyright © 2010 owner Clinton Callahan grants permission to use. www.nextculture.org

A communication persists until it is received.

TRANSMITTED

ORIGINAL URGE   ENCODED   DECODED   FINAL IMPRESSION

THIS COMPLETION LOOP WAS KILLED BY A ROADBLOCK.

This *completion loop* has been destroyed by a *communication roadblock* so that the listener does not have to feel what they would feel if they actually heard the communication. The listener blocks conscious adult communications with advice, opinions, solutions, judgments, criticisms, positive aphorisms, and humorous distractions, none of which completes the communication. Since the communication is not confirmed by the listener, the speaker is unsatisfied, and the communication must be repeated. The ultimate consequence of incomplete communications is war.

Dissatisfaction is one of the most common outcomes of modern communication. The ultimate result of unsatisfactory communication is war.

It does not have to be this way. A world without war begins with you completing both the information and the energy of communications, even if you have feelings in the process. A world without war begins with you learning to consciously feel.

MAP OF COMMUNICATION: COMPLETED
World Copyright © 2010 owner Clinton Callahan grants permission to use. www.nextculture.org

A communication persists until it is received. An adult completes communications through receiving them. A communication is received when both the energy and the information is heard *and* confirmed. By completing a communication, you end the *doing* of communication and take a step closer to the original intent of *being* in love together.

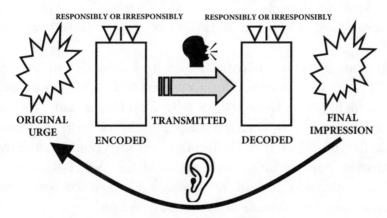

COMPLETION LOOP
You as the listener repeat back in your own words what you heard the speaker say. If the speaker confirms the accuracy of what you repeated by saying *Yes*, it signals that this communication has been completed. Then you can both go to the next deeper level of intimacy together.

THE MAGIC OF CHOOSING RESPONSIBILITY
In the adult ego state you have the ability to *responsibly decode an irresponsibly encoded message*. This is nothing less than miraculous.

PRACTICE COMPLETING COMMUNICATIONS

Now it is time to practice. It is astonishing to experience the effectiveness of communicating with feelings. Yesterday, for example, our five-year-old Merlin came stomping up the stairs in tears, sobbing, "David hit me in the head with a pillow!" David is Merlin's eleven-year-old brother.

Rather than jumping into the fray and stomping back downstairs with Merlin to scold David, as used to be her pattern, Marion, Merlin's mother, squats down, looks Merlin straight in the eyes, and with an even voice repeats back, "David hit you in the head with a pillow." (It is not a question. It is a simple statement, repeating back what Merlin said.)

What is Merlin's response? He says, "*Yes!*"

That *Yes* is like the successful *Bing!* tone in a video game. The *Bing!* signifies that Merlin's message was received by his mom, and now that particular message is gone forever! Merlin is now free to go to his next deeper level of intimacy.

Merlin says, "I knocked down David's castle because it was too high!"

Marion's previous tendencies would have produced an outburst like, "It is not okay to knock down someone else's castle just because it is too high! It took David a lot of time to build that castle. You can knock down your *own* castles, but not David's!" or some such communication roadblock (See Thomas Gordon's marvelous book *Parent Effectiveness Training* for a complete list of the Twelve Roadblocks to Communication). Instead, Marion uses a completion loop: "You knocked down David's castle because it was too high."

What does Merlin say? "*Yes!*" (*Bing!*) Again Marion completes Merlin's message. Again Merlin has been heard and he can go to the next deeper level.

"David put my Teddy on top of the castle so I couldn't reach it!"

Marion's scolding would have been *completely* inappropriate if she had followed her first impulse rather than completing Merlin's communication. Luckily, she didn't fall into that trap as she had done hundreds of times before learning to use completion loops. Marion continues using completion loops, "David put your Teddy on the top of the castle so you couldn't reach it."

"Yes!" (Bing!) "I will *never* play with David again!"

"You will never again play with David."

It is unbelievable but at this point, no *Yes!* comes from Merlin because Marion completed all of his urgent communications and he is already headed back down the stairs to continue playing with his beloved brother. Marion did not waste her energy, Merlin's energy or David's energy, and love is happening. This is the value of using completion loops.

Now you practice.

The times to most effectively use completion loops are when a person comes to you with a problem or with something to share, which could be far more often than you might realize. If you use completion

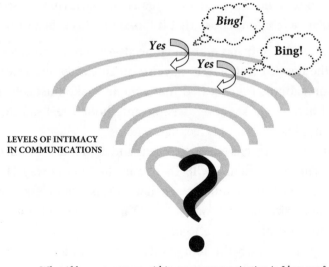

MAP OF COMMUNICATION LAYERS

World Copyright © 2010 owner Clinton Callahan grants permission to use. www.nextculture.org

What is the central message within every communication? You can approach it through completing successive communications at the level they are given to you. When a communication is completed a person cannot help but say, *Yes*, meaning, *Yes, you have understood me!* This is a *Bing!* You have succeeded! With each *Bing!* you drop to the next deeper level of intimacy.

Bing!

Yes

Bing!

Yes

LEVELS OF INTIMACY
IN COMMUNICATIONS

What if the core message within every communication is *I love you*?
How often have you blocked communications at a superficial level
and missed out on the deeper message?

loops appropriately, they are invisible. If you use completion loops inappropriately people might comment, "Is there an echo in here? I just said that. Have you become a parrot?" Listen to your feedback. Competence comes through practice.

FOUR BODY COMMUNICATION

Each of your four bodies has its own communication mode. You can recognize this in yourself quite easily.

Your *physical body* has physical needs and communicates actions and sensations: I'm hungry. Let's eat. I'm tired. I want to go home. You're stepping on my foot!

Your *intellectual body* has intellectual needs and communicates information from the mind. There are two kinds of information to communicate.

- Objective information, such as facts, rules, and precisions: What time is it? This is the wrong way. It costs sixteen dollars and starts at 7 P.M. I already read that book. This is not mine.

- Subjective information, such as opinions, beliefs, compliments and complaints: I can't do this. He's a real angel. They are so rude. You are a fabulous cook. That is too loud. This is beautiful.

Your *emotional body* has emotional needs and communicates feelings from the heart: I feel glad to have so much clarity about feelings and communications. I feel scared that I might make mistakes. I feel angry that I had no classes about feelings in school. I feel sad that my father does not know about his feelings.

Your *energetic body* has energetic needs and communicates inspiration, vision, commitment and will: There must be a better way. Human beings have access to more intelligence than this. Is it hopeless or not? I want to connect with teams. I want to create and implement sustainable culture. I know it is possible. Let's go!

Once you distinguish the four kinds of communications coming from your own four bodies, distinguishing the four kinds of communications coming from someone else's four bodies becomes simple. Significant miscommunications result from thinking that a person is expressing from their emotional body when in fact they are expressing from their intellectual body, and so on. Such confusions are so common as to be normal.

Take a breath before speaking—a few second's pause to identify which of your four bodies wants to speak, or which of the other person's four bodies is talking to you. This simple but profound practice permits you to clarify your own needs and to more appropriately respond to another person's needs. Waking up to the four kinds of messages takes you a long way toward successful and satisfying adult communications.

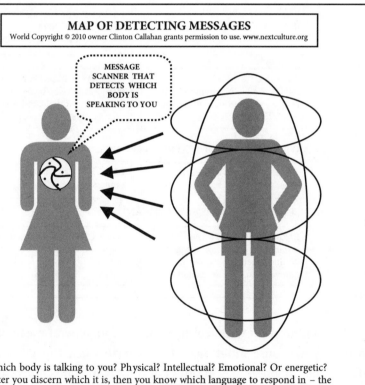

MAP OF DETECTING MESSAGES

World Copyright © 2010 owner Clinton Callahan grants permission to use. www.nextculture.org

MESSAGE SCANNER THAT DETECTS WHICH BODY IS SPEAKING TO YOU

Which body is talking to you? Physical? Intellectual? Emotional? Or energetic? After you discern which it is, then you know which language to respond in – the language of actions, ideas, feelings, or aspirations. You can detect which body is addressing you with your internal *Message Scanner*. It seeks to detect: Why are they talking to me? What do they need? The answer is simple. There are only four choices:

1. Do they want me to do something? This is the body speaking.
2. Do they seek or offer information? This is the mind speaking.
3. Do they want to share a feeling? This is the heart speaking.
4. Do they have a vision? A wish? This is the soul speaking.

MAP OF FOUR KINDS OF MESSAGES

World Copyright © 2010 owner Clinton Callahan grants permission to use. www.nextculture.org

THE URGE TO COMMUNICATE COMES FROM AN EXCESS OR LACK.

1) PHYSICAL MESSAGES EXPRESS NEEDS.

EXCESS NEEDS: to go play, to exercise, to move, to cool off, to go out, to use the bathroom	LACK NEEDS: tired, hungry, thirsty, sick, need physical contact, feeling cold

2) INTELLECTUAL MESSAGES EXPRESS INFORMATION.

EXCESS OF OBJECTIVE INFORMATION: facts, details, maps, clarity, rules, costs, times	LACK OF OBJECTIVE INFORMATION: requests, inquiry, questions, confusion
EXCESS OF SUBJECTIVE INFORMATION: opinions, reasons, assumptions, projections, beliefs, complaints	LACK OF SUBJECTIVE INFORMATION: being adaptive, insecurity, withhold, following expectations

3) EMOTIONAL MESSAGES EXPRESS FEELINGS.

EXCESS FEELINGS: such as anger or joy	LACK FEELINGS: such as sadness or fear

4) ENERGETIC MESSAGES EXPRESS WANTS.

EXCESS OF SPIRIT: vision, inspiration, discovery, design, leading, creativity, curiosity, innovation, experimentation	LACK OF SPIRIT: existential angst, seeking, boredom, lethargy, hopelessness, waiting, following, depression

Communicating with feelings does not in general mean stomping through your house shouting, "I feel angry because this place is such a mess!" Then again, it may. It does not usually include confronting your boss, colleagues, customers or suppliers with your needs and boundaries, although occasionally it might. It is not normally about trying to change your parents, your neighbors, or even your city council, although it could be.

Some people fear turning on their feelings because they imagine themselves morphing into an emotional storm trooper. But quite the opposite is true. Lowering your numbness bar and communicating with conscious feelings permits you to make boundaries or ask for what you need when your fear, sadness or anger rises to only 3 or 5 percent intensity. It is when your numbness bar is set to 80 percent numb that by the time you finally notice you are feeling something you explode out of control.

Communicating with feelings has a lot to do with distinguishing between present feelings and past or foreign emotions, and then trusting and using your feelings to create a world that works for everybody. Aligning yourself with the energy and information of your adult responsible feelings moves you along the path of unfolding and fulfilling your destiny. And that path might not always look or feel like you thought it would, particularly when it comes to reenlivening intimacy through clearing your resentments.

ASSUMPTIONS, EXPECTATIONS AND RESENTMENTS

Assumptions, expectations and resentments are related. It all starts with assumptions. *Assumptions* are like beliefs, in that (1) *any* person can make *any* assumption about *anything*, and (2) there is no connection between an assumption and reality. It is a trick of the mind. We whip up our own delusion and then we think it is true.

There is a great scene in the first Jackie Chan *Rush Hour* movie. Jackie has flown to America from Hong Kong to help with a police investigation, but he doesn't say anything when he arrives so his new partner assumes he can't speak English. When it is finally revealed that Jackie Chan *does* speak English and has been listening in on his partner's conversations all along, his partner angrily blurts out, "I assumed you did not speak English!" Jackie looks him calmly in the eyes and replies, "I am not responsible for your assumptions."

Bingo! Nobody else can be responsible for the assumptions under which you operate.

And if you do make an assumption, it is natural to expect it to be true. This is how an assumption becomes an *expectation*. An expectation is a solidified assumption.

For example, let's say that you assume your partner will remind you to take out the garbage on the night before garbage day. Then, since the assumption is in your mind, you regard your assumption as the truth. If your assumption is *true*, then you *expect* your partner to remind you. If they fail to meet your expectation, you conclude that your failure to bring out the garbage is *their* fault. In your mind, they betrayed you. This betrayal is the reason behind your resentment.

A *resentment* is your story (supported with evidence!) that your partner betrayed you by failing to fulfill your expectation. It just stabs you in the heart, doesn't it? Resentment is feeling betrayed by having an expectation that is not fulfilled.

But *you* are the source of the assumption upon which your expectation was based, so *you* arranged the whole betrayal yourself. It is *not* your partner's fault at all. The whole deal is *your* fault. If you did not make that assumption you would not have had an expectation with which to arrange the betrayal, and then there would be nothing to support your resentment. It is *all* your creation.

What is your purpose for doing all that?

What is your payoff for arranging a strategic betrayal to substantiate a resentment?

What does the resentment give you?

Answers to these questions reveal the workings of your own personal underworld.

Having even one small resentment is enough to block intimacy in a relationship. When you are near the person you resent, or even think of them, you no longer perceive the authentic person as they are. All you perceive is your resentment about that person projected onto them as if they were a movie screen.

So what does the resentment actually give you? It gives you a wall to block intimacy.

Why would you go to such lengths to create a wall to block intimacy with someone you supposedly want intimacy with?

Because you are afraid of letting yourself be seen.

It is your Box, actually. Your Box is afraid to let someone closer to you than the edges of your Box. If they did come closer they would turn around and see that your entire personality is just a show, a performance. They would see that your mask is not authentically you and the Box's game would be up. The Box thinks that it could then no longer protect you with its mechanical defense strategies. Someone would be inside your castle walls. This, of course, is what your heart and soul have actually been longing for, but it freaks out your Box. The Box has not been trained. It has not been assured that it still has a place even when you are intimate beyond its ability to control. Out of fear for its own survival the Box arranges for you to experience feeling betrayed to protect its high status in your world.

Resentments are an aspect of Box Technology that you could have been learning about since childhood. Back then it would have been easy. Your internal sensors could have been developing for years. By now you would easily be able to detect the Box's tendency to resent, and special energetic muscles could have been strengthened for making movements to avoid the Box's assumptions and expectations. By now you have believed the correctness of your Box's resentments for so long that even hinting at bringing them into question seems earth-shattering. Clearing a resentment would make you a heretic in your own church!

Soon we will explore how to clear resentments. Then you can do the experiment of being more intimate than your Box allows while assuring your Box that it is still loved and that it will be okay afterward. The point now is to recognize that in daily life you make many, many unconscious assumptions, even about things you never suspected you could make assumptions about.

The quantity of assumptions you continuously make is astonishing. It is quite a useful exercise to make an in-depth inventory of the assumptions you are making.

For example, you might assume that the person across from you likes you or does not like you, wants to talk with you or does not want to talk with you, wants to know about you or does not want to know about you, wants to be with you or does not want to be with you. You might assume that you will succeed or you will not succeed, that things will be the same tomorrow as they are today or that they will be different tomorrow, that there is a reason to live or that there is no reason to live, that what you could do or say would make a difference or would not make a difference, that it is important to try to make a difference or useless to try to make a difference, and so on.

The list of assumptions is endless, and also important, because you might be making many false assumptions that you assume are true assumptions. You might also be basing your life decisions on your own false assumptions. The invitation here is to learn to recognize the sensation of making an assumption so that your assumption making becomes conscious, and also to develop the practice of testing anything that even smells like an assumption to decide if you still want to keep that assumption or not.

BEING RIGHT OR BEING IN RELATIONSHIP

A resentment is a fully justified position taken by the Box when it asserts without question that it is right and the other person's Box is wrong. The righteousness can be recognized in your own arrogant attitude. The real question is, can you admit it?

At the point of recognizing and admitting that you are holding a resentment toward another person you get to make a choice. The choice is between keeping your resentment and being right about it, or clearing your resentment and having that person back in your life.

You are choosing between being right and being in relationship.

For the Box the choice is clear: be right! After all, your Box keeps you safe by blocking against intimacy. But if you decide to choose intimacy your Box does not get to have its way.

Clearing resentments is high drama, an adult action of communicating with responsible feelings. To the Box, clearing resentments may seem like suicidal self-betrayal. Everything that the Box invests in to sustain its unconscious, irresponsible, Gremlin survival strategy is revealed and disempowered through clearing a resentment. That is why I had to wait so long in this book to talk about this. You will apply everything we have so far been practicing in order to responsibly clear a resentment. Before we begin, though, one more distinction is needed.

CONFLICT RESOLUTION VS CARING COMMUNICATION

There is a difference between *conflict resolution* and *caring communication*. This distinction turns out to be a key for unlocking resentment, the destroyer of intimacy.

Most of us carry within our hearts some resentments about other people—especially about our closest friends and colleagues—and almost none of us rid ourselves of these resentments. Either we don't know how to get rid of resentments, or we don't want to.

If you do not want to get rid of a resentment, that is understandable. Resentment comes from an unfulfilled expectation. The Box's displeasure at having its expectation ignored is justification enough to protect itself against having another expectation ignored by the same person again; therefore, the resentment.

It is logical to think that your resentment will never dissolve until the other person changes their behavior. But the other person's behavior is measured against your own expectation of how they should have behaved. So your resentment can actually only dissolve when *you* dismantle *your own* expectation.

But your resentment is justified! The conflict is the *other* person's fault. After all, *they* disrespected *your* expectation. To you there is a conflict between what you *expected* and what they *did*. Wishing to resolve your resentment you might first think of using conflict resolution techniques: things like mediation, discussion, compromise, negotiation. Or, if you are avant-garde, you might try some form of brainstorming. But neither conflict resolution nor brainstorming techniques will create satisfactory results. This is because dissolving resentment is neither cerebral nor strategic; it is visceral and happens through surrendering the Box's entire game. There are no possible negotiations. Dissolving resentment is total capitulation.

From the Box's perspective, dissolving resentment is certain death. The Box *loves* resentment because then it can square off against a clearly identified enemy. All of your Box's familiar defense mechanisms jump into active mode and have permission to do whatever it takes to protect you from this evil adversary. Bye, bye relationship. Hello war.

Dissolving resentment involves you taking radical responsibility for creating the resentment in the first place:

Your resentment comes after feeling betrayed. Your resentment's purpose is to protect you from ever being betrayed by this same person again.

You felt betrayed when your expectation was unfulfilled.

Your expectation was based on an assumption.

You assumed that your assumption was correct.

But that was merely another assumption you made.

Anybody can assume anything about anything.

You assumed something about this other person that was obviously not true, or they would have behaved differently and you would not have been offended.

Start by identifying the assumption(s) you made. For example, *I assumed they would / would not do that. I assumed they would keep their promise. I assumed that by now they knew this about me. I assumed that they sense how I feel. I assumed they were aware of this already.*

Now assume that your assumptions are wrong. Assume that what you thought was true is not actually true.

Take it one step further. Find the purpose behind why you made your assumptions.

Find out if your Box made assumptions in order to build resentments with the other person so as to block the possibility of intimacy with them. Consider that your Box strategically concocts such conflicts in order to retain its unquestioned authority in your life.

Through taking radical responsibility for having created your assumptions and expectations you find perhaps the only effective way to vanish your resentment: to admit your woundedness through *caring communication*. The way out of war is vulnerability.

Caring communication is the procedure whereby you step sideways, away from your resentment and you admit your woundedness. *You* get off your position of being right. You hit bottom by revealing your innermost feelings of fear, sadness, and anger, whatever is driving you to try to avoid intimacy.

Caring communication means you tell these stories even if you look unprofessional, immature, stupid, silly, weak or childish; even if it proves you are a failure or an idiot.

While you tell your stories, the other person listens to you and says nothing except to deliver a few completion loops to show that they have heard and compassionately understand how it is for you. The listener asks no questions and gives no justifications, analysis, rescuing or suggestions. There is listening, acceptance, and respect.

CLEARING RESENTMENT

Carrying a resentment is like carrying a stinking bucket full of shit rotting you from the inside out. There is no defense for this. If you have resentment, you have no dignity.

It would have been easier to share your feelings, lose face, be liquid, and look bad when your feelings were fresh. Now they are old and infecting your whole system. Through your own weakness you still carry them with you. You have sacrificed intimacy in order to carry resentment. It is time to admit this.

If someone wants to be with you, what they get instead is this bucket of festering feelings. You cover it over with a show, an intellectual concept. Clearing your resentment starts with letting your mask fall down and standing in the bucket. Start with: *I don't know . . .*

The intellect is impervious to almost everything but you. Between you and life is your intellect. To get some air you can drill holes through the brick wall of your intellect by revealing confusions. By drilling enough holes the wall can crumble from the inside and life can gush in. It is not that the intellectual construct is negative or bad—it is just false. Someone wants to be with you and you only offer them reasons and concepts from your mind?

That's the great thing with relationships—there is a living human being who wants to be with the *you* that is alive and true no matter what it knows! But what is alive and true does not fit in your intellect. Almost no part of relationship happens in the intellect. If you want closeness, learn to put your intellect aside. To do this, you need the courage to not know who you are. Again, start with: *I don't know . . .*

Your mind has learned to think your feelings away. Now learn to stop doing that. Let your mind be completely overwhelmed with the swirling abundance of feelings that is present in your body. Then admit that you are so wounded that you would rather be in resentment than in vulnerable contact with another human being.

Your task is to keep going deeper and to share how that is for you. Communicate just as it is, making no sense, in full embarrassment, without explanation, without trying to package your communication to make it understandable. It does not have to be understandable. Admit defeat; crumble into the liquid state; hit bottom and stay there without knowing how. Share your pain; unmask your mechanicality and your helplessness; permit yourself to be known.

When the other person lets in what you have revealed about yourself, the original communication that you had previously imprisoned behind your resentment is finally expressed, heard, and completed. The message has been received. There is no more energetic charge between the two of you. In this moment a miracle happens. What had only a few moments before seemed to be a solid conflict, mysteriously resolves itself without the actual conflict being addressed at all. Respect this moment. Notice the shift. Do not rush through it. The true cause of the conflict has been dissipated through re-establishing intimacy with caring communication. Often the listener says nothing at all to complete the process. The quality of *being with* and spacious listening are alone sufficient.

EXAMPLE OF CLEARING A RESENTMENT

Detecting a resentment in yourself often begins by noticing that you are in conflict over something. In this example we imagine that the school has sent home a paper with your child saying they are going to give free flu vaccinations to all the students. Your partner seems to agree to this without question, yet something is churning in your guts about it. You don't say anything but you feel deep resentment that your partner doesn't mention anything to you about it. The surface manifestation is that you shut down at the dinner table, being harsh and ungenerous with the kids and uncommunicative with your partner.

MAP OF HOW TO CLEAR RESENTMENT
World Copyright © 2010 owner Clinton Callahan grants permission to use. www.nextculture.org

Almost none of us can rid ourselves of resentments. Either we don't know how, or we don't want to. The result is a life of loneliness, conflict and war.
1. Conflicts are natural when you carry resentments.
2. Resentments are your betrayal stories about your unfulfilled expectations.
3. Expectations originate in false assumptions.
4. Expectations are strategic intimacy killers to avoid being hurt.

Why remove expectations? Because you are starving for intimacy. *Even one small resentment is enough to block intimacy* . It seems to you that resentment cannot dissolve until the other person changes their behavior. But you measure their behavior against *your* expectations. Dismantling the assumption / expectation / betrayal / resentment / conflict chain occurs when you take responsibility for its root cause: your fear of intimacy.

CLEARING RESENTMENT THROUGH CARING COMMUNICATION

1. As soon as you sense resentment ask the person you resent if they will meet with you for half an hour so you can take responsibility for blocking the relationship. Ask them to simply listen. Tell them that by the end you will be fine. It may help to read these instructions together out loud as you begin.
2. Do not worry about how to do this. It cannot be figured out. Start feeling and talking. Use *I statements*: "I feel angry, sad, scared, glad. " Do not use *You statements*. "You always . . . ," "You never . . . ," "You did this to me . . . ," "You should . . ."
3. This is not about them. This is about *you* giving up your charade, *you* hitting bottom, *you* getting off it, *you* revealing your innermost feelings through admitting why you avoid intimacy. Tell your stories with radical honesty, even if you look unprofessional, immature, stupid, silly, weak or childish, even if it proves that you are a failure or an idiot.
4. While you tell your stories the other person listens to you and says nothing. Now and then they can deliver a completion loop to show that they compassionately understand how it is for you. The listener asks no questions and gives no justifications, analysis, rescuing or suggestions. There is a space of acceptance, respect and pure listening.
5. Your task is to keep going deeper and to communicate just how it is for you, in full embarrassment, without explanation, without trying to make it make sense. Admit your defeat. Crumble into the liquid state and stay there without knowing how. Share your pain. Unmask your mechanicality and your helplessness. Let your weak and vulnerable self be known.
6. When the listener lets in what you have revealed about yourself the communication has been completed. Your message has been received when it vanishes and there is no more charge between you.
7. In this moment the resentment mysteriously resolves itself without the conflict necessarily being addressed at all. Respect this moment. Notice the shift. Do not rush through it. The true cause of the conflict has been dissipated through re-establishing intimacy. Often the listener says nothing at all. The quality of *being with* and spacious listening are alone sufficient.
8. Out of the ashes a phoenix arises. This is a mystery. Let it be that way.

A subtle conflict erupts between you and your partner after dinner about who will clear the table and wash the dishes tonight. It is normally no problem. You notice the unusual conflict energy in you. The red warning light has gone off in your mind. If it was not the dishes, it would have been something else. You are a conflict waiting to happen. The conflict is just a manifestation of something deeper. So you stop it, midsentence.

You say, "Something is going on with me. I don't know what it is. Could you listen to me for a half hour?"

Your partner says, "Yes, at eight-thirty, in the living room, after the little one is in bed."

The pain in you is so intense that you feel numb. You would rather explode than wait, but you know that waiting is the right thing to do. So you say, "Okay. Thanks."

Since you are in a gnarly emotional state you set yourself to doing simple physical tasks in the meantime, such as sweeping the garage, wiping water spots off the chrome and mirrors in the bathroom, scouring the slime off the shower floor, pulling weeds in the garden, picking up toys around the house and putting them away as if they were sacred objects, classifying nails in the workshop, knitting, or hand sewing. This way the time goes by and you do no harm to anyone. It is not the time to go jogging, overeat, drink, eat sweets, or complain to a third person. These are all standard ways to dissipate or stuff away feelings. You will need your feelings.

Eight-thirty comes and you meet. You sit close to each other on the couch. If you have done this before your partner may arrange to have simple physical contact; for example, legs touching. Your partner says nothing and sits waiting attentively. A box of tissues is within reach.

You start out on the wrong foot. "You always make me do the dirty work! I am the one who has to be a problem and disagree with the system. You never really care what they are doing to our kids, do you?"

Your partner interrupts. "I notice that you are using *You* statements instead of *I* statements. It might help you to use *I* statements. I also notice you using words like *always* and *never*. These are perfection words that the Box uses to engage in low drama and to block feelings. Please see if you can express what is under these words. I also notice some accusation in your question. This would be a time to take responsibility rather than to accuse. This is a time to explore what is going on for you by using feeling statements. I am listening."

(Ah, your partner has been reading this book!)

You take a deep breath, center yourself and say, "Okay. Thanks for the feedback. This evening I read the letter from the school about giving our kids flu vaccinations and I felt really scared. I don't know what it is, but this huge, mindless money-grabbing system could eat our children and not care one bit!" (Tears are rolling down your cheeks but you don't mind.) "I have been doing some reading online. There are things going on that the mainstream media hides from us. This vaccine letter is from a group of medical doctors owned by large pharmaceutical companies, the ones who make the vaccines. First they make the flu viruses and then they make the vaccines. The population drops off while the pharmaceutical companies make billions. I hate it. I hate it that they would do this to our kids and not care. I hate it that I have to guard my family against the school and the government and the medical professions that are supposedly there to serve us and protect us. And I hate it that I don't know anything for sure." (More tears.) "So many people don't know and just act like stupid sheep doing whatever they are told without question. It drives me crazy with anger and frustration to not be able to just trust. And I need you to connect with me on this and not just go along like the others."

There is a pause. Your partner is still looking at you, still listening to what you are saying, letting it in, digesting it, saying nothing, being with you with all this. After a moment your partner repeats back, "You need me to connect with you."

You start again. "Yes!" (Bing!) "I need you to talk with me and think these things through. I am not willing to let my kids be vaccinated by the government and the pharmaceutical industry just because they want to do it. I don't care what they say. I don't believe their bullshit. When I was a kid, I got sent to school too. Nobody explained anything to me. Just one day they took me to school and there I was and I didn't get it. I was so scared and my parents didn't understand me. I didn't want to leave my nature play to go sit in chairs with these other kids all day. It was torture, insane. It made no sense. What did I do wrong? My parents, even the teachers, couldn't understand my questions, so I stopped asking. It seemed like my parents did not really care what the system was doing with me. They were busy with their own lives and all I could do was survive mine. And that's the point. Our kids are merely surviving, too. They don't actually get to live their lives now. They must do what the teachers tell them to do and their years are going by. Each day they spend in school is one less day they have to learn what they'll need to be effective in the coming changes. And I don't want them vaccinated! I was afraid you would argue with me about this. I was afraid you would not talk with me. I need us to work together. I don't have any answers. I just feel so scared and frustrated by what's going on in the world these days. I am so sad that our kids do not have a bright future with plenty of fresh water and healthy oceans and beautiful coral reefs to snorkel around. I am so sad that the tigers and elephants and bears are dying off and going extinct. It is not right. And what can I do to stop it? There is so much going on. Can we talk about this more?"

Your partner says, "You want to talk with me more about this."

You say, "Yes! But not now. It doesn't have to be now. I just need to know that you won't sign this vaccine paper and send it back in. And if the administrators want to know why, I can explain it to them. You don't have to talk to them about it. Okay?"

Your partner says, "Yes. It's okay with me, as long as you talk to them. You are right, though. I was not even thinking about this. I won't sign the paper. Maybe you could write a letter to send in with the kids so they don't have to try to explain it to their teachers?"

You say, "Yes. I'll write it now and I'll explain all this to the kids at breakfast. I feel glad we got to talk. I was really resentful at you for not bringing this up with me. It felt like I was being betrayed by my parents again, getting thrown back into the jaws of the system. Whew, this is big for me!"

At this point, hugs would be appropriate.

USE FEELINGS TO MAKE OR CHANGE BOUNDARIES

Sometimes the action step attached to a feeling is to make or change a boundary. Before you can make a boundary you will first need to experience the distinction that the boundary expresses. When I first started working with distinctions I thought that distinctions occurred in my mind. I thought that if I understood or could explain a distinction then

I *got* the distinction and other people would *get it* too. I also thought that if I complained loudly enough, blamed severely enough, sulked darkly enough, exploded destructively enough, or went away permanently enough, the other person would *get it*. Now I think differently. Now I think that a true distinction occurs simultaneously in all four bodies, not only in the intellectual body, and that it is utterly simple: as clean, sharp and well-aimed as a samurai's blade.

For example, a boundary is a distinction, so making a true boundary is an action that takes place simultaneously in all four bodies. If the boundary is "No Gremlin feeding in our relationship," it goes like this:

- The boundary occurs in your *physical* body as a clear perception of unique domains, distinguishable one from the other, such as: "Low drama Gremlin feeding creates one quality of relationship. High drama love, respect, discovery and intimacy creates an entirely different quality of relationship. I clearly experience the difference. Stop letting your Gremlin feed on our relationship. I am not a plaything of your Gremlin."

- The boundary occurs in your *intellectual* body as a communicatable concept, such as: "Gremlin plays I win–you lose games that show up as power struggle, competition for attention, or I'm right–you're wrong. Adult men and women play Winning Happening games where we creatively collaborate to serve Bright Principles. I am willing to play Winning Happening games with you and nothing else."

- The boundary occurs in your *emotional* body empowered by all four feelings, such as: "If my boundary that Gremlin feeding is excluded from our relationship is not tacitly honored, I feel angry because I want it to be upheld. I feel sad because I lose something if it is not respected. I feel scared because other boundaries might not be upheld. And I feel glad because I have clarity about the boundaries I need to make to have the kind of relationship I want with you."

- The boundary occurs in your *energetic* body as a declaration of how the world is for you; in other words, as a component of who you are as a being, such as: This boundary is so. It actually exists. When I say, *No Gremlin feeding in our family*, I mean absolutely none. I am not in any kind of doubt about it. My clarity about this boundary requires neither explanation nor force of command. It just is. That is my boundary, and it is not my problem anymore."

If a boundary is not simultaneously made in all of your four bodies, it will not function as a boundary. If you think that you have made a boundary and it is not functioning as a boundary (e.g., your partner keeps doing Gremlin behavior with you, your child keeps whining at

RAGE STICK These men are using a special stick and cushion to practice making boundaries with all four bodies, physical, intellectual, emotional and energetic. After practicing a few times the stick transforms into an energetic sword of clarity, carried everywhere and used to make distinctions and boundaries easefully but alertly in daily life.

you, the customer or boss keeps intruding in your space or violating your requests, you keep feeling betrayed by your friends) then you are making boundaries only in theory, not in fact.

The Box has full control of your mind. The Box can cause you to forget anything it wants you to forget in an instant and you won't even notice that you forgot it. A boundary made from the mind is a puff of smoke in a hurricane. Where a boundary first starts becoming solid is when it spreads into your other three bodies.

When you *become* a boundary in all four of your bodies the other person or persons to whom the boundary applies will instantly and automatically *get it* in all four of their bodies. For example, many people have reported that when they declare a personal space around their body and *become the boundary* and then walk through the shopping mall, no one bumps into them anymore. Their personal space is respected unconsciously by all the other shoppers no matter what kind of shopping frenzy they are in. A true boundary is sensed previous to words and ideas.

By the time your boundary occurs in your energetic body you have become the boundary. "Not in my house. Sneaking, flirting, lying, whining, deceiving, Gremlin feeding, these are beneath our dignity. That does not happen here." Once you become your boundaries they wordlessly shape the quality of the space. They establish the context of the current gameworld and it really cannot happen there. It cannot. The space won't permit it. High drama will not support there being a *situation* without someone being at source for the Is-Glued story that creates the situation. Who the source person is for a low drama becomes transparent in a high drama space where you do not agree to fool yourself.

Along these lines, you can develop the habit of making boundaries out at the edge of your territory rather than waiting until the metaphorical enemy is storming your castle gates. If you wait until they are beating down your front door before you make a boundary, it is a little too late. Your hesitation indicates that you have been fogging yourself about what is really going on. Gremlin gets a payoff for procrastination. Gremlin gets to say, "It's not fair." "But I didn't know." "They are so inconsiderate." With each complaint Gremlin grants its own license to

RAGE STICK Eyes open, looking straight ahead, no one in front of you or behind you, everyone going with you, shouting from deep in your guts before
you know what you are going to say. This is how to practice making clear, adult
boundaries.

take immediate revenge in an ordinary low drama. Remember, this is
high drama. High drama is *not ordinary*. High drama is *extraordinary*. If
you try your usual Gremlin behaviors you will crash out of high drama
quicker than you can say, "Oh my God! I can't believe I did it again."

Your adult feelings are the gateway to accessing the masculine and feminine archetypes that are hardwired into your body and have been ready to turn on ever since you were about fifteen years old. The process of initializing your archetypes for your use is called *stellating*.

RAGE STICK The rage stick and cushion has multiple further uses. It is the way to get your dignity back in the final healing process from childhood abuses, whether they were psychological, emotional, physical or sexual abuses. It is the sword for cutting the childhood connection binding you to your parents, finally freeing you to live your own adult life. And it is part of stellating the high drama warrior and warrioress archetypes. This is an example of High Level Fun!

7. STELLATING FEELINGS

(NOTE TO THE READER: If you have skipped ahead to this chapter without carefully studying the previous six chapters, it's a clever idea but I don't recommend it. Learning to consciously feel has similarities to learning to use dynamite, which is actually quite simple. Drill a hole in the stone, tamp in a few sticks with their primers, hook up your wires, and slam home the detonator. But they make you take lessons and get a license before letting you blast with dynamite. It's for your own good. That's because if you leave your dynamite sitting too long the nitroglycerin can leak out and explode just by pulling a stick out of the box. If you don't leave a lightning gap in your wires then static electricity could set off the charge by surprise. You might walk away from your set up thinking everything is fine and, KABOOM! Short fuse... I am not saying anything like this will happen if you skip over the previous chapters. But I am saying that the world of conscious feelings operates under different laws than the world of numbness, just like lighting dynamite is different from lighting birthday candles. Before you try stellating feelings, I strongly encourage you to study the first six chapters of this book. It's for your own good.)

NINTH DISTINCTION: FEELINGS CAN STELLATE ARCHETYPES

The ninth of the Ten Distinctions for Consciously Feeling says that Phase 1 and Phase 2 of feelings work is part of a formal rite of passage into adulthood that awakens (stellates) archetypal structures and talents that have been lying dormant within you, waiting to be initialized and directed toward fulfilling your destiny.

(I just noticed that nearly every word in the previous paragraph originates beyond the concept limits of ordinary society. Do not be dismayed if almost none of this makes sense at first. The distinctions, maps and tools explained in this chapter are intended to last you a lifetime. Each one is a doorway to further experiences and discoveries. Try to be okay with not necessarily being able to grasp all of it at the first go-round. Instead, get what you can, use what you can, and come back later to get more when you want it.)

Modern human beings are raised to behave as planets but we are designed to be stars. A planet absorbs more energy than it radiates. For example, the Earth would be dead and lifeless without the sun's energy blasting it 24/7/365. The Earth does not produce enough of its own energy to power the biological experiments it is doing.

Modern society conditions us to stay planets for our whole lives, orbiting around the energy, information, products and services marketed to us by institutions and corporations. We are, for the most part, ignorant consumers, dependent on a complex supply chain of food, clothing, energy and entertainment that we cannot produce ourselves. American city children can easily identify one hundred corporate brand logos but only three kinds of trees. These same children ask, "Why do milk cartons always have pictures of cows on them?" (Really.)

A child does its parents no honor by remaining a child.

TECHNOPENURIAPHOBIA (TPP)

The word *technophobia* was invented in the early 1960s, and means *the fear of technology and its effects*. In 2006, just four decades later, I had to invent the word *technopenuriaphobia*, the *fear of the lack of technology*. We are now so dependent on modern technology that we carry a profound fear of losing it. We are justifiably concerned that without modern technology we would quickly die.

Children today—and I dare say we too—were born and raised high up on a technological ladder of progress. We learned that if we want light in a room, we flick a switch and there is light. If we want it warmer, turn up the thermostat. Cooler? Turn on the air-conditioning. Food? Get it from the refrigerator, freezer, cans, fast food joints, or grocery stores. Entertainment? MP3s, CDs, DVDs, or surfing the Net. Talk to someone? Use our cell phone. Go somewhere? Take a car, plane, or train. Garbage? Drop it in the trash can. We dedicated ourselves to working toward *the good life*: total comforts, total easefulness, totally supported by technology. It is all so easy, fast and clean. But . . . if it breaks down? (*When* it breaks down . . .) The fading mirage reveals our weaknesses. Without modern technology we can no longer survive on our birth planet.

We are trained to consume, copy, conform, obey, adapt; be conventional, play the game, follow the program, give our authority away; distrust our own instinct, intuition, and innate talents; repress our feelings and ask no questions.

We are trained to live as planets, absorbing.

We are designed to live as stars, radiating.

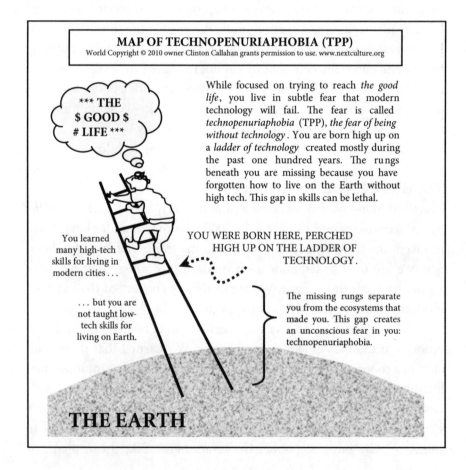

MAP OF TECHNOPENURIAPHOBIA (TPP)
World Copyright © 2010 owner Clinton Callahan grants permission to use. www.nextculture.org

*** THE
$ GOOD $
# LIFE ***

While focused on trying to reach *the good life*, you live in subtle fear that modern technology will fail. The fear is called *technopenuriaphobia* (TPP), *the fear of being without technology*. You are born high up on a *ladder of technology* created mostly during the past one hundred years. The rungs beneath you are missing because you have forgotten how to live on the Earth without high tech. This gap in skills can be lethal.

You learned many high-tech skills for living in modern cities . . .

YOU WERE BORN HERE, PERCHED HIGH UP ON THE LADDER OF TECHNOLOGY.

. . . but you are not taught low-tech skills for living on Earth.

The missing rungs separate you from the ecosystems that made you. This gap creates an unconscious fear in you: technopenuriaphobia.

THE EARTH

Stars emit more energy than they consume. The sun, for example, glows with internally generated heat and light. It sources its own liveliness. Human beings are designed as stars, to lead, discover, explore, create, generate, experiment, and to declare the way things are. We are designed to develop new social systems, solve impossible problems, communicate in new ways, create new forms of thinking and relating, and share all these with others.

The process of changing from a planet to a star is called *stellating*. The idea is simple: light yourself energetically on fire from the inside. The heat of combustion comes from the conflict between your clarity

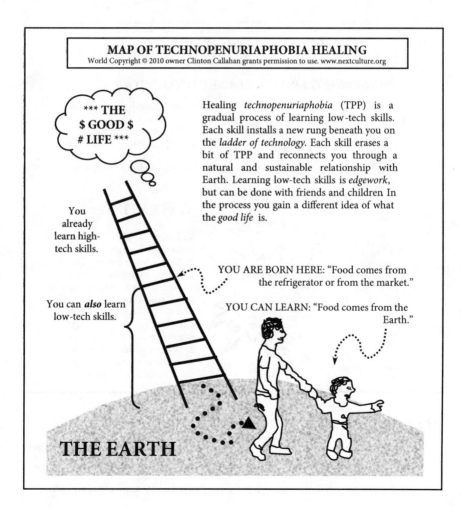

MAP OF TECHNOPENURIAPHOBIA HEALING
World Copyright © 2010 owner Clinton Callahan grants permission to use. www.nextculture.org

*** THE
$ GOOD $
# LIFE ***

Healing *technopenuriaphobia* (TPP) is a gradual process of learning low-tech skills. Each skill installs a new rung beneath you on the *ladder of technology*. Each skill erases a bit of TPP and reconnects you through a natural and sustainable relationship with Earth. Learning low-tech skills is *edgework*, but can be done with friends and children In the process you gain a different idea of what the *good life* is.

You already learn high-tech skills.

You can *also* learn low-tech skills.

YOU ARE BORN HERE: "Food comes from the refrigerator or from the market."

YOU CAN LEARN: "Food comes from the Earth."

THE EARTH

about what you see is possible and your clarity about what you see is happening. The result is two clashing clarities occupying the same space at the same time. The friction produces a nearly intolerable impetus that moves you to create what you came here to create.

You came here with a plan. Your plans were approved, so you were born. Are you fulfilling your plans? For example, my plans are to empower facilitators of the shift to next culture. Writing this book is part of fulfilling my plans. Writing this book is excruciatingly intense for me. I want it done, and it is not yet done. There is a fire in me about this. This book comes out of that fire.

MAP OF STELLATING ARCHETYPES
World Copyright © 2010 owner Clinton Callahan grants permission to use. www.nextculture.org

CHANGING FROM A PLANET INTO A STAR

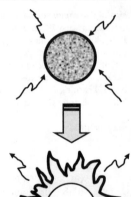

PLANET:
Consuming
Absorbing
Copying
Criticizing
Judging
Complaining
Following
Pretending

Planets absorb more energy than they radiate. Stars radiate more energy than they absorb. Human beings are trained to live as planets, but we are designed to live as stars.

STELLATING:

Stellating is the initiatory process of changing from a planet into a star. This process involves deep emotional work done safely and sustainably over a minimum of two years. Each one of the four feelings stellates into one of the four archetypes. The result of stellating is living in service of your destiny principles.

STAR:
Producing
Creating
Appreciating
Leading
Exploring
Experimenting
Declaring
Generating
Causing
Discovering

RITE OF PASSAGE

Stellation is an essential element in a formal *rite of passage* from childhood into adulthood. A rite of passage is the activation process that empowers a person with the wisdom of responsibility and consequence.

During childhood, the Box learns to defend itself. At age fifteen, the Box is designed to change its purpose, from childish defensiveness to adult expansiveness. Modern culture assumes that the shift happens automatically when we turn eighteen or twenty-one years of age. It does not.

For 100,000 years human beings knew that a formidable rite of passage was required to initiate a man or woman into responsible adulthood. We seem to have forgotten. The result is that modern society lacks responsible adults. Parents do not know what being adult means. Our governments, militaries, businesses, educational institutions, and religions are being led by adolescents in older bodies. This explains why the annual international budget for promoting war in 2007 was over 1,339,000,000,000 (US dollars), and the annual international budget for promoting consciousness expansion in the same year was zero.

Modern policies sponsored by modern leaders in modern countries underwrite starvation for the poor third of humanity while the rich third pays billions for liposuction to surgically remove extra globs of fat from their bellies, waists and thighs.

Modern leaders are so committed to child level responsibility that they choose to fight each other over finite territory and resources instead of creatively collaborating to cultivate the beneficial potential of each human being on Earth.

You *do* need to fight, but the true battles are *internal*. Fight to pay attention and stay unhypnotized. Fight to take back your authority. Fight to keep the promises you make to your children and your partner. Fight to build the matrix upon which your consciousness can grow. Fight to make unusual efforts of generosity and kindness.

Fight through your prejudices to forge critical connections with other people so as to nurture the emergence of a world without war. Fight with fierce discipline and unquenchable commitment by your own authority, not at the whim of some politician or corporate executive! The noble fight *is in you*. This is where the archetypal warrior takes risky, inspired actions. Modern wars are little boys with guns. It is time to grow up.

Adult responsibility is a new agreement between an individual and the universe, after which the adult's life is about serving conscious Bright Principles greater than themselves.

An adult takes responsibility for attention, center, presence, purpose, outcome, space, energy, time, costs, feelings, thoughts, possibility, consequences, the Box, communication, relationship, the greater community, and also responsibility for the level of responsibility that is being taken. If you do not know what some of this means, it is because modern society is not grounded in adulthood—you have not been taught. No one has shown you how to apply the technology of responsibility. Not knowing about a thing, however, does not protect you from that thing seriously affecting your life.

Rite of passage may have been abandoned by modern culture due to a misunderstanding. We did not recognize that there is a difference of purpose between a traditional rite of passage as used by original cultures for 100,000 years, and the kind of rite of passage needed today. This difference can now be explained.

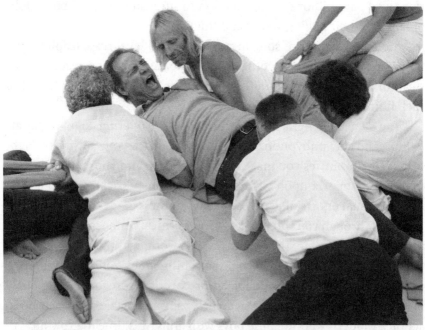

RAGE HOLD The author is being held by four men in a classic *rage hold*—everybody's first step towards stellating anger. A rage hold is so safe that feelings repressed since infancy can be experienced and expressed in such a way that they get completed. The rage hold is one element of a twenty-first century rite of passage.

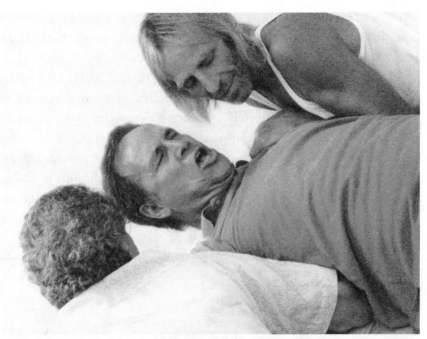

RAGE HOLD Through a sequence of steps you permit your rage to gradually increase in intensity and maturity of expression. A first attempt might reach 5 percent intensity of baby rage. Your next effort may get up to 15 percent child rage.
Getting past 50 percent intensity involves using loud angry adolescent words.
Anger past 80 percent is anger beyond understanding. You gain the capability to
hold space for other people's feelings up to the intensity of anger that you yourself have experienced. When you can freely experience and express 100 percent
archetypal anger for no reason and can let it flow through you unrestricted until it
stops by itself, your nervous system reorders and you have stellated the warrior
or warrioress archetype. Then it is no longer *your* anger. It is a force of nature,
anger coming directly from its own archetypal territory. For the rest of your life
the energy and information of archetypal anger is turned on and available for
your use in every instant.

TRADITIONAL VS ARCHETYPAL RITE OF PASSAGE

The traditional rite of passage used by original cultures differs from the
archetypal rite of passage needed today by what is done with your *assemblage points*. Assemblage points are core reference frames around which
you construct your Box. (I borrow the term from Carlos Castaneda's
reports about Don Juan Matus's Yaqui Indian teachings in the book

Journey to Ixtlan.) Each Box design orbits around a few foundational assertions about the world and life. If an assemblage point is shifted the entire Box reflexively reshapes itself.

The human mind is capable of adapting to such a stunning diversity of cultures that it should be clear that the original placement of assemblage points is completely arbitrary. Rearranging the position of an assemblage point can establish an entirely new framework of reality in which the Box can operate. In a traditional rite of passage the assemblage points are lifted out of their original (childhood) positions and repositioned so as to weld a person into complete identification with the tribe's longstanding customs and worldview. This strategy con-

RAGE HOLD *Be quiet, be a nice boy, be a good girl, be cool, stay in control, don't be a problem*—it takes great courage and stamina to break these long obeyed rules. This photo shows proper rage hold form. A person lies on top of each arm and leg placing one hand over and one hand under each knee and shoulder. Two additional people hold folded towels for the rage hold person to grab onto. Don't pull too tightly, but give the person some resistance to fight with. There are two rules: don't hurt yourself, and don't hurt anybody else. Holding someone in archetypal rage is like riding a greased pig. Hang on!

strains new adults to think, feel, and behave strictly within the norms established by that particular culture. They are bonded to their clan. The new adults have no option but to continue doing things in ways the old culture has already found to be sustainable for perhaps thousands of years, assuring the continued survival of the tribe.

In cultures that need to change only gradually, if at all, traditional rites of passage make sense. For the twenty-first century's hyper-evolving circumstances, something completely different is required: *an archetypal rite of passage.*

An archetypal rite of passage does not weld your assemblage points into the local culture. An archetypal rite of passage instead anchors your assemblage points into your own personal set of Bright Principles, your archetypal lineage, and your high drama archetypes: (for men) King, Warrior, Magician, Lover or (for women) Queen, Warrioress, Sorceress, Lover. These archetypes are forces of nature that are more powerful than culture. The procedure for stellating these archetypes is well understood, although not by modern culture.

The difficulty of explaining archetypal rite of passage to someone in modern culture is that modern culture is patriarchal. Patriarchy promotes the patriarchy, not the transformation of the patriarchy. Any rite of passage created within a patriarchy will avoid noticing that *the patriarchy is itself irredeemably adolescent.*

No patriarchally ordained rite of passage can lead to greater responsibility. This means that an archetypal rite of passage to adulthood must be sourced from outside the realm of patriarchy, in *archearchy.* Archearchy is a new form of human society beyond matriarchy and patriarchy, where deep masculine and deep feminine archetypes reign in dynamic harmony. Archearchy is already being lived, for example, in Possibilica <www.possibilica.org>.

It is deceptive to assume that you can design and manage a rite of passage for yourself by yourself. This would be like trying to midwife your own birth. The suggestion is to undertake a rite of passage in close association with guides.

A guide is someone more experienced and further along in their rite of passage than you are. Since rites of passage are not sponsored

RAGE HOLD Having so much safety and support from people feels wonderful. The rage work itself feels like a butterfly struggling to get out of a cocoon. The alternative is staying trapped in the cocoon forever, never to realize your life purpose. The outcome of breaking free of childhood patterns is becoming a Pirate Sorceress Warrioress Queen Goddess Woman (or a Pirate Magician King Spiritual Warrior Man). This result is astonishing, beautiful and attractive.

by modern culture, your guide will be someone centered in a context that is greater than the context of modern culture. This does not mean, however, that you should commit to the first Tibetan Shaolin Kabalistic American-Indian Hindu Atlantean Tantra Priest Psychic Sufi Healer Shaman Kundalini Buddhist Drummer from Africa who comes along . . .

Nonetheless, I can encourage you to begin your own archetypal rite of passage now, even if you have not found a guide, because of the *Law of Precession.* The Law of Precession says that as soon as you start making authentic efforts, the universe provides sideways coincidences to make your efforts more productive—including providing the appropriate guide *when you are ready.*

FEELINGS AND ARCHETYPES

Each of the four feelings ignites one of the four archetypes, as shown on the Map of Feelings and Archetypes. Anger ignites the doer / maker. Fear ignites the creator / designer. Sadness ignites the communicator. Joy ignites the leader / visionary.

The procedure for igniting archetypes is to consciously choose to experience and express 100 percent maximum archetypal levels of feelings in their pure form (unmixed), in total safety, for no reason, letting it get bigger and bigger and letting it go and go until it stops all by itself.

Stellating is neither a reaction to anything nor the release of emotions. Stellating is not catharsis—the discharge of accumulated energy.

PUNCHING Through physical metaphors such as punching a cushion safely and respectfully, your whole body learns to make use of the energy available in the adult ego state. You naturally replace victim behaviors with the ability to say, *No!* or *Stop!,* the ability to make effective decisions, the ability to change plans, make and keep agreements, take intelligent risks, and expand your capacity for passionate living and loving.

LIFTING As an adult woman emerges and stands on her own two feet it is a time of celebration. Giving this woman a *lifting* welcomes her into the culture of adult women. The typical behavior of regarding other women as *the enemy* or as mistrusted competitors can slide into the past. A new partnership and camaraderie between women arises, full of support and wonder in the further exploration of adulthood and the unfolding of archetypal capacities. (The equivalent ritual of men lifting men recognizes successful rite of passage steps for men.)

Archetypal feelings do not come from you. They already exist in the four territories of archetypal feelings. You intentionally choose and enter a specific territory—anger, sadness, fear or joy—and become the space through which the archetypal feeling is experienced and expressed into the world.

Stellating is authentic adventure.

Stellating archetypes is one aspect of an underworld journey, the appropriate preparation for the Hidden Purpose Process, wherein a group of people in the company of a trained spaceholder (for example, a Possibility Trainer) consciously enters their own personal shadow world to retrieve the bright jewel of clarity. Specifically, the clarity retrieved from the underworld is the set of four, five or six Shadow Principles that your Gremlin serves.

Once your hidden purpose is distilled (for example, in a Possibility Lab or Next Culture Lab training), you gain a choice as to which purpose you serve with each action: your hidden purpose or your true purpose (as shown on the Map of Possibility in Appendix C). Before gaining this clarity, you had no conscious choice. Choices were made unconsciously for you by your Gremlin. Having a conscious choice is worth working for. (This is my opinion.)

After a sustained experience of 100 percent maximum fear (or rage, or sadness, or joy), your internal relationship to the feeling is changed. When asked the question, "Which is bigger, you or the fear?" (for example), the remarkable answer is, "I am bigger." The answer is irrefutable

---

MAP OF FEELINGS AND ARCHETYPES
World Copyright © 2010 owner Clinton Callahan grants permission to use. www.nextculture.org

ANGER DOER / MAKER (WARRIOR OR WARRIORESS)	**SADNESS** COMMUNICATOR (LOVER)
JOY LEADER / VISIONARY (KING OR QUEEN)	**FEAR** CREATOR / DESIGNER (MAGICIAN OR SORCERESS)

Before learning how to feel consciously, maturely and on purpose, your feelings will be using you to serve your *hidden purposes*. By learning to consciously feel, your feelings become rocket fuel for serving your *true purposes*. Associated with each of the four feelings is an archetypal structure that is hardwired into your body and ready to turn on at about age fifteen. Each of the four archetypes is initialized individually through a guided process of intentionally experiencing and expressing 100 percent maximum of an archetypal feeling until your relationship to that feeling shifts. Archetypes arrive responsible, adult, clear, and bigger than your 100 percent big feelings. Once initiated, the four archetypes are available for the rest of your life. Without stellating your archetypes during a formidable and authentic rite of passage, you remain functionally adolescent.

---

because it comes from direct experience rather than theory or concept. Through the stellating process, you become bigger than your fear.

It is now *your* fear. You own it. You never have to be afraid of fear again because through the stellating you have become bigger than 100 percent maximum archetypal fear.

You contain the fear. It does not contain you. You own the fear. It no longer owns you. Nothing could ever be scarier than this fear, and even while experiencing it you are okay.

PUNCHING Ordinarily you might not permit yourself to experience high intensity feelings due to the fear of hurting yourself or someone else. In conscious feelings work you are safe. You learn to start and stop feelings for no particular reason, only because you decide to start or stop. You detect what percentage big each feeling is, and you learn inner navigating so your feelings are pure and not mixed. Conscious feelings work changes your relationship to feelings. Feelings become a vast source of clarity, insight, intuitive intelligence, and focused energy for taking effective linear and nonlinear actions.

LIFTING Lifters stand directly across from a partner, one grasping the wrists of the other under the body, supporting the shoulders, back and buttocks. The person holding the head does not touch the ears, holds the head and not the neck, and does not rest the head against their chest. The spaceholder of the lifting asks, "Is anything uncomfortable?," and adjusts positions accordingly. Then the space-holder says, "Let yourself weigh ten thousand pounds. Let yourself be held in the arms of the women (men). Let your thoughts go. Welcome to women's culture (men's culture)." Then ask for silence. A lifting lasts two to five minutes. After placing the person gently back on the floor, all sit around them in a circle and give them a moment to assimilate this fabulous experience. Then ask them to slowly open their eyes, sit up, and connect with one or two of the lifters.

In any moment, for no reason, you could return to the territory of fear and tap its full wisdom and power for the rest of your life, and you would be okay. You can also now make it safe for others to experience and express their 100 percent maximum archetypal fear. You can help others through their rite of passage into adulthood. This could even be your life's calling.

Through stellating fear, the creator / designer / magician / sorceress archetype is turned on in you and is ready for action. The creator is the one who can step past the limits of the known into the terrifying unknown. Even though you are fully afraid, you can still function professionally, speak, think, feel, make intelligent decisions, etc. This is a completely different understanding and relationship to fear than is held in modern culture.

Over a period of about two years all four of your archetypes can be turned on in a safe and stable way and can be educated in the use of their tools and possibilities.

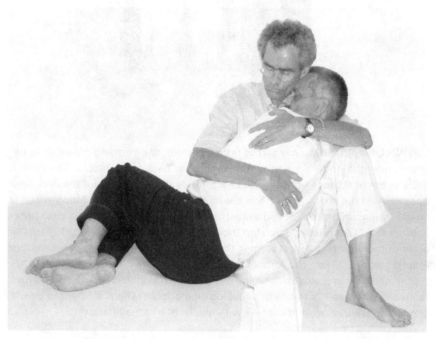

HOLDING One thing modern culture seems to have abandoned in its busy lifestyle is touch. Children in pre-industrial cultures are held almost constantly on the mother's body until they are six months old. For 100,000 years this is how human beings were raised. Modern mothers and fathers are encouraged to not physically bond with their children. This causes a deep wound. You can satisfy your lack of human contact through exchanging *holdings*, men with men, women with women. A ten to fifteen minute holding once a week for three months removes a crusty old scar and builds a foundation for the healthy adult.

During stellating your four bodies are accelerating to a new velocity of stillness, a new vastness of instantaneous presence. This shift is like changing from being an ordinary conductor of electricity in which you have ordinary resistances, to being a superconductor of electricity that has zero resistance. It is like shifting from subsonic to supersonic speeds without moving. A completely different set of physical laws becomes valid. What you considered to be reality before is still true. It just is not sufficient anymore for working at the archetypal levels.

HOLDING The holder sits on a mattress or padded carpet, braces her back against a wall, and wraps the other woman in her arms so she can feel her heart beating. Notice that the woman being held is completely allowing herself to be held. She is not holding the holder. Notice how the holder is not holding her own clasped hands. Instead she is holding the other woman with both hands fully open. This makes for better contact.

HOLDING Notice how the woman being held has her forehead tucked up into the other woman's neck. There is skin contact. The two of them have their eyes closed. There is no talking, patting, stroking or rocking. The one woman is simply letting herself be held, and the other woman is simply holding her. While holding, it can make it more comfortable if you brace your elbow on your knee as this woman is doing.

ARCHETYPAL TOOLS AND THOUGHTMAPS

If you understand the previous sections and follow the recommendations it is possible for you to stellate your feelings and turn on your archetypes. In case you manage to get yourself stellated I wish to supply you with a few tools and thoughtmaps that may become immediately relevant in your new condition. Please be warned that the following sections may at first seem bizarre.

Modern society has sensitized its citizens to be terrified of anything that does not originate in the thoughtware of modern culture. By now you have a built-in detector that categorizes things as *weird, kooky, strange, esoteric, witchcraft, new age, or fantasy*, often before you even notice you have categorized it. The message from modern culture is that weird, kooky or esoteric things must be avoided at *all* costs because they obviously brainwash people into joining a sect.

I am telling you that *the following tools and maps do not come from modern culture*. Your *kook detector* may at first go off the scale. I have been personally using some of these tools for over thirty-five years. Some of them I invented and some I learned from books, workshops or friends. They have been tested and found to be practical, simple, and remarkably effective by tens of thousands of people. These people use archetypal tools every day to bring more love and harmony into their relationships and more fulfillment into their lives. But the tools *definitely* come from beyond the thought limits of modern culture; otherwise, you would have learned them in grade school.

You can skip over these sections and come back to them later if you want. It does not matter. But if you have stellated your feelings and start entering archetypal energies and spaces you should be warned that different laws suddenly apply. Making turns when moving at light speed with a group of people, for example, is very different from making turns during ordinary meetings and conversations. In rarefied archetypal atmospheres these skills and tools can be as important and useful to you as a shoveling is to a gardener.

The tools include:

- The bubble and grounding cord
- The Disk of Nothing
- The Black Hole
- Holding double space
- How to be killed and not die

If you eventually need additional tools or skills there are more where these came from.

BUBBLE AND GROUNDING CORD

Once you reclaim your own authority and place your *being center* on your *physical center*, you are then *centered*, as shown on the Map of Being Centered in Chapter 3. The sensation of being centered is being less intellectually rigid and more responsively alert. You are capable of interacting with both local and general conditions and you can make relaxed gestures within a smaller-sized present. In simpler terms, you could say that when you are centered you are in the *here and now*.

Being centered in the here and now also brings you more directly into contact with your own feelings. When you know what you are feeling you can easily sense what other people are feeling. At this point it becomes important to be able to distinguish between your feelings and another person's feelings. Here are two energetic tools that help to discern whose feelings are whose: your bubble and your grounding cord.

Both the bubble and grounding cord are tangible. You can tell when they are functionally present and when they are not by using the same sense organs that you use to sense the mood in a conversation when you first join a group of people. The bubble and grounding cord are not distinctions of thought but rather distinctions of sensed space. To establish each of these distinctions you use Is-Glue to make a *declaration*. A *declaration* is a creative energetic gesture establishing that something *is* the way that you say it is. (That last sentence was a declaration.) (So was that one.)

You (as well as most everyone else) unconsciously use Is-Glue to declare things all day long. You say, "The weather IS beautiful." "I AM a specialist." "I CAN help you." "It IS not coffee break time yet." "I (DO) want to stop giving examples of declaring now," and so on. Most declaring fabricates unconscious stories to support the reality that is painted for you by your Box. With a small effort you can convert your faculty of declaring into a conscious skill. Then it becomes a simple thing to consciously declare your bubble and a grounding cord.

It helps me while declaring things consciously if I snap my fingers or tap my finger on my leg in the moment that I use the Is-Glue in my declaring. I call this *using my clicker*. I encourage you to use your clicker in the same way. Click! and it's there.

To make your bubble, simply click your clicker (tap your finger on something or snap your fingers) while at the same time asserting, "This is my bubble," either out loud or to yourself. The bubble is a pliable, durable, energetic distinction defining where your personal space starts and stops. It extends about half an arm's distance from your body all around you: over your head, under your feet, and around your back.

Click your clicker again and vanish your bubble. Click your clicker again and make your bubble once more. Can you feel the difference? Making your bubble is that easy and that fast, taking almost no time and no energy. It only requires a clear declaration to create it and then a bit of your attention to keep it there. As long as you remember your bubble it is there.

Inside of your bubble is your personal psychic and energetic space. Outside of your bubble is public space. The moment you first make your bubble could be the first moment in your life that you have clearly established and can definitely experience your own personal private space. Take a deep breath and relax a bit. Enjoy your privacy and safety. This is *your* space, and your space *only*.

Psychic etiquette says that inside of your bubble is *your* space and that no one else's energy or information belongs in your space. It also says that your energy and information does not belong in anybody else's space. Therefore, your first action after establishing your bubble (and your grounding cord) will be to clean other people's energy and information out of your bubble and fill it up with your own energy and information extracted from everybody else's bubbles.

You make your grounding cord in the same way that you made your bubble, by clicking your fingers and declaring, "This is my grounding cord." Your grounding cord functions like a lightning rod. It is a protective connection that *grounds* you by connecting your physical center (halfway between your hip bones and halfway back in your abdomen) straight down to the center of the Earth (even when you are in a tall building, a moving car, an airplane, swimming, etc.). Your grounding cord should be four or five centimeters in diameter (about two inches across) and should have a flexible resilience like rubber hose or thick rope. Different people have different-colored grounding cords, and the color may change from time to time. It does not matter what color your grounding cord is. Just be sure that you observe whatever color it is when you declare it into existence. Click again and vanish your cord. Click once more and establish it again. Can you feel the difference? This could also be the first time that you are truly grounded. Having a bubble and a grounding cord is a great feeling. As long as you remember them, they are there. At first it may require using 30 or 50 percent of your attention to hold your bubble and grounding cord in place. Later, after some practice, you can maintain your bubble and grounding cord with no more than 2 or 3 percent of your attention.

To practice, start like this. First thing when you wake up in the morning, Click! Click! Make your bubble and make your grounding cord. Any time during your day or night that you notice they are not there, Click! Click! Make them again. There is almost no time when it is not appropriate to have your bubble and your grounding cord.

Cleansing your bubble a few times a day is far quicker than brushing your teeth, and is at least as useful. To cleanse and simultaneously refill your bubble, use your clicker to declare a new personal-space bubble at your center. Click! Your new bubble starts out the size of a pea, but it quickly inflates as you retrieve your own golden energy and information from other people's bubbles wherever they might be in all time and all space. In a few seconds your new bubble expands with your own golden energy and information, flushing out anybody else's energy and information that is presently in your space, sending it directly and immediately back to them where it belongs. As your newly clicked bubble grows from your center your body and your bubble fill to overflowing with your own golden energy and information. The excess energy flows down your grounding cord into the Earth, cleaning the grounding cord as it goes. Voila! Your old bubble is vanished, replaced by your new bubble that is cleansed and refilled.

Now keep your bubble and go listen to another person. Every communication contains both energy (feelings, intention, spin, attitude, purpose, etc.) and information (opinions, facts, ideas, needs, requests, gossip, beliefs, etc.). With your bubble and grounding cord in place it is easy to distinguish whose energy and information is whose. Just because somebody in front of you is having a feeling, even someone you know intimately, does not make it *your* feeling. It is *their* feeling. Let them have their feeling in their bubble. You listen and be with them with their feeling, but their feeling is no longer touching your body. Their feelings stay outside of your bubble. You can be in compassionate contact with them and listen to their feelings while your space remains completely free and clear.

The same with problems. You can listen and respect people with their problem, but the problem does not come inside of your bubble. A problem may hit your bubble and get sucked down by your grounding cord like lightning through a lightning rod, but it is not your problem. Respect people and their problems, and let people have their own problems.

The same is true in reverse. When you have a feeling or a problem it is yours. You do not have to try to spread it on other people and make it into their feeling or their problem. Now you can take responsibility for having a feeling or a problem and you can take the necessary actions to deal with it without making the people around you suffer.

DISK OF NOTHING

Other people's hungry Gremlins may try to push your buttons to trigger an automatic reaction from your Box to get you out of the adult ego state and into a Gremlin feeding frenzy. If they can trigger your Box's reactive defense mechanisms, then you are hooked into a low drama with them and their Gremlin can eat your life energy for lunch.

Being centered and having a grounded bubble are very useful, but some Gremlins are so insidious about finding trigger hooks that an additional tool can be extremely valuable at times. No matter how rude or abusive the insult, criticism, insinuation, moan, or complaint, you do not have to react. The tool for protecting yourself from flying Gremlin barbs is called the *Disk of Nothing*.

The Disk is flat, about ten centimeters in diameter (four inches across), and rimmed with a thin golden tube. The back is solid silver. The front surface is a bluish liquid mirror, something like an activated stargate (from the film *Stargate*).

The Disk of Nothing is lightly clipped to your tool belt, meaning it is ready for instantaneous use. And that's the point, actually: to use it instantaneously.

In the same moment that a comment is hurled in your direction, whip out your Disk of Nothing and hold it up between you and the approaching hook. The hook goes deep into the nothingness of the Disk of Nothing and cannot touch you. There is nothing in the Disk for the psychoemotional barb to hook onto, so you don't get hooked. The Disk of Nothing helps you stay present and unhookable.

It doesn't matter if the insult comes from the front, the side, the back, the telephone, an email, a letter, lights on, lights off. Whatever form the hook takes, let it land in the Disk of Nothing instead of in you. Then you are protected. Even while someone is shooting insults in your direction you can stay in contact with them, listen to them, and feel with them.

BLACK HOLE

Your Box is designed to manage exchanges between you and your environment so that it can stay in control, perform its usual filtering actions, and succeed with its original survival strategy.

But each Box has a limit as to how much energy it can tolerate before going into overload. More often than you know, communications arrive with higher emotional energy levels than your Box is designed to manage. Without you knowing it the Box protects itself by blocking high-energy communications, causing you to end the communications before they are received. These can be messages that contain too much anger, fear or sadness for your Box to manage. But they can also be messages with too much joy, love, happiness and excitement for your Box. If your Box shuts down these messages then you miss out on them too.

The *Black Hole* is a tool that allows you to safely receive and complete communications with more emotional energy than your Box can ordinarily manage.

The Black Hole is a 20-centimeter-diameter (about 8 inches) hole in the floor that sucks in an infinite amount of energy. Energy has mass, as explained by Einstein's famous equation $E = Mc^2$, where E is energy and M is mass. But information is weightless; it has no mass.

So the Black Hole distinguishes between the energy and the information of a communication. While the high-energy blast is coming toward you, the Black Hole fiercely sucks all the energy out of the communication before the communication even touches your bubble. All that remains is the information. The energy is sucked down into the Earth, and the pure information comes through your bubble to you. Your Box can completely relax its defenses, which are ineffective against so much energy anyway, so you stay open and in total contact with the person delivering the communication. The Earth uses the excess energy like organic fertilizer.

If the communication is powered by anger, for example, then the *energy* of the anger is absorbed into the Black Hole, but the *information* of the anger, such as "I feel angry because . . . ," peacefully comes to you. You can then use a completion loop to repeat back to the speaker what you heard them say. Through using the completion loop you permanently complete the communication and it vanishes forever. This takes you to the next deeper level of intimacy with the speaker. Using the Black Hole opens the door to receiving whole new dimensions of communication.

As soon as you detect a high-energy communication coming your way, simply click your clicker (snap your fingers, or tap your finger on an object) to declare, "Here is my Black Hole." Make the Black Hole in the floor just in front of your bubble. Remember, the energy gets sucked into the Black Hole *before* it even touches your bubble. There is no force or pressure needed to protect yourself against the discharge of energy. You are protected and can completely relax while you receive the information. This is a fantastic tool!

If a high-energy communication is coming by phone or by email, you can click a mini–Black Hole into existence three or four centimeters in diameter (one or two inches across) on your desk or in the space between your ear and the telephone to suck down all the energy.

You can also use the Black Hole to cleanse a meeting room after it has been used for an intense gathering. As soon as you notice energetic residue, click your clicker and declare a one-meter diameter Black Hole (one yard across) in the center of the floor. In an instant, this giant Black

Hole will suck all the old energy remnants out of that space and reset it to its pristine state, ready for your use. Then vanish the Black Hole. You can perform the whole cleaning operation without even slowing down your pace while walking in and setting up the room.

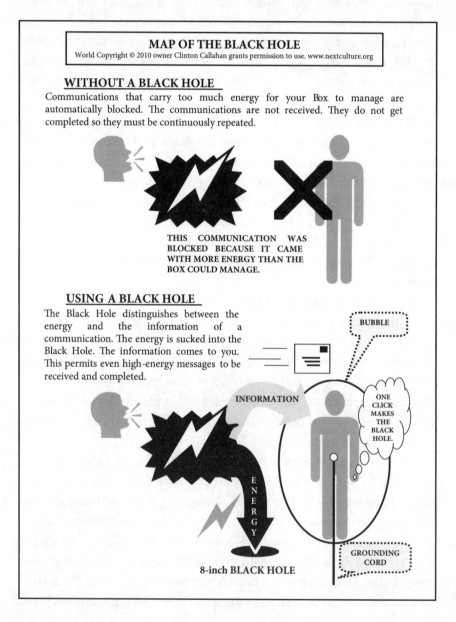

MAP OF THE BLACK HOLE

WITHOUT A BLACK HOLE

Communications that carry too much energy for your Box to manage are automatically blocked. The communications are not received. They do not get completed so they must be continuously repeated.

THIS COMMUNICATION WAS BLOCKED BECAUSE IT CAME WITH MORE ENERGY THAN THE BOX COULD MANAGE.

USING A BLACK HOLE

The Black Hole distinguishes between the energy and the information of a communication. The energy is sucked into the Black Hole. The information comes to you. This permits even high-energy messages to be received and completed.

BUBBLE

INFORMATION

ONE CLICK MAKES THE BLACK HOLE.

ENERGY

GROUNDING CORD

8-inch BLACK HOLE

Also, sometimes during certain meetings, conferences, funerals, political rallies, or public confrontations, huge clouds of pent-up emotional fear, anger, or sadness are released. If the emotional energy gets too concentrated it can generate back pressure that resists more energy being expressed and causes people to explode, panic or go a little berserk. In these conditions you can vanish the energy down a giant Black Hole with a few clicks. You may need to make Black Holes ongoingly under certain conditions. The results can be miraculous.

As soon as you are done using a Black Hole, I recommend that you vanish it with another click of your clicker. Leftover Black Holes may be where those second socks and missing earrings have disappeared.

HOLDING DOUBLE SPACE

The clarity of conscious, adult, responsible anger can be used to make precise energetic distinctions. A particularly useful anger distinction is to declare and hold energetic space. Making your bubble and grounding cord is an example of holding energetic space for yourself. After you can make and hold your personal grounded bubble space with some level of competence, you are prepared for the next application of conscious anger. This would be to split off an additional bit of your attention to declare and hold energetic space in a room for the purpose of serving a group of people with your Bright Principles.

Every room, no matter its size or shape, has the equivalent of physical walls, ceiling and floor. These surfaces define the boundaries of the *physical* space. Physical space is relatively rigid and does not change shape without the building being damaged or remodeled (or folded up, for example, if it is a tent).

Within the physical boundaries of a room you can click your clicker and declare into existence the four walls, ceiling and floor of an *energetic* space by asserting, "This is my energetic workspace." As long as you use a bit of your attention to remember it, the distinction stays there. You are then the spaceholder of an energetic space.

When you spacehold a box-shaped energetic workspace while at the same time spaceholding your personal grounded bubble, you are holding two spaces at the same time: one for the purposes of the team, project, or meeting, and one for you. This is called *holding double space*.

Traditional forms of practice such as tai chi, archery, meditation, dressage, or gymnastics begin with a starting position—what in fencing is called *en garde* and in ballet is called *first position*. From this beginning position all other positions and moves in that form can originate. In Possibility Management, first position is being centered and holding a grounded and cleansed double space.

The set of Bright Principles (the conscious purpose) of a workspace can also be declared with a click of your clicker: *This space is in the service of integrity, clarity, teamwork, efficiency, nonlinear possibility, and easefulness*, or whatever is needed to serve the meeting's outcome.

More than one person can hold the same space at the same time if they have the same purpose. In this way you can hold space for a meeting even if the official leader of the meeting is not holding space.

With a click of your clicker you can expand or shrink the size of the energetic space you are holding. You can click and hold space for an entire business building, a city, a continent, a planet, a galaxy, even an entire universe, or all universes, for that matter. Try it yourself. Each click changes the size of the space for which you are taking conscious responsibility.

Or you can shrink the size of the space you are holding to being smaller than the size of the physical space. This is useful, for example, at those times when you are in a restaurant with your partner or friends and you would like to have a private space of intimacy. Keep your grounded personal bubble, then click your clicker and declare an energetic workspace so that it surrounds just the people with you at your table. Now things are beginning to get interesting.

Through your practice of holding double space you get to remain centered in your grounded, cleansed personal bubble while at the same time holding and navigating space for a project or team. This practical expression of clarity gives you tremendous abilities to serve.

WALKING AT THE SPEED OF LOVE

There is a particular form of holding double space that adds fascinating dimensions to a man-woman relationship. It works best when both people are engaged in the rite of passage process, so that the extraordinary adult space is familiar, and so that feelings work has stellated at least a couple of your archetypes, particularly the archetypal anger of the warrior and warrioress.

Begin your experiments while walking down the street together, in the shopping zone or through a park. First of all, agree to be walking together at the *speed of love*. It could take a while before you figure out what this is.

When absorbed in ordinary modern culture you naturally walk at the *speed of mind*. The speed of mind is quick because you already imagine yourself to be where you are intending to go, so you are not actually being where you are. Love has a very different speed, and walking at the speed of mind leaves love far behind. This could be one reason why you do not experience as much love in your life as you might like to. The speed of love is much, much slower than the speed of mind.

To walk at the speed of love, hold hands and let your feet move at the speed that love moves them. It is slightly slower than a stroll, a little faster than not moving at all, and it meanders a bit, like a brook through a meadow. If you are accustomed to walking at the speed of mind this could drive your mind crazy for a while. Learn to walk together at the speed of love. This alone is already fantastic.

DECLARING EXTRAORDINARY AND ARCHETYPAL SPACE

When you are comfortable walking together at the speed of love, use your clicker to declare and hold a box-shaped space of adult level responsibility just like you learned in the previous sections. The adult space provides you with conscious feelings and extraordinary love, where love is there because you are there responsibly sourcing love. (For more about this topic, you may be interested in reading my book *Radiant Joy Brilliant Love*.) All around you is the ordinary world, with its ordinary level of resentment, jealousy, greed, low drama, and ordinary love, where love is scarce and people go around looking for someone to love them. In the middle of that ordinary field, you have now created a sanctuary of extraordinary adult relationship, completed communications, respect, listening, and extraordinary love.

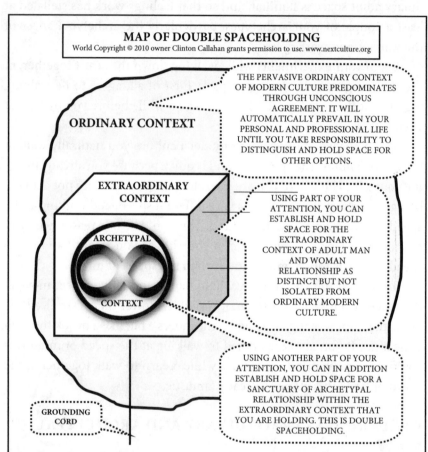

MAP OF DOUBLE SPACEHOLDING
World Copyright © 2010 owner Clinton Callahan grants permission to use. www.nextculture.org

ORDINARY CONTEXT

THE PERVASIVE ORDINARY CONTEXT OF MODERN CULTURE PREDOMINATES THROUGH UNCONSCIOUS AGREEMENT. IT WILL AUTOMATICALLY PREVAIL IN YOUR PERSONAL AND PROFESSIONAL LIFE UNTIL YOU TAKE RESPONSIBILITY TO DISTINGUISH AND HOLD SPACE FOR OTHER OPTIONS.

EXTRAORDINARY CONTEXT

ARCHETYPAL

CONTEXT

USING PART OF YOUR ATTENTION, YOU CAN ESTABLISH AND HOLD SPACE FOR THE EXTRAORDINARY CONTEXT OF ADULT MAN AND WOMAN RELATIONSHIP AS DISTINCT BUT NOT ISOLATED FROM ORDINARY MODERN CULTURE.

USING ANOTHER PART OF YOUR ATTENTION, YOU CAN IN ADDITION ESTABLISH AND HOLD SPACE FOR A SANCTUARY OF ARCHETYPAL RELATIONSHIP WITHIN THE EXTRAORDINARY CONTEXT THAT YOU ARE HOLDING. THIS IS DOUBLE SPACEHOLDING.

GROUNDING CORD

Distinguishing and holding more than one space at the same time is done through anger's clarity, not through force. Begin by distinguishing the sensations of ordinary, extraordinary and archetypal spaces so that you can detect where you are and what is possible for you there. Then practice consciously splitting your attention three ways at the same time: (1) Being aware of what is happening in ordinary space, (2) declaring into existence the clarity of extraordinary space, and then (3) establishing the safety of the archetypal masculine holding space for the archetypal feminine. Your double spaceholding is now in resonance with an archetypal symbol. Continue holding these two spaces simultaneously, keeping them distinct from each other and distinct from the ordinary world. Each space has its own laws. Holding the outside layer of extraordinary adult space makes it possible to hold the inside layer of archetypal masculine-feminine space even when you are walking down the street with your partner in public. You will not already know how to do this. Just keep trying, and learn to navigate through practicing.

Wait for the extraordinary adult space to stabilize for you both. Whether that takes three minutes or three years does not matter. It is time and experience wondrously enjoyed together.

When the extraordinary space stabilizes—almost like balancing on a high wire—the man additionally splits his attention, clicks his clicker, and declares an additional bubble around the two of you inside of the cubic sanctuary of adult space: *There is now archetypal space for us.* It is the archetypal masculine nothingness holding space for the archetypal feminine everythingness.

Keep breathing.

How can the masculine *nothing* hold space for the feminine *everything*? To find that answer, ask yourself this question: Which is bigger: nothing, or everything?

Experience tells you that nothing is bigger. If the nothing weren't bigger, where would the everything fit?

This means that whatever comes up from the Feminine, the Masculine can assert, *I am bigger than that* (speaking from the archetypal *I*). This declaration does not come from a position of already knowing. He speaks from not knowing, and continues holding the archetypal space with his split attention. Navigating this double spaceholding in the midst of ordinary busyness is a form of living art, each nuance of which can be deeply experienced and pleasurably enjoyed.

BULLSHIT AND COWSHIT

There are two kinds of shit: bullshit and cowshit. This can prove to be a most useful distinction. Men do *bullshit*, saying things that are relevant but not true, such as, "Honey, I'll fix the toilet on Saturday," "Darling, I'll be home at seven," or "Sweetie Pie, I'll help Stevie with his math before the weekend." These are very relevant things to say, but coming from the man, they are just not true. This is called bullshit.

Women do *cowshit*, saying things that are very, very true, excruciatingly true, absolutely, undeniably, totally true . . . but are just not relevant.

Such as, it is Friday evening around nine o'clock, the kids are handled and the couple is headed up to the bedroom. The man steps through the door behind his woman. She turns around to him and says, "I noticed that you completely ignored the laundry basket full of clothes at the bottom of the stairs. What do you think? I'm your slave? I washed those clothes. I folded those clothes. The least you could have done is carry them up the stairs for me. But no, you were thinking of yourself again." Thunk! Thunk! Thunk! Each statement is an arrow in the man's chest. Everything she says is true. Irrefutably true . . .

But at this particular moment it is just not very relevant. This is cowshit.

HOW TO BE KILLED AND NOT DIE

Certain times when the woman is doing cowshit may not be the best times for the well-trained, beyond-patriarchy Possibility Management man to use his centered and grounded bubble, Sword of Clarity, Disk of Nothing, *and* the Black Hole to protect himself. If he uses those things then he may not appear to be authentically touched by what his woman is saying. She may sense that her message is not being thoroughly received.

In such times you may not appear to be vulnerable enough for her to be vulnerable with you. Then she has to pull out her high powered bow and arrows to soften you up a bit more: "That's probably the same reason you didn't get the brakes checked on the car this week" (Thunk!), "or take the insurance papers in," (Thunk!) "or pay the credit card bills" (Thunk!). "I mean, what exactly *have* you been doing all week anyway while I was taking care of the kids, doing the shopping and cooking the meals? Watching our investments online while they sink even further below sea level?"

The point is, some women end their day with a quiver full of these nasty little arrows and they just need somewhere to deposit them. If you put on your stainless steel armor and deflect the arrows untouched or turn yourself invisible, she feels unheard. On the other hand, if you let the arrows slam repeatedly into your heart and react emotionally from your parent or child ego state or from your Gremlin, you are dead. And the other little guy is dead, too—the one who was so excited about it being nine o'clock on Friday night . . . remember?

What can be quite useful in this situation is to know how to be killed and not die—how to be authentically touched and at the same time not deflate little john.

So here is how. First, get killed. Let yourself feel the bright pain of each arrow as it pierces your well-meaning heart.

Let yourself get killed knowing that whatever can get killed was not real in the first place. Decide that it is fine to let those parts that are so easily offended get lasered like an ant under a magnifying glass in the hot sun. It may hurt tremendously. Let yourself feel the sadness, the fear, the anger. You do not have to say anything at this point. Just feel the truth of what she is saying. Admit the truth of it. Stay in the present moment. Minimize your *now* so that your timescale for what *being present* means is very small: about two heartbeats long.

Keep breathing in this *minimized now* timeframe. Keep looking in her eyes and keep listening until she is finished. Stay in the exact present moment and watch how what she says slides out of the present into the past while you don't. You stay in the present. As she stops talking, you keep breathing and you keep being with her. Notice how the sound echoes have faded completely away. It takes at most three seconds for all that sound to fade out of the space and into the past, where nothing has any power anymore.

The only place those things she said to you still exist is in your mind as a memory. Recognize that the words that were spoken are no longer in the present . . . *but that you are.*

You are still here, with your grounded bubble, Sword of Clarity, Disk of Nothing, and Black Hole. Keep breathing. You are still here. You were killed. And you are still here. You did not die.

Here is a very small *now*, and you are still in it, here and now. And so is *she.*

She is in the *now* with you.

As you keep breathing in the very small time span of *now* and stay in contact with your woman, the word *she* begins to resonate with a very interesting sensation: a sacred, precious, tingling. This amazing *she* is still here with you *now* in the present moment, and you were indeed killed but you did not die. And *he* did not die either, the little guy. You and he are still together here in this small present moment with *her*, where touch happens, where contact happens, where what was just spoken has drifted into the distant past of more than three seconds ago, and you and she are still here in this now, where loving and kissing is happening. And what a great thing it is to be killed and not die, wouldn't you say?

FEELINGS MADE INTO SUFFERING

A relevant question has perhaps come to you. Why bother to feel pain? Isn't it masochistic to consciously feel pain? The answer becomes clear through making a distinction between consciously feeling pain, and consciously suffering.

First of all, feelings are physical sensations that cover the full spectrum from pleasure to pain. Even with laughter, muscles cramp up all over your body, loud sounds strain your throat, tears come out of your eyes, and you may need to exert great efforts to keep from peeing in your pants. I have even fallen out of my chair because I was laughing so hard. Laughter can be quite painful.

The feelings of anger, sadness, fear and joy may each become painful beyond a certain intensity. But the point at which to call a physical sensation painful is subjective. For example, each person has their own judgment about what is too loud music, too many blankets, too hot tea, too fast driving, or too much ice cream.

Our assessment about what level of intensity constitutes pain may have been set during childhood and may still be distorted by childhood memories.

The adult human body, however, is designed to experience and express full-out rage, horrifying terror, gut-wrenching grief, and extended ecstatic joy. One hundred percent maximum archetypal feelings are our birthright, acquired through rite of passage into adulthood. The thousands of people who have stepped beyond the limits of modern culture and engaged a rite of passage for themselves can confirm this. They experience and express archetypal feelings at maximum intensity. When this happens in our trainings, afterward I ask, "Are you okay?" The one who just experienced and expressed archetypal feelings checks themselves out, and sure enough, although it is beyond belief, they discover, *Yes, I am okay.* And they *are* okay. They could do it again whenever they want and also then be okay. This pain is not suffering.

On the other hand, any person can Is-Glue a victim story to any emotional pain to create a low drama. For example: "You cut in front of me in line, you asshole!" (emotional anger) "She didn't remember to call me back." (emotional sadness) "I'm not prepared to visit that horrible client!" (emotional fear) "I'm sure looking forward to going on vacation so I can finally relax!" (emotional joy).

Through Is-Gluing stories to feelings human beings change pain into suffering. We are the only animal that can do this.

Reasonable questions might arise at this point. For example: How can I become more sensitive to feelings through lowering my numbness bar, and at the same time be more relaxed and present? How can I be more vulnerable if it is going to hurt more?

The answer has to do with gratitude: I can appreciate painful experience, no matter which of the four feelings the pain is, because my feelings are some of the most precious experiences of being alive.

Appreciating experience in its original neutrality permits you to use conscious feelings for creating high drama. To consciously create high drama it helps to distill your destiny.

8. DISTILLING YOUR DESTINY

(NOTE TO THE READER: In this chapter you will be clarifying the four, five or six Bright Principles of your destiny. If you have skipped ahead to this chapter without carefully studying the previous seven chapters, it's a clever idea but I don't recommend it. Learning to consciously feel has similarities to rock climbing, which is actually quite simple. Slip into a harness, design your approach, chalk up your hands and its monkey time. But they make you take lessons and get a certificate before letting you climb El Capitan. It's for your own good. That's because if you shout "off belay" when you mean "on belay" you could scream ten meters and wrench your back. If you thought your rock face is grade IV 4.2 but it is actually VI 5.8 you could be in for hard knocks. If your carabiner isn't fully locked when you've got your climbing rope clicked into your quickdraw the wrong way you might need more than a new brain bucket (helmet). I am not saying anything like this will happen if you skip over the previous chapters. But I am saying that the world of conscious feelings operates under different laws than the world of numbness, just like rock climbing is different from stair climbing. Before you rope up for distilling your destiny I strongly encourage you to study the first seven chapters of this book. It's for your own good.)

"I want to be true to that in me which seeks to fulfill its promise."
– Etty Hillesum, *An Interrupted Life*

This chapter contains a process through which you can distill out of your life the four, five or six Bright Principles of your destiny.

What are Bright Principles?

Bright Principles are forces of nature. Each Bright Principle is a facet of the bright jewel of responsibility, the practical manifestation of consciousness, as shown on the Map of Possibility. (The term *responsibility* here means *adult responsibility* as described on the Map of Child and Adult Responsibility in Chapter 5.)

MAP OF POSSIBILITY

This is a map of what is possible right now.
What you are doing right now is creating conscious or unconscious stories about what is.
Without your storymaking, *what is* would have no meaning. This is not bad – it is how it is.
The world is rich in evidence, so you can make up any story about anything.
You do not make up stories for no reason. Every story has a purpose.
You are either aware of the purpose of your story or you are not.
If you are aware of the purpose of your story, then your actions serve conscious purposes.
If you are not aware of the purpose of your story, your actions serve unconscious purposes.
This map is not about good or bad. It is about conscious or unconscious creating.

CONSCIOUS PURPOSE

THE BRIGHT JEWEL OF RESPONSIBILITY
CREATES A RESPONSIBLE GAME :
"WINNING HAPPENING," "I WIN AS YOU WIN."
ABUNDANCE THROUGH TAKING RESPONS-
IBILITY FOR SOURCING THE RESOURCES.
SERVES YOUR TRUE PURPOSES (DESTINY).
YOUR BRIGHT PRINCIPLES.
USES THE ENERGY AND INFORMATION OF
FEELINGS TO CREATE HIGH DRAMA.

UNCONSCIOUS PURPOSE

THE SHADOW JEWEL OF IRRESPONSIBILITY
CREATES AN IRRESPONSIBLE GAME:
"I WIN, YOU LOSE," "HA - HA! I GOT YOU!"
SCARCITY THROUGH AVOIDING TAKING
RESPONSIBILITY FO R THE RESOURCES.
SERVES YOUR HIDDEN PURPOSES.
YOUR SHADOW PRINCIPLES.
USES THE ENERGY AND INFORMATION OF
FEELINGS TO CREATE LOW DRAMA.

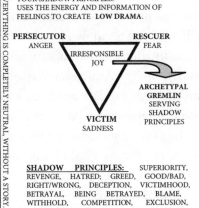

(center vertical text: WHAT IS, IS, AS IT IS. (Desjardins/Prajnanpad). JUST THIS. (Lozowick) — EVERYTHING IS COMPLETELY NEUTRAL, WITHOUT A STORY.)

BRIGHT PRINCIPLES: KINDNESS, DIGNITY, GENEROSITY, LOVE, CLARITY, RESPECT, ACCEPTANCE, POSSIBILITY, INTEGRITY, COMMUNICATION, TEAMWORK, DISCOVERY, FRIENDSHIP, COMMUNITY, EMPOWERMENT, TRANSFORMATION, GROWTH, RADIANCE, TRUSTWORTHINESS, HIGH LEVEL FUN, ETC.

SHADOW PRINCIPLES: SUPERIORITY, REVENGE, HATRED; GREED, GOOD/BAD, RIGHT/WRONG, DECEPTION, VICTIMHOOD, BETRAYAL, BEING BETRAYED, BLAME, WITHHOLD, COMPETITION, EXCLUSION, RESENTMENT, DENIAL, EXPECTATION, DISRESPECT, ETC.

This map is inside of you. Each of us has a bright world and a shadow world. This map is not about good or bad, only about the kinds of results you want to create. The king or queen of your underworld is your Gremlin, which feels glad when someone else feels pain and serves Shadow (*hidden purpose)* Principles. The king or queen of your upperworld is archetypal man or woman, who feels glad when someone heals, learns, changes or succeeds, when the game is about winning happening and serves Bright (*true destiny)* Principles. When you have gained clarity about both your hidden purpose and your true destiny, what you get is the possibility of making a conscious choice about what you are creating right now. This can be a most useful choice.

Responsibility is consciousness in action: the actions you take have a level of responsibility that reflects your level of consciousness.

There is no deception possible about your level of responsibility because the results never lie. For example, if you come late to an appointment, no matter what your excuse is, the result is that you are responsible for being late. You are the source of the consequences in your life. Consequences cannot be avoided. To quote an old saying, "You can't fool Mother Nature." For example, it's a fool's game to think you can externalize business costs. What goes around, comes around. Profit is an illusion.

ARCHETYPAL WORLDS

Archetypally speaking, there is a middleworld, an upperworld and an underworld. You normally live your everyday life in the middleworld. You shift from world to world according to whether Bright or Shadow Principles motivate your actions, communications and relationships.

If you do not consciously choose to serve Bright Principles, you unconsciously choose to serve Shadow Principles.

Bright and Shadow Principles are both diagrammed on the Map of Possibility. But the map is general, merely a concept. You cannot consciously navigate your everyday moment-to-moment thoughts and actions through Bright and Shadow Principles until you clearly distill out those Principles from your life.

The *Distilling Destiny Process* is how you find your Bright Principles and, except for the final check, you can do it yourself by following the instructions in this chapter.

The *Hidden Purpose Process,* on the other hand, is how you find your Shadow Principles. The Hidden Purpose Process is a two-hour chaotic, loud, intense group experience navigated by a highly experienced facilitator. "Intense" meaning the maximum of what you could imagine a journey into the archetypal underworld might be like. Needless to say, the Hidden Purpose Process is not something you would try at home on your own from a book.

I equate your distilled Bright Principles to your *destiny*, the significance of which is that you do not have to wait to find out what your destiny turns out to be. With clarity about your Bright Principles you can live as your destiny in action right now.

The Distilling Destiny Process has four parts. The whole thing might take you a couple of hours. Not all four parts need to be done at one sitting. The four steps are:

Part 1: Discovering Your Destiny

Part 2: Choosing Your Destiny

Part 3: Adding Mass to Your Destiny—Your Practices

Part 4: Implementing Your Destiny—A Project

Parts 2, 3 and 4 bring Part 1 out of intellectual curiosity into authenticity. To do Part 1, reserve a half hour of private time and sit at a writing desk with several sheets of paper to answer the Distilling Destiny Questions.

PART 1: DISCOVERING YOUR DESTINY

The following Distilling Destiny Questions have no right or wrong answers. Your answers are for you alone. Answer as many of these questions as you can, keeping in mind that you are not looking for the linear answers to the questions. You are looking for the themes, principles and values that have been at work in your life. The questions lead you to recognize these overall patterns.

You do not need to write complete sentences. Neither do you need to answer all of the questions. Just write the ongoing principles and values that the questions reveal. The purpose of these questions is to help you identify what really matters to you.

The Distilling Destiny Questions (Reminder: Don't write answers to the questions that are printed in straight type. *Do write answers to the questions in italics.*)

1. What was your favorite story as a child? Who are you in that story? *What do you resonate with in this character? What turns you on about him or her? What qualities do you have in common with this character?*

2. What is your favorite film? Who are you in the film? *What do you love about this character? What inspires you about him or*

her? What qualities are the same between you and the character? His or her attitudes? His or her way of being? What decisions, conflicts, solutions are the same?

3. Where are your favorite places to be? *What in you is expressed at these places? What in you comes alive there? What is stimulated? Fulfilled? Amplified?*

4. What are your favorite things to see? To smell? To touch? *What delights you about these experiences? What inspires you about them? What values do you appreciate about them?*

5. What are your favorite fantasies? Where do you go when you daydream? What is happening there? *What attracts you to that? What happens for you there? What is your need? What is it that you want to be true? What are you longing for?*

6. What are the best times you ever had? What happened? *Why was it so good? Why do you classify it as the best of times?*

7. What are your biggest successes? *What motivated you to try so hard? What value did it have? What did you get?*

8. What awards have you received? What honors? *What in you was recognized? What was your purpose?*

9. If you were fully rested and had a week of unscheduled time, and money was not a consideration, what would you do? Who would you do it with? *Why would you do this? What would you get out of it?*

10. What are your favorite possessions? Why are they favorites? *What do they mean to you? What do they represent to you? What in you is expressed by these objects? What do they stand for? What do they touch in you?*

11. What are the most valuable experiences or adventures you ever had? *Why do you consider them valuable? What did you enjoy? What did you learn?*

12. If you had 100 million dollars, no strings attached, no taxes, what would you do with it? *Why? What is the value for you in*

doing this? What would it accomplish? What is the worth of that to you?

13. What have you made with your own hands? *What did you get from doing this? What motivated you to make the effort?*

14. What are your hobbies? *What do you enjoy most about them?*

15. *In what ways do you have substance?* (Just write the first answer that comes to mind.)

16. *If there were a group of people who were undefended, what would you defend for them? What would you care enough about to take a stand for on their behalf?*

17. If your parents were to brag about you to their neighbors, *what would they say?*

18. *In what ways are you authentic?* (Just write what comes to mind.)

19. *What do your friends really love about you?* (Be honest!) *What do they see in you that makes them want to be your friends?*

20. *What qualities are you famous for? What is your reputation about? What are the qualities about you that are legendary?*

21. If you had fifteen minutes of free worldwide TV exposure, so everyone could understand you in every language, *what is the most important message that you would want to communicate to people? What core message do you want people to know?*

22. *What traits or characteristics or values would you want your children to inherit from you?*

23. If you went to a costume party, what favorite character would you like to be? *What do you admire and respect about this character? What does this character communicate to you?*

24. Who are your heroes in history? *What do you admire and respect about them? What radiance do they have that you notice and appreciate?*

25. If you painted your own self-portrait, *what characteristics would you want people to experience when looking at the painting?*

What mood would you want them to have? What possibilities would you want them to gain?

26. When you die, *what words would you want printed in your obituary in the newspaper? What do you want them to say about your life?*

DISTILLATION INSTRUCTIONS

After you have answered the questions review what you wrote and circle the four to six main Principles that have been revealed running through your life, the central themes that really matter to you, the qualities that resonate deeply with your inner wish to be alive. Try to avoid using your mind to analyze what you wrote. Instead, use your body to sense core Principles that have the most resonance for you in the long term.

After you have circled four to six Bright Principles copy them to the bottom of your page. These Bright Principles have been with you since you were born. You could even say that you were born to enliven these Principles in the world.

Sometimes we think that what we *have to do* is different from what we *are supposed to do*, which is different from what *really turns us on to do*. In fact, these three things *are all the same thing*. This becomes clear when you distill your Destiny Principles out of your life. No matter what you do you are serving the purpose of bringing your Principles to life. This is what really matters to you.

When you make yourself conscious of what really matters to you and write it down on paper, what you are looking at is your destiny.

In your list of Bright Principles it turns out that there is a pattern. What matters to you fits together as a whole, balanced and complete portrait. Certain elements will be included. Your list of Bright Principles should include at least one heart Principle (such as Love, Friendship, Family, Togetherness, Oneness, Acceptance, Joy, Harmony, Community, Communication, Teamwork), at least one sword Principle (such as Integrity, Clarity, Trustworthiness, Impeccability, Reliability, Respect, Commitment, Discipline), and at least one soul Principle (such as Possibility, Transformation, Healing, Beauty, Empowerment, Adventure, Leadership, Service, Creativity, Growth, Patience, Vision).

The Principles cannot be too general. For example, if the theme *ecology* runs throughout your answers, ask yourself, *ecology in relationship to what? For what purpose? To what end?* For example, ecology could reflect a resonance with any of these Bright Principles: Balance, Fairness, Beauty, Elegance, Respect, Sustainability, Harmony, Efficiency, Connectedness, Exchange, Innocence, Evolution, and so on. Sense into it and figure out precisely which specific Bright Principle the theme of ecology represents for you.

Take your time with this. Strive for an accurate reflection of your inner motivation, your true purpose for being alive.

Over the years that we have been Distilling Destiny with people we have learned to avoid particular Bright Principle formulations because Gremlin can grab hold of them, create theoretical loopholes, and then twist you into serving its own shenanigans. For example:

- *Honesty.* Gremlin can say, "But I'm just being honest with you . . ." while dumping a mountain of destructive criticism, blame and hatred on your head. Instead, use Clarity, Vulnerability, Integrity, Openness, Courage, or Transparency.

- *Freedom.* Gremlin says, "Yeah! Freedom from responsibility! Freedom to not keep my promises! Freedom to betray!" Instead, use Abundance, Choice, Creation, Nonlinearity, Possibility, Diversity, or Appreciation.

- *Power.* Remember, Bright Principles are the way you serve *other* people. You may have been attracted to power your whole life, but serving Bright Principles is about empowering other people, not yourself. Gremlin can take Power twice around the block before you blink an eye. Instead, use Empowerment, Encouragement, Clarity, Commitment, Persistence, Teamwork, Fulfillment, Enthusiasm, Inspiration, Discipline, Healing, or Wholeness.

- *Justice.* Gremlin is perfectly justified to take revenge in the name of justice—after all, has it not been written *An eye for an eye and a tooth for a tooth*? Instead use Fairness, Sharing, Connecting, Relationship, Understanding, Being With, or Communication.

- *Trust.* Trust is actually a decision, not a Bright Principle. You don't have to collect enough evidence before you can trust, or wait around until you have a certain warm internal sensation before you can trust. You can simply decide to trust or to not trust. Instead of trust, you can represent and serve the Bright Principle of Trustworthiness. Then you empower others to become trustworthy.

- *Intensity.* Gremlin devours intensity by jumping from one stimulation to the next: food, drink, emergency, confrontation, risk, accident, entertainment, online sex, drugs, business deals, competition, shopping, etc. A commitment to intensity is Gremlin's excuse for more, more, more. If you are oriented toward intensity, instead serve the Bright Principles of Integrity, Commitment, Discipline, Impeccability, Ruthless Self-Observation, Accountability, Vulnerability, or Community. Truly embracing any of these Bright Principles will bring you to levels of intensity far beyond the intensity of self-indulgence

- *Being Special.* Gremlin *loves* to be special. Then it has a reason for doing *anything* it wants, because it's special: special needs, special requirements, special privileges, etc. Gremlin claims that *everyone* is special. He is just *a little more special* than all the others. Instead, use Self-Respect, Diversity, Appreciation, Impeccability, Elegance, Gentleness, Generosity, or Kindness.

Try writing your list of Bright Principles over and over again until they come together in their most clear and powerful natural order. Remember, you are making a working draft. Your destiny principles will continue to refine themselves and evolve over time as you apply them in daily situations. When your Bright Principles feel round and resonant you have distilled your destiny.

PART 2: CHOOSING YOUR DESTINY

It may surprise you to learn that *your destiny is optional!* Most civilized people unconsciously choose not to enact their true destiny. (NOTE: Many of these distinctions about what really matters to you come from

Robert Fritz's amazing little book *Creating*, a book I highly recommend.) You have distilled your destiny Principles, but you have not *become* your destiny Principles. Here are some considerations to ponder before it would be possible for you to consciously choose to align to your Bright Principles.

While reading over your Bright Principles, get in touch with the part of you that might resist serving these Bright Principles, thinking it to be an overwhelming burden. Specifically, what makes it seem like a burden to you? Write down your thoughts and ponder what you wrote. Such ideas have been at work in the back of your mind your whole life. Do they still truly apply to you now? Would you like to change your mind about any of these now? If so, go ahead. Then write down your new perspectives.

After distilling your Bright Principles, you can see that the Principles have always been there. What behaviors or excuses do you use for explaining why *what really matters to you* does not show up first and foremost in your life? Typical excuses might include: I don't know how. I can't. I'm not good enough. I'm not allowed to. I'm too old, too young, too stupid. People will hate me. I am a bad person. I am crippled. I am addicted.

Perhaps you experience your destiny as an incredible opportunity and good fortune. If so, what still stands between you and *being* your destiny? Write that down.

Which is bigger, your commitment to what matters to you—or your commitment to what stands between you and what matters to you? Write out your answer, with examples.

What would have to be different in your life in order to have *what matters to you* come first? First before low drama. First before finding excuses. First before mere survival.

Do you see that you are already involved in sourcing these Principles in the world? They have been functioning, perhaps unconsciously, for your whole life. Even so, you are in no way obligated to commit to your destiny. Living your destiny consciously is completely optional. Choosing your destiny is a moment-to-moment choice. Only by consciously choosing to make your life about fulfilling your destiny can you truly commit to it. You have the power to choose this because you have free will.

The formal commitment to serving your Bright Principles is more compelling than the force of your psychology (your Box's demands).

Principles are a force of nature. If you actually choose to be your destiny in action, your life will not be about you anymore. Many people who commit to serving their destiny are unexpectedly moved to locations and moved to take actions that their Box would ordinarily never have chosen. Think seriously about this choice.

Your Principles are not about *you*. Your Principles are not there for *you* to be empowered, for *you* to have more joy, money, power, fun, or more love in your life. They are there for serving humanity and the Earth.

Your Principles are your calling card, the sign over your door. Your Principles are what you represent as a service for other people. People come to you when they need what your specific Principles can provide for them. You become the eyes, ears, mouth, hands, feet and heart through which your Principles and your archetypal lineage can do their work in the world.

If you decide to choose your destiny, then your Box no longer has majority vote in your day-to-day actions. Your Principles have majority vote. Your life is not about you anymore; it is about serving something greater than yourself. You become your Principles. Your self-image, comfort zone, worldview and old stories about yourself are released and slowly drift to a decreased level of importance.

Then when you are brushing your teeth and you look in the mirror, what you see is not your personality character any more. What you see is your Bright Principles. For example, I don't see some guy named *Clinton*. I see Integrity, Clarity, Possibility, Love, Transformation, and High Level Fun. It is a completely different view of who I am. The same will occur for you when you walk down the street and catch a reflection of yourself in a storefront window or a mirror. It is not the old you anymore. It is something else, with a much greater potential for service.

CHOOSING YOUR DESTINY PRINCIPLES

Now that you know what your destiny Principles are and what will occur if you choose to be your Bright Principles, you can either choose your destiny or not.

Do you choose your destiny? Yes or no?

If yes, then write the words *I am* in front of your list of Bright Principles and memorize them. Make an appointment to stand before an assembly of respected individuals and say out loud to them, "I choose my Bright Principles. I am _____," filling in the blank with your distilled list of Bright Principles. The Principles should be spoken in such a way that they land firmly in the space, in the entire universe, not with a rising voice as in a question, but each one announced individually with a falling voice as in a statement. This is a declaration. You declare yourself to be your Principles. If your Principles have been well spoken, your witnesses will tend to automatically respond by saying, "Thank you."

Your Bright Principles need to stay forever on the tip of your tongue. Whenever someone asks you, "Who are you?," you can instantly say, "I am _____," and announce your Bright Principles.

Again, the Principles that you have distilled are a working draft. They will most likely evolve and reorganize themselves during months and years of use. Two might meld into one, or together become a new Principle. One Principle might fall away. Then suddenly two more show up as long-lost friends.

After having distilled your Bright Principles and your Shadow Principles what you get is a choice in each moment as to which Principles you serve. This is a choice worth having.

PART 3: ADDING MASS TO YOUR DESTINY—YOUR PRACTICES

At first your destiny does not have many votes in your life, overshadowed as it has been by the busyness of daily life. Weighing your destiny Principles against your customary comforts and habit patterns, your destiny has relatively little mass. Twenty, thirty, forty or fifty years of avoidance habits usually outweigh the possibility of acting in this moment in accordance with your destiny.

Part 3 of the Distilling Destiny Process is about reorienting your daily life around practices that build mass for your destiny. To begin, take twenty minutes to write a list of twenty practices for yourself that add votes in favor of being your destiny in action. A true practice has qualities of being doable, measurable, clear, simple and distinct.

- For example, a practice for adding mass to the Bright Principle of Clarity would be: *Three times a day I will tell another person, "I feel (mad, sad, glad, or scared) because _____ and my need is _____."* This practice uses the intelligence and impulse of feelings to clearly communicate and ask for what you need.

- A practice for adding mass to Integrity would be: *By November 18 I will search through my house, attic and basement to dispose of memorabilia from previous relationships to make respectful space for my commitment to my present partner.* This brings Integrity to life in your relationship.

- A practice for adding mass to Self-Respect would be: *On July 13, from one o'clock until eight o'clock, I will have a Mother Graduation Party for me to recognize that I have completed my job as mother to my nineteen-year-old son. I am no longer known as Mom. I take back my womanly name of Virginia.*

Make a list of twenty practices for yourself. Ask two or three qualified friends for specific feedback and coaching about your list. Tell them what your intention is so they can add an additional five practices for further expanding your Box and building mass for your destiny. Be sure to have them check that you wrote down exactly what they said, not what you understood them to say. The Box is *so* clever at defending itself. Trust your coaches.

PART 4: IMPLEMENTING YOUR DESTINY—A PROJECT

Bringing integrity to your destiny automatically results in a project. Otherwise, the whole procedure for distilling your destiny has been imaginary. The project brings the fruits of your destiny to life. Being your Bright Principles will move you to accomplishing something on their behalf.

Your opinion about your project does not matter. Neither does anyone else's opinion matter. It is none of your business what your project is. The project is the business of your Bright Principles. You chose to be the space through which your Bright Principles serve the world. How they do that is none of your business.

Your project is at hand. It is not somewhere else, some when else, depending on someone else. Your project is immediately here.

Your destiny is about changing the world for the better. (Everybody's destiny is about changing the world for the better. You are no exception.) Changing the world for the better is done right here, with what you have right now. You already have everything that you need to implement your destiny right now, and right now . . .

Your project could be something that lasts for a few days or for a week. It could be something that you start now and that lasts far beyond your lifetime. Again, it is none of your business what your project is. It is your Principles' business. Just keep putting one foot in front of the other and do the work.

As soon as you have written down some impressions of what your project might be, no matter how immense or trivial it seems, arrange to have a meeting with a coach. This coach should have some expertise in the field of your project. They should already have some skill in what you are destined to accomplish. Do not ask your coach *if* this project can be done or not. *Of course it can be done.* The Principles are sourcing it. Instead, ask your coach to give you connections to resources for ways to make this happen.

As uncomfortable as this might at first seem, your destiny is a public conversation. Your destiny takes place in public, not in private. You are meant to live your project out loud, with all four feelings and in all four bodies.

If you create what you have always created, you will get what you have always gotten. Your project will tend to take you out of your old patterns. Your project is about evolution: yours and humanity's. Your project will expand your Box. Your continued transformation happens in relation to bringing your destiny project to life.

Here is a suggestion. Adjust the method of implementing your project to the result that you want to create. Do not do the opposite. Do not shrink your project goals to match the methods or resources you already know about.

You needlessly tolerate an immense amount of mediocrity in your life because you match what you want to do with what you already know how to do.

Instead, let yourself not know how and go ahead anyway.

Radically rely on your destiny Principles to arrange things in the world so that the project is successful. After all, *it is not your project!* It is the project of your Principles. Let the Principles handle the hard stuff. You may remember the old saying, *God works while man plays!* Your job is to play full out, to have High Level Fun!

That's not so bad, is it? It could be far worse! If you simply put one foot in front of the other and keep moving and don't look down, you will stay in motion. While you are in motion, the Principles can navigate your actions through precessional events and unpredictable coincidences. If you stop moving then it is far more difficult for the sideways forces of the Principles to cause nonlinear course corrections.

Keep moving. Don't stop simply because you cannot see the whole series of actions that will take you to your goal. Instead, take whatever actions you can see to do, and then, after the actions, reassess what you can see to do. The preceding section is pure gold. What if you read it again?

FURTHER DISTINCTIONS ABOUT IMPLEMENTING YOUR DESTINY

Whatever behaviors and excuses arise that prevent what matters to you from showing up first in your life are simply your Box defending its known position and territory. Your destiny will generally take you into the unknown. It can help immensely if you just change your mind about the looming fears and discomforts of consistently heading into the unknown. If you change your mind and decide it is not so bad, you can more easily get used to it.

It can also be quite useful to acknowledge and say exactly what you want independent of whether you think it is possible or not to get what you want. You are better off knowing what you want even if it is impossible to get it, since the alternative is lying to yourself about what you want.

Perhaps you have the habit of manipulating yourself into doing what you already want to do. Stop doing that. There are plenty of other people out there trying to manipulate you. You do not have to do it to yourself.

Getting specific is the one thing that the Box does not want you to do. The Box tries to avoid specifics because specifics imply commitment. Avoiding commitment is how the Box keeps a back door open, guards secret loopholes, stays in control and keeps everything the same way it has always been for you. Creating new results is done by focusing on specifics.

If you have followed the Distilling Destiny Process all the way through, by now you have distilled, chosen, amplified and implemented your Bright Principles. In doing that you have made yourself a source person for next culture.

9. NEXT CULTURE

CULTURAL RELATIVITY

Culture is the gameworld in which a group of people agree to live together. Historically, we established culture to function as a survival Box modeled after our personal Box, to give us group identity, group security, and so on. Cultures typically included the claim: *ours is the only true and right culture.* For example, in most aboriginal languages there is no difference between the word for "human being" and the word for "a member of our tribe"—meaning that unless you speak *our* language, wear *our* clothes, and subscribe to *our* worldview, customs and rituals, you are *not* a human being. Therefore, we are justified in having you for lunch—*as the main course . . .*

Gremlin easily morphs the credo: *ours is the only true and right culture,* into the belief: *our culture is better than your culture if we can kill you.*

This conviction fueled Alexander the Great's annihilation of Persia. It inspired the church-sponsored *conquistadores* as they wiped out millions of inhabitants in the Americas. It sanctioned Christian missionaries to utterly decimate South Pacific islanders. *Our culture is better than your culture if we can kill you . . .* it numbed the Australians, Japanese, and Americans while they slaughtered their original populations; and the Hindus and Muslims to ceaselessly murder each other for centuries. The insanity continues to this day, exemplified by America/Israel/England contaminating Iraq, Afghanistan, Kosovo, Bosnia, Lebanon and, most recently, Gaza with illegal radioactive Depleted Uranium genocide weapons.

A heavily subsidized brainwashing scandal asserts that Western-style globalization is the crown jewel of human development, relegating all other cultures to the category of wannabes (third worlders) or brutes (original wisdom cultures). America has by far the greatest military budget in the world; Gremlins with trillions, marching acrross the globe, thinking: *our culture is better than your culture if we can kill you.*

Untangling yourself from the debilitating arrogance woven into Westernized perception distortions can take decades—especially for the third worlders to regard themselves with self-esteem even if they don't have a sofa and a microwave. The fact that 20 percent of the world's population is sucking down 80 percent of Earth's natural resources should tell you something about the scam going on. There could soon be some surprises coming for the "elites." For one thing, the "uncivilized" 80 percent will still know how to live when the planet goes cold turkey on oil, while the 20 percent who are oil addicts will stare slack-jawed and wide-eyed into raw terror. Oops.

Despite all its deluded self-congratulations there *is* one thing truly commendable about modern civilization, and that is its tourism industry. Since World War II millions of people have been tantalized by brochures showing tropical palms swaying over white-sand beaches, cheap air flights, and shrewd travel guides like those from Lonely Planet <www.lonelyplanet.com>. (I was lucky enough to find one of Lonely Planet's first editions of *Southeast Asia on a Shoestring* in the early 1980s. Its wise travel hints to secret hideaways served me as a true treasure map during two and a half years of fabulous vagabonding.) Captured by the thought of romance and adventure, average Joe's were convinced to leave their hometowns and become travelers.

By "traveler" I do not mean the pink-skinned groups riding in air-conditioned buses staying in three-star rather than five-star hotels. Those would be *tourists.* I mean *travelers,* the ones who carry a small backpack, live in local accommodations, eat local food, wear local clothing, speak with people in local language phrases, and allow themselves to be deeply touched by the abundant and graceful expressions of the human spirit.

Because so many people in modern times acquired a joyful wanderlust the word "foreigner" lost its millennia-old connotation of *dangerous* or *threatening* and took on more of a sense of allure. For example, in Munich it used to be that you could only find restaurants that served meat, potatoes and beer. Now the international restaurant section fills nineteen pages in the Munich phone book!

The value of intercultural journeying is that the traveler cannot avoid culture shock, the mind-blowing realization that the society you were born and raised in provides merely one of an unlimited number of possible answers to the questions of how to live a dignified and satisfying life.

Kurt Vonnegut Jr stressed the importance of developing *cultural relativity*, the ability to be comfortable in the realization that, while your own culture may make sense in your own mind, it may appear quite ridiculous to someone else and vice versa, *and* that this is perfectly okay. You can even laugh about it together and then learn to explore and appreciate the differences. Keep in mind that the phrase *cultural relativity* was originated in 1948 in an article in *American Anthropologist* by Virginia Heyer, a student of the German American anthropologist Franz Boas. This is shockingly recent! The clarity that *all* cultures are arbitrary fiction is still not fully grasped by modern civilization. Human dignity is truly in its infancy.

Human potential is limitless. Think of how small a part of the range of possible human behavior is elaborated or emphasized in any one society. Why shackle yourself to this tiny window of opportunity?

By encouraging people to travel to foreign cultures for entertainment and education, modern civilization set the stage for a whole new class of cultures to emerge—cultures that are aware that their culture is a consciously fabricated gameworld rather than the absolute truth.

James P. Carse classifies gameworlds into finite and infinite games. (See his book *Finite and Infinite Games*). Finite games are played to win, and when someone wins, the game is over. Infinite games are played to continue playing the game. Modern culture is an *I win, you lose* finite game, rapidly approaching the condition of *game over*. Modern culture does not recognize itself as a fictional gameworld. Nor does it empower its players to change the game, quit the game, or go play a completely different game whenever they choose.

Next-culture gameworlds are consciously created infinite games in which participants are ongoingly empowered to serve Bright Principles without winners or losers.

If you assume that your game is the *only* game in town and your rules are the *only* true rules, you trap yourself in a rigidly defended culture Box, unable to adapt to changing conditions and terrified that someone might prove your game wrong. This explains why modern culture is so offensive and defensive and so unrelational. It has to protect its illusions.

Next cultures recognize themselves and each other as but one of an unlimited number of possible gameworlds, each with its own language, customs, music, foods, architecture, clothing, rituals, handicrafts, celebrations, thought patterns, religious ceremonies and indescribable feel. The domain of possibilities for life experience and relationship is wide open and multiplying. There is so much to be explored and appreciated.

Cultural relativity destroys your certainty of control while providing you with the stability of diversity. After awhile globilization and *monoculture* become the horror, and *cultural diversity* the delight. People who find comfort in seeing Wal-Bucks and McPizzaKings replicated in every town around the planet live a hair's breadth away from the stark raving madness of having their culture proved fictitious. But the truth is that *all* cultures are fictitious.

REACHING YOUR OWN PERSONAL CHOICE POINT

You could well be at your own personal choice point right now, standing on the fringe of modern culture and deciding whether to return to the cultural marshmallow zone and stay numb, or to leave the numbness behind and consciously feel the pain of what we humans have unconsciously collaborated to create. It is shocking and painful to find yourself standing on the fringe of something you were told has no fringe. You perceive two drastically different perspectives (see the Map of Having Two Views at the Fringe).

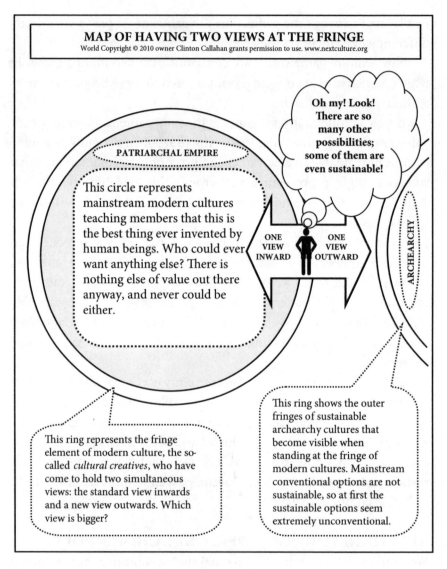

The two perspectives seem to exclude each other. Sometimes it may seem that you pop back and forth from seeing exclusively one perspective or the other. Sometimes you hold an overview and seem to hold both perspectives at the same time. It is not comfortable standing on the fringes.

There are two things to consider when making a decision as to whether or not to lower your numbness bar and feel more:

1. It does not matter what other people think, feel or do about your decision to feel or not to feel. The choice is yours alone—it is extremely personal.

2. The choice affects *every* aspect of your life—there will be enduring consequences to whatever you choose.

For me, personally, the consequences of choosing to feel are still unfolding. For example, even though the fatal trajectory of modern consumerism was already recognized, documented, and published in 1972 (read *Limits to Growth: The 30-Year Update*, by Donnella H. Meadows), I managed to stay completely ignorant of it all until December 2007 when I was fifty-five years old. Denial fogged my view for thirty-five years, then drifted silently away to reveal a staggering clarity. The catalyst was my decision to consciously feel. My deep and long-held delusions are still shattering in the aftershocks.

The chasm between what I thought was happening and what is actually happening spans wider than a heart can embrace. I considered the human race to be approaching a global celebration of modern civilization with its flashy entertainment and amazing technology. I thought we had a Star Trek future. What I find instead are fear-based, small-

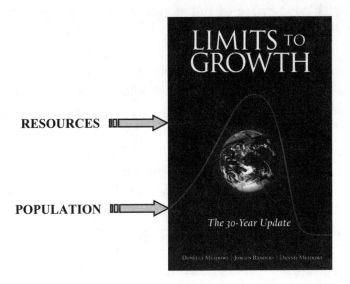

minded, greedy, corrupt political, religious and business leaders all around the world playing adolescent power games, forcing the extinction of a potentially intelligent species.

The outrage, grief and horror of simultaneously perceiving, like Janus, both the past and the (lack of a) future ignited enough emotive force to reflexively eject me from modern culture.

At first I thought that lowering my numbness bar was a grave mistake (read Appendix D: *Bambi vs the Collapse of Civilization*, by Tim Bennett). I felt completely alone, captive of a specter that hungrily devoured the happy world I had known my whole life. I was in the solitary confinement of recognizing that modern culture is a sham, a dream world, where up until that moment, I had been one of the willing dreamers. I was awake trying to get back into the dream and no one could help me. No one could disprove the stark evidence of the imminent collapse of civilization. No one could turn the alarm clock off.

NEW CIRCLE OF FRIENDS

After a few months the thought-shrapnel stopped flying with such deadly force in my mind. I found myself considering new questions. For example, if what I had been holding as reality is false, what then is actually possible? What is wanted and needed of me in these new circumstances? In what ways will serving my destiny principles unfold now?

As soon as I dared to ask these questions out loud I found people around me who understood—people who, in fact, had been asking such questions themselves for some time and who were already shifting to other contexts in which workable answers to these questions become obvious.

These people collaborate in meetings that tend to have a circular seating arrangement. They interact using new meeting softskill technologies such as Open Space, Possibility Team, Dialog, Forum, Phoenix Process, World Café, The Problem Is the Solution, Appreciative Inquiry, Swarmsource, and the U Process. They genuinely understood what I asked and freely shared what they had so far discovered or invented in the new contextual territories. They welcomed my participation. (They may also welcome yours!)

I was astonished about what I was learning. Half the books in my library were replaced. I wanted to talk with the authors, but how dare I? Hesitatingly at first, I called or emailed writers of the blogs, websites and books that most inspired me. More often than not these individuals were open to contact and enthusiastically encouraged me to keep going.

I was afraid to express my true thoughts and feelings, but since I had already rewired my mind so that *fear equals fear*, I could *write while feeling tremendously afraid*, and I produced a few articles conveying my strongest opinions. To my surprise, these articles were published on world-class alternative news websites such as www.truthout.org, www.democraticunderground.com, www.thepeoplesvoice.org, www.stwr. org, www.informationclearinghouse.info, www.climatetruth.org, www. mwcnews.net, www.worldproutassembly.org, www.novakeo.com, www. countercurrents.org, www.dissidentvoice.org, www.opednews.com, www. globalresearch.ca, www.commondreams.org and www.alternet.org.

A whole new breed of DVDs accumulated in a stack beside my desk—eco-docs, like *What a Way to Go: Life at the End of Empire*; *The Corporation* (YOU <u>HAVE</u> TO SEE *The Corporation!*); *An Inconvenient Truth*; and *The 11th Hour*. Most filmmakers turned out to be real people, and also contactable.

These preliminary trial-and-error experiments gave me the courage to phone, email or visit whomever I had the impulse to speak to anywhere in the world. As a result, my world expanded.

Suddenly I was accompanied. I found myself in astonishing new circles of friends, people I never knew existed before. These people meet, live or work together outside of modern culture in adventurous new social forms—gameworlds that recognize themselves as gameworlds. There are ecovillages, nongovernmental organizations, conferences, festivals, cohousing neighborhoods, global campuses, virtual universities, trainings, demonstrations, multimedia projects, workshops, pilgrimages, camps, fairs, outdoor programs and informal private circles. The diversity of social forms reflects the richness of human culture that emerges when people relocalize their authority.

The first step in relocalizing your personal authority is stellating your feelings.

TENTH DISTINCTION: ARCHEARCHY IS SUSTAINABLE CULTURE

The tenth of the Ten Distinctions for Consciously Feeling says that stellating feelings turns on masculine and feminine archetypes in you that become the active elements in *archearchy*, a new and truly sustainable culture, oriented more toward *being present* and *being with*, and less toward consuming, owning, having, going and *doing*.

Previous to five thousand years ago human cultures functioned in various forms of matriarchy, where feminine forces shaped societies. Then patriarchy took over, with empire as its goal and competitive hierarchical structures as its means. In 1985 patriarchal empire exceeded planetary sustainability and thereby doomed itself to extinction. The future of humanity rests in archearchy, cultures that emerge from the harmonious and intelligent interplay of responsible adult feminine and masculine archetypes. Rather than the matriarch or the patriarch prevailing it is stellated archetypes that prevail. The way to participate in the feminine-masculine synergy of archearchy is to grow up.

This book is about how to grow up. The degree to which you engage your rite of passage into responsible adulthood is up to you. This book provides extraordinary clarity for applying the natural strength and intelligence of feelings to enhance your personal and professional life, yet a singular distinction stands in the foreground:

Understanding feelings is one thing.

Experiencing feelings is something else entirely.

What this means is, if you experientially apply the Ten Distinctions for Consciously Feeling during a few months of daily practice it tends to produce a momentous yet possibly unexpected result: your capabilities expand beyond what can be explained or contained by modern culture. In such a case it may behoove you to gain more insight about what sort of cultures evolve beyond the thought limits of modern culture.

Let us review.

You were culturally trained to be a single fighter in a capitalist patriarchal empire. The successful man is a strong, numb, cunning, powerful and rich lone wolf. The successful woman seduces that man and molds him to suit her own purposes (see the film *Charlie Wilson's War*), or else she learns to be a better man than the men and beats them at their own games (see the film *The Devil Wears Prada*). A few people appear to win in this fierce competition. The rest of us are supposed to watch TV.

You were told in a gazillion ways that having a "negative" feeling means something is wrong with you and that a mythical steady-state happiness can be achieved if only you would be a *good* citizen living a *good* consumer life, asking no questions except, "Do you take credit cards?"

The happiness myth flies in the face of intense burnout shouldered by many who follow modern society's program: go to school, get a job, work, work, work, retire, die. The great deception—that you can be a *happy consumer* or a *happy soldier*—remains hidden because cognitive dissonance beats personal experience every time. If not, you can easily obtain a prescription for brain drugs to fog over the gap, or you can simply commit suicide.

This book says that you have far more intelligence than modern society knows what to do with. It says that it is your birthright to use maximum awareness to perceive what is going on and maximum creativity to ongoingly invent diverse cultures that celebrate and continue unfolding your natural gifts and those of your family and friends. It says that you have an important and true destiny serving people through your personal set of Bright Principles even if your vocation can only be classified on the IRS tax forms under the category *other*.

Once you have stellated your feelings in Phase 1 of your rite of passage, Phase 2 builds solid ground for the responsible adult context during your daily life. Sooner or later that responsible adult context starts having majority vote. In those moments your actions originate a new culture. New culture is needed right now. The need correlates to a massive shift taking place in the human thought field.

EPOCHAL CULTURE SHIFT

Ready or not, twenty-first century humanity is in the middle of an epochal culture shift. It happened once before, more than five millennia ago, when goddess-worshipping child-responsibility matriarchal cultures were gradually replaced by warrior-clan adolescent-responsibility patriarchal cultures (see the Map of the Present Epochal Culture Shift).

This ivory figurine (right) was carved 25,000 years ago and found near Brassempouy, France in 1892. The transformance art (left) is by Libor Balák, Antropark, Copyright 2007 <www.loborbalak.wz.cz>. Human hardware has remained essentially unchanged for at least the past 100,000 years. It is human thoughtware that evolves to make human cultures what they are.

The goddess of Laussel, Dordogne, France, was carved some 27,000 years ago during the age of original wisdom cultures. She was found in 1911 still covered in ochre. Photo courtesy of *The Cambridge Illustrated History of Prehistoric Art by Paul G. Bahn,* © Copyright 1998.

MAP OF THE PRESENT EPOCHAL CULTURE SHIFT

Cultures naturally tend to evolve, but during a rare *epochal culture shift* the entire paradigm of a culture changes context. Just as children are capable of maturing into adolescence and then into adulthood, modern adolescent civilization is now faced with changing mode into a responsible adult context. Self-induced climate change forces humanity to instantly grow up or risk a return to animalism. The paradox is that *"we"* cannot make this shift because *there is no "we" when it comes to taking responsibility.* Only *"I"* can take responsibility. **Each personal shift makes a difference**. As you build your capacity to enter responsible adulthood, *the portion of culture that you source shifts with you!* There is almost no time left to go through this rite of passage. Your continued development depends on you using your personal knacks to facilitate the growth of others during their transition into archearchy. It can help to know that your natural knacks are probably beyond the understanding of modern culture.

<u>BABY CULTURES</u>   <u>CHILD / ADOLESCENT</u>   <u>ADULT CULTURES</u>

hunter gatherers   agriculture technology corporocracy   kindness generosity relationship

10,000   5000 years ago   Present   Future

MATRIARCHY	PATRIARCHY	ARCHEARCHY
TRIBE	CIVILIZATION	COMMUNITY
INDIGENOUS	GLOBALIZATION	LOCAL & DIVERSE
ORIGINAL WISDOM	HOMOCENTRIC	TERRACENTRIC
"MAN IS THE EARTH"	"MAN OWNS THE EARTH"	"EARTH OWNS MANKIND"
NATURALISM	IMPERIALISM	COLLABORISM
SURVIVAL	CONTROL	TRULY LIVING

PEAK OIL
2008

Graph of Oil Use vs Time   ..and then it's gone forever.

<u>CHILD MODE</u>	<u>ADOLESCENT MODE</u>	<u>ADULT MODE</u>
Cared for by Mother Nature.	"Cared for" by patriarchal mega-authorities.	Cared for by radically responsible self.
Organic design.	Technical design.	Conscious design.
Essence.	Personality.	Holistic being.
Naiveté and belief.	Control and security.	Personal development.
Innocence.	Cynicism.	Love.
Survival, being.	Consume, possess, do.	Relationship community.
Economy of subsistence.	Economy of power.	Economy of presence.
Natural pop. control.	Unlimited pop. growth.	Conscious population.
Unconsciously sustainable.	*Not sustainable*.	Conscious sustainability.

Some researchers suggest that climate changes six thousand years ago caused general crop failure and out of the ensuing chaos warrior cultures emerged, thriving by capturing and consuming ever more resources and the slave labor of those who could not defend themselves against the improved *guns, germs and steel* (see Jared Diamond's book of the same name). Although recently the slave labor has been augmented by oil-powered machinery, laborers must work in town, and their villages are being paved over by megacities at an outrageous pace. The five thousand–year strategy of empire building continues today.

Now modern culture has exceeded planetary parameters. The culture shift to post-civilization will occur far more suddenly than the thousands of years it took to change from nomadic tribes to nation states. This is because modern civilization has so precariously extended its reliance on fossil fuels. After oil peaks, the fall may come swiftly, but the outcome is not entirely bleak. For the first time since the ascendan-

Millions of people have been displaced during Shanghai's fifteen years of mega-expansion. Photo courtesy of Shoestring.

Courageous geniuses invent next culture in sustainable culture ecovillages. Photo courtesy of Tamera Archive <www.tamera.org>

cy of the patriarchal paradigm some five thousand years ago, human beings have a chance to try again. What could that look like? Who is leading us there?

LEADERSHIP BEYOND THE STATUS QUO

Decades ago scientists well understood that humanity would overshoot Earth's sustainable limits. However, avoiding that calamity would involve changing modern culture's status quo. One of the toughest things in the universe to change is a society's status quo. Even though the science-backed forecasts were far worse than horrific, they made no difference. (Pragmatic scientists might do well to also study Box Technology, the science of changing the status quo.)

Forty years later, now that 100,000-year-old glaciers are melting even faster than the scientists predicted, now that the ocean is measurably rising and storms are flooding low-lying cities, now that methane chimneys are bubbling out of Siberian seas and lakes, now that the oil supply is peaking and the world economy is collapsing, there are large and irreparable cracks appearing in the status quo. Our Titanic civilization, long assumed to be unsinkable, has hit reality and is going down.

Shocking in their finality, these fissures also represent true opportunities for personal, institutional and societal change. Liberation from the status quo is a gift not to be taken lightly. A working strategy for social entrepreneurs is taking hold: in the same moment you detect a crack, move through it, even if what you move into is the unknown.

One part of your Box may be attracted to coinventing archearchy or you would not be reading this book. Another part may have your foot hard-pressed to the brakes. This part may be creating *really good* excuses to block Box expansion for fear of no longer fitting within mainstream society, reminding you that your neighbors might notice your strange new behavior and report you to the authorities. Considering Inquisitions and witch burnings, such fears are well founded.

And . . .

What I want you to know is that there are *already* whole societies of people living wonderful lives beyond the reach of modern culture, ready and waiting to welcome you if you should ever decide to visit. They have been waiting to welcome you for a long time (see the Further Unlearning section at the back of this book).

If you sense *external* forces of resistance that are trying to keep you from changing, you do not have to face those resistances head on. You do not personally have to convince all of modern society to change. This is important to remember. It's not your job.

If the forces of resistance approach you personally, you can *spin*. To "spin" means to keep your center and, at the same time, to energetically *whirl* yourself—to hold no positions, rebuff no attacks, be a *yes*, agree with the forces of resistance, and yet keep moving in the direction you need to go. When you spin, external resistances have nothing to grab onto. When they can't see you anymore they will forget you were ever there.

If you sense *internal* forces of resistance trying to keep you from changing it could simply be your residual hesitation to experience feelings. It can help to recognize that feelings are integral to every process of change; for example:

- Sadness about letting go of the familiar, knowing its time has passed.

- Anger that change is so difficult.

- Fear that whatever you try, the change may be too little too late.

- Joy that you now have a real chance to live out your destiny.

Let yourself deeply and thoroughly feel these feelings. Communicate them to others in many different forms: singing, art, theater, sculpture, music, dance, poetry, public talks, meetings, workshops, essays, blogs, and transformational acts of kindness, generosity and compassion. Use the vigor and diverse intelligences of your feelings to establish entirely new forms of personal behavior, organizational design, project goals, and societal context. This is what you and your feelings were born for!

Practicing the suggestions in this book strengthens your leadership. A leader is simply the one who goes first. Even though parallel cultures with higher than mainstream levels of responsibility have been operational since the 1960s and before, almost none of them implement the clarity of thoughtmaps and processes provided in this book. Those cultures hunger for these ideas and could well be waiting for *you* to trust your own leadership and bring these ideas to them. Didn't you ever, just once, want to be *the chosen one*? Well, here is your chance!

There is no hurry for you to go there, of course. At the same time, why would you want to wait? If a part of you comes to life while I am speaking like this why not let your heart and soul move you to take actions in these directions? You don't even need a reason.

IS HAVING FEELINGS STRANGE? OR NORMAL?

It can be both disturbing and astonishing to experience conscious feelings. You will either make it through the shock and adjust to your new experiences, or you will rebound back into mainstream.

If your personal experience does not fit within modern society, what are you supposed to do? Your first impulse after consciously feeling may be to try to get yourself back together the old way, put the happy face back on, and reanimate your familiar act. At least your old behavior seemed acceptable to your friends and relatives even if it was not so entirely acceptable to you.

Experiencing the undeniable reality of authentic feelings confronts you with an option you did not have before. Modern culture rejects feelings. Other cultures thrive on feelings. *Who chooses in which culture you live?*

What if, regardless of circumstances and evidence, you continuously choose next culture?

WHAT IS NEXT CULTURE LIKE?

Next culture already exists; yet, in contrast to modern culture, next culture is relatively invisible. Learning to perceive next culture begins with recognizing what next culture is not. Next culture is not marketed in three-second sound bites. It does not seek to sway your political opinion and get your vote. It does not explode in blood and suicide bombers across the headlines of CNN. It does not announce itself like drunken World Cup champions. Next culture is a finer signal easily overlooked amid all the modern noise and hubbub. The following Map of Comparing Cultural Attributes can offer some clues.

THE GNAWING QUESTION

How has humanity so seriously messed up its future? How have we come to the edge of ruining the only life-supporting planet in this neck of the universe?

The short answer is that our cleverness exceeds our intelligence; we did not grow up before we got smart. Global leaders are stuck at the childish *Me! Me! Me!* level, and the rest of us have not matured beyond sheep. We have not taken responsibility for our individual authority.

The long answer is that as soon as the human nervous system evolved to the degree of sophistication that it held enough consciousness to become self-aware, that consciousness sought clarification about its most urgent question: *Who am I?*

There are two obvious answers.

The first answer we find when we are babies: *I am my body*, because we feel sensations. We identify ourselves as our body, and our body

MAP OF COMPARING CULTURAL ATTRIBUTES

You are under a spell if you think modern culture is *present culture*. There is no *present culture*. Humans are a biology experiment of planet Earth, living in hundreds of thousands of cultures around the globe. One particular culture has turned cancerous and is devouring the ethnosphere, teaching its victims to think that it alone is *present culture*. Can you free yourself of this memetic virus? We moderns are a minority of arrogant fools consuming 80 percent of Earth's resources and hiding our greed by marketing the story that *everyone can consume like us forever if they adopt modern culture*. Are you under this spell? Can you break out of it? The term *cultural relativity* was not known until 1948. Human cultures are *so* immature. Can you grow up?

MODERN CULTURE:

PATRIARCHY: That was the old days. We are modern! There are women presidents!

MONEY: Everybody needs money! How can you live without money?

GOVERNMENT: There are 192 members of the United Nations. Whoever has the most guns tells the UN what to do.

OWNING LAND AND BUILDINGS: Everyone and everything has a price. If you can afford to buy it, then you can own it.

OWNING RESOURCES: God gave man dominion over all things.

TV: But it has important news and educational documentaries. I don't watch the commercials anyway.

CARS: How could we live without cars? Are you nuts?

SUPPLY CHAINS: A 3000-mile Caesar salad? What's that?

PROFIT: Free market competition is good. The WTO and World Bank help the poor countries.

SCHOOL: What would kids do if they were not in school? School teaches the three Rs and prepares us to get a good job.

RITE OF PASSAGE: When kids can drive, vote, drink and smoke, they are adults.

GMO: You can't stop progress.

OVERPOPULATION: It's all those Africans, Indians and Chinese. They should do something about their overpopulation, but it does not affect me.

PEAK OIL: It's just oil companies trying to make more profit. We can replace oil with solar, wind, waves and free energy.

GLOBAL WARMING: It's probably caused by solar variations, but no one really knows.

METHANE CLATHRATES: What's that?

NUCLEAR POWER: Cleaner than coal.

NEXT CULTURE:

PATRIARCHY: Is thinking that our culture is better than your culture if we can kill you. Next culture is not matriarchy; it is *archearchy*: the collaboration of masculine and feminine archetypes. Any culture that respects human dignity and sustains the diversity of life is of equal value.

MONEY: Next culture supports each person to develop and give fully of their special talents for the benefit of all. When people give their talents they are ecstatic and there is abundance. The abundance is a magnet that attracts whatever is needed by the village. Who would work for anything but love of the work?

GOVERNMENT: How can anyone else authentically represent me? Only I can speak my own voice. Responsibility is localized.

OWNING LAND, BUILDINGS, RESOURCES: Human beings are owned by the Earth. Resources are borrowed from the future.

TV: Looking outside of ourselves for our center comes from the false assumption that we are not already that which we seek.

CARS: Moving faster than the speed of love leaves love behind. Ego is as intelligent as bacteria.

SUPPLY CHAINS FOR PROFIT: Profit is a false paradigm. In a closed system, *externalizing costs* is suicidal. Irresponsibility is an illusion.

SCHOOL: Creative, loving intelligence does not grow in a production line. Each person is unique.

RITE OF PASSAGE: People remain children unless they have a formidable rite of passage to adulthood. Putting children in leadership positions?

GMO: Diversity leads to stability. GMO is suicide.

OVERPOPULATION: Humanity now consumes 2.5 planets of resources. Overpopulation affects everybody.

PEAK OIL: Has arrived but not soon enough to avoid GLOBAL WARMING that releases the planet-killer time bomb METHANE CLATHRATES.

NUCLEAR POWER: Produces uncontainable toxic wastes in the interconnected planetary ecosystem. It's more stupid than poisoning your own drinking water.

requires instant gratification, unable to care about others, the future, or the big picture.

The second answer we find when we are children: *I am my Box*, because we have thoughts and feelings. We identify ourselves as our ego (the Box), and ego is an unconscious mechanical survival strategy with no more intelligence than bacteria.

Nothing dissuades us from the certainty of our answers because they both seem indisputable. Nevertheless, both of these indisputable answers are wrong. The wrongness does not reveal itself except through an authentic rite of passage into adulthood.

Disidentification from our body and disidentification from our Box are two key elements of an authentic rite of passage into adulthood. Very few of us gain freedom from being identified with body or Box because very few of us go through a true rite of passage to adulthood. We remain lifelong adolescents.

Philip K. Dick, the science fiction author, framed his longing to grow up thusly: *I wish to encounter a disinhibiting factor that will trigger my anamnesis.* He wished to find a way to remember who he truly was. Most of us have such longings, but we allow society to discourage us from truly committing to them.

Having no rite of passage equates to having no entrance to the path of self-discovery where you would learn to elegantly and effectively function as what you actually are: nothingness, a space of possibility through which the Bright Principles that you serve can creatively benefit humanity.

Instead you consign yourself to reacting to circumstances as a psychoemotional ego-mind trapped in an individual body, competing against other adolescents stuck in the illusion of separation, all struggling for survival in a capitalist patriarchal empire. The boring details predictably play themselves out until we arrive at today's news headlines. Authentic rite of passage to adulthood would eradicate modern civilization and replace it with something better.

The gnawing question comes down to this: Will humanity implement the shift to sustainable cultures in time to save ourselves from the consequences of our immaturity? Or not?

The race is on. Which will win?

- The tipping point for climate change, peak oil and the collapse of civilization?

or

- The tipping point for a paradigm shift from patriarchal empire to radically responsible archearchy?

Talk is cheap and the frightening deadline for action is quickly approaching. What are our chances?

CULTURAL CREATIVES EXIST

People thinking outside of mainstream culture and applying their discoveries for the benefit of humanity are called *cultural creatives* (from Paul Ray and Sherry Anderson's book of the same name). This wildly diverse nongroup of social entrepreneurs has become what Paul Hawken, in his book *Blessed Unrest*, calls "the largest social movement in history."

Cultural creatives are paradigm shift in action.

How many cultural creatives are there? Such individuals frequently organize their projects into nongovernmental organizations (NGOs). Wikipedia reports the present number of international NGOs at more than forty thousand, each with its own support staff, field agents, network of volunteers and clients. The number of national NGOs is far higher. For example, Russia has 277,000 national NGOs. India has somewhere between one million and two million! Ray and Anderson estimate the present number of cultural creatives at fifty million and climbing. Clearly, fifty million cultural creatives working hard to reinvent social reality is a formidable change force.

But is it formidable enough?

Comparing these fifty million cultural creatives to a world population pushing seven billion reveals that only 0.7 percent of the world's people are working toward next culture. 99.3 percent work to sustain the mainstream, or are Gremlins doing whatever they can to survive.

What is the critical mass number of people needed to reach a tipping point for a paradigm shift to radically responsible archearchy?

If we use the seesaw model of a simple scale, at least 51 percent of the world's population needs to be thinking, perceiving and acting with greater responsibility than their leaders before next culture gains majority vote. Building from fifty million to three and a half billion (a factor of seventy times more) will probably take more time than the few years we have before the demon of peak oil calls down the Four Horsemen.

People are stubborn and serve agendas and purposes that are often hidden even from themselves. Consciousness expansion seems to have a speed limit. On the surface, our present ideas appear to have worked well enough so far. If it works, why bother to fix it? Exchanging current ideas for new ideas is neither comfortable nor easy. Embodying new culture would change everything: agriculture, city planning, schools . . .

Think about it. How long would it take for teachers to change their classrooms into safe havens for learning how to love, how to communicate authentically with feelings, how to create high drama in service of each individual's Bright Principles? The truth is that it could happen in one day.

The nation of Estonia proved this.

On one day, May 3, 2008, more than fifty thousand people (4 percent of the Estonian population) suddenly changed their behavior and removed *ten thousand tons* of garbage that for decades they themselves had scattered throughout their forest lands. True, operation *Let's Do It!* required intelligent fore planning, but it also awakened teams to their ability to self-organize—and it worked! It was the most ambitious volunteer action in modern times. *The entire territory of Estonia was cleaned up in five hours.* In the same way, teachers across the land could self-organize a new curriculum in one day and transform the relevancy of school.

CRITICAL MASS VS CRITICAL CONNECTIONS

It makes total sense to think that a paradigm shifts only when a critical mass of individuals begins using new thinking. When the tipping point is reached the new paradigm takes over. Even though this critical mass model seems so logical it turns out not to be the only source of sudden change.

Since 1973, Margaret Wheatley has been exploring how living systems organize and reorganize themselves <www.margaretwheatley. com>. In the article she wrote with Deborah Frieze *Using Emergence to Take Social Innovations to Scale*, she explains: "In spite of current ads and slogans, the world doesn't change one person at a time. It changes as networks of relationships form among people who discover they share a common cause and vision of what's possible. This is good news for those of us intent on changing the world and creating a positive future. Rather than worry about critical mass, our work is to foster critical connections. We don't need to convince large numbers of people to change; instead, we need to connect with kindred spirits. Through these relationships, we will develop the new knowledge, practices, courage, and commitment that lead to broad-based change.

"But networks aren't the whole story. As networks grow and transform into active, working communities of practice, we discover how Life truly changes, which is through *emergence*. When separate, local efforts connect with each other as networks, then strengthen as *communities of practice*, suddenly and surprisingly a new system emerges at a greater level of scale. *This system of influence* possesses qualities and capacities that were unknown in the individuals. It isn't that they were hidden; they simply don't exist until the system emerges. They are properties of the system, not the individual, but once there, individuals possess them. And the system that emerges always possesses greater power and influence than is possible through planned, incremental change. Emergence is how Life creates radical change and takes things to scale."

Emergence has a life-cycle. It begins when individuals form a network to share information. When these individuals desire something more substantial than a mere network they commit to support each other as practitioners in their lineage. When this community of practice makes critical connections with related communities of practice they weave a powerful system of influence that facilitates the emergence of global scale change.

During a private conversation with Meg Wheatley at the 2010 Authentic Leadership In Action conference in the Netherlands

<www.aliainstitute.org>, Meg provided practical advice in response to my question about how to best make critical connections. She said, "Stop looking to the elders or founders of a community of practice. Stop trying to connect at the top. These people are often too busy, too tired, and too crystallized in their ways. Instead connect further down in the organization with the people who are actually implementing the ideas. Rather than trying to get something from them, focus your intention on providing them with practical support from your resource base. In the moment they accept what you are offering, the critical connection is made."

The classic example of emergence causing a large scale system to reorder is the Berlin Wall suddenly vanishing on November 9, 1989. The thing to recognize is that the Wall did not suddenly vanish. Many interrelated communities of practice worked for years in parallel to reweave local conditions so the old systems that built and maintained the Wall were no longer relevant.

This is happening again, only on a much grander scale. After five thousand years, the entire system of civilization has proven itself to be a fatally flawed paradigm. The parasitic system of multinational corporations and national megagovernments has become irrelevant. Next culture *is* emerging. And you have a part to play.

YOU ARE A CULTURAL CREATIVE

Your Phase 1 and Phase 2 feelings work makes a far bigger difference than you may have suspected. Your feelings work is cultural transformation happening personally and promptly, even by reading this book. If you simply read this book all the way through it builds a landing strip in you for new understanding to arrive for the rest of your life.

If while reading this book you do 25 percent of the recommended experiments, your attitudes and daily life behaviors could possibly begin to change.

If while reading this book you do 50 percent of the experiments, some of your friends and acquaintances may not be able to resist behaving differently in response to your new invitations to relationship.

If while reading this book you do 75 percent of the experiments, you will naturally emit memetic waves that modify the morphogenetic field of what is possible for humans. You will embody a new common understanding. You will hold space for a new cultural context. Your experiential clarity reshapes how the world looks to you, and this impacts all that you do, even washing the dishes.

In addition to your feelings, you have imagination, premonition, inspiration, intuition, nonlinearity, direct experience of your experience, and clarity about your Bright Principles. Your awareness manifests itself through your actions. You were born in these times with a real purpose. Consciously using the intelligence and impulse of your feelings enlivens that purpose. You are implementing you. In doing so, you serve as an agent of change, a cultural creative.

This book does not tell you what you should or should not do. If you apply the clarity and drive of your feelings, your actions take your relationships, family and work into a higher complexity of order. By reclaiming your center and avoiding being hooked into emotional reaction patterns, you will find yourself with an abundance of energy resources that were previously consumed by low drama. This energy is now available to use for serving a purpose greater than mere survival. As your Gremlin learns to trust that you will conscientiously feed it, he remains alert and dedicated to accomplishing the interesting jobs you provide.

With your extra attention and energy you can expand your immediate circle of friends by connecting heart and soul with other agents of change. There are fifty million cultural creatives out there in the world, working independently at the fringes of modern culture. When you connect with them by phone, email, and in-person conversations, you weave strands in a system of influence for the emergence of *next culture* on planet Earth.

The emergence of next culture is self-organizing—*as long as you do the jobs that the universe drops onto your bench.* The universe does not waste resources. If the universe puts a job on your bench to do, even if you have never done it before, the universe already knows that you can do it. In my experience, you can trust that. In my experience you can trust the universe about this more than you can trust your Box's screaming reaction attacks.

FACILITATING THE SHIFT TO NEXT CULTURE

If you have read this far then one of the jobs on your bench is helping the people around you during their shift into next culture. You are ahead of them. You have been going first. You have begun feeling your feelings about the disintegration of the known. Somebody has to feel because most people won't. When circumstances collapse and denial can no longer numb their senses the shock will hit them and they will not be prepared. It is then that they will need your help.

MAP OF FIVE PHASES OF EMBRACING CHANGE
World Copyright © 2010 owner Clinton Callahan grants permission to use. www.nextculture.org

It is shocking to adjust to change. Whether you must deal with the restaurant being out *of clam chowder or the planet being out of oil*, you will go through these five phases of embracing change. These five phases do not necessarily occur in a linear order, nor are they necessarily completed the first time through. You may randomly slip from one phase to another during your journey toward acceptance. There is no right way to do this. Depending on the significance of the change, a healthy acceptance process may take anywhere from two minutes (e.g., the store is closed) to two or more years (e.g., death of a loved one, divorce, culture change). It helps to trust the process and to share what you are feeling with others who listen well.

1. DENIAL – Fear. Shock. Avoidance. Paralysis. Trying to ignore the change: *This is not happening to me! Something is wrong. It's not true.*

2. OUTRAGE – Anger. Threatening. Demanding: *How dare you! This is not okay with me! Stop it, now! It must stay how it was before!*

3. BARGAINING – Mixed feelings. Using the mind. Trying to be clever. Maneuvering: *There must be a way out. Let's make a deal. Undo this.*

4. DESPAIR – Sadness. Giving up hope of making any difference. Depression: *Oh no! Oh God! This is too much for me.*

5. ACCEPTANCE – Being where you are. Choosing what is. This is the first moment of regaining your power to take responsible actions. There is joy.

Which stage are you in now? And now?

This thoughtmap was originated by Elisabeth Kübler-Ross in her book *On Death and Dying*, first published in 1969. She named it The Five Stages of Grief or The Grief Cycle, and applied it to thanatology. It turns out that her clarity about humans adjusting to change applies to all transitions. <www.ekrfoundation.org>

If you arrange to meet with people in an ongoing group you can use this book as a guideline for learning to consciously feel. While going through the changes it will help to have one more thoughtmap, the Map of Five Phases of Embracing Change, originally developed by Elisabeth Kübler-Ross.

IT DOES NOT HAVE TO BE PERFECT

If you do 100 percent of the experiments in this book . . . *Hey, buddy!* Don't *kid* yourself! *Nobody* does 100 percent of the experiments in this book. Not even me. Perfection is not necessary in order to do the jobs that the universe places on your bench.

You are not perfect. The material world is not perfect. If you wanted to you could decide right now to stop using the fear that you might not do it perfectly as an excuse to avoid doing the jobs on your bench.

Face it. No matter how expertly you declare and hold space for your Bright Principles to do their work in the middleworld the spaces will *never* be perfect. The floor of your meeting room might not be vacuumed. There might be rambunctious kids around. You might not be as eloquent as you think someone else could be. You might get hooked by an inferred insult. So what? This is the middleworld. It can't be perfect.

It is admirable to strive for impeccability, to start on time, to identify potential low dramas and slide past them, to be kind, to avoid Gremlin feeding during meetings, to energetically clean a space with a Black Hole after you end a meeting, and so on. These practices will develop over time as you become more and more sensitive to the consequences of *not* doing them.

It helps tremendously to know that since your work spaces *cannot* be perfect, they also do not *have* to be perfect.

If you declare your work space to exist for the purpose of serving your Bright Principles then the work that you do in that space, even though it is not perfect, will be *as good as it gets*.

It turns out that *as good as it gets* is good enough. As Lee Lozowick says, "Good enough is good enough!"

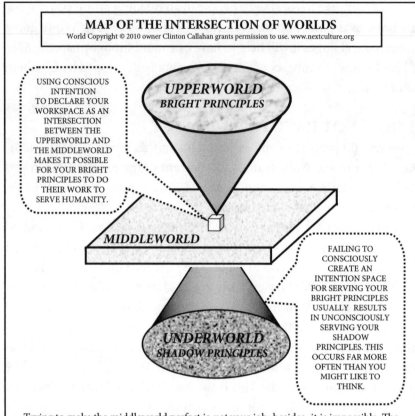

MAP OF THE INTERSECTION OF WORLDS

World Copyright © 2010 owner Clinton Callahan grants permission to use. www.nextculture.org

USING CONSCIOUS INTENTION TO DECLARE YOUR WORKSPACE AS AN INTERSECTION BETWEEN THE UPPERWORLD AND THE MIDDLEWORLD MAKES IT POSSIBLE FOR YOUR BRIGHT PRINCIPLES TO DO THEIR WORK TO SERVE HUMANITY.

UPPERWORLD
BRIGHT PRINCIPLES

MIDDLEWORLD

FAILING TO CONSCIOUSLY CREATE AN INTENTION SPACE FOR SERVING YOUR BRIGHT PRINCIPLES USUALLY RESULTS IN UNCONSCIOUSLY SERVING YOUR SHADOW PRINCIPLES. THIS OCCURS FAR MORE OFTEN THAN YOU MIGHT LIKE TO THINK.

UNDERWORLD
SHADOW PRINCIPLES

Trying to make the middleworld perfect is *not* your job; besides, it is impossible. The middleworld is inherently *imperfect*. Your job is to call Bright Principles into your work space. Your work then manifests as an intersection of worlds. You become the space through which the Principles that you serve can do their work in the middleworld. What happens in this space will never be perfect. But it will be as good as it gets. And it is good enough.

WHAT TO DO

There is a next culture. When you discover it yourself, your first urge may be to try to tell others about it. But the others won't be able to hear you, just as you could not hear the ones who tried to tell you before now. People can only shift to next culture when their matrix is ready to hold the new distinctions.

Your next urge might be to try to transform modern culture into next culture.

It can save you a big headache to realize that paradigms are unique species. One paradigm cannot be transformed into another paradigm, because *a paradigm is what it is*. Paradigms cannot shift, but you can. Consciously feeling your feelings changes you. It builds energetic matrix in you personally that permits you to suddenly function in a different paradigm. No one can do this for you, and you can't do it for anyone else.

Awareness expands from feeling more and more deeply the pain of consequences. What can you do to facilitate the shift to next culture? Feel the pain of consequences.

For example, if a businessman feels the outrage, anxiety and sadness he causes in local citizens when he gets control of public water rights and raises domestic prices to make a profit, he could not proceed. By feeling the pain of consequences the businessman would no longer be in the same paradigm where quarterly stock reports make sense. He would be in a new paradigm.

If a sales rep or manufacturer of plastic disposables feels the grief and shame of selling the plastic bottles and grocery bags that contribute to the Texas-sized dead zone of partially decomposed plastic choking life out of the albatross chicks on Midway Atoll in the North Pacific (see <www.midwayjourney.com>), she could not go to work in the morning. She would find another profession.

If a hamburger flipper at a McFastfood chain store feels the maniacal greed behind clearing tropical rainforests one acre per second, exterminating species faster than the dinosaurs died out sixty-five million years ago, merely to plant more soy beans to feed more beef cattle for the hamburgers he is serving, he could neither work there nor eat the fast food himself.

If a miner, manufacturer, transporter, or user of uranium weaponry felt the relentless agony of parents who gave birth to a baby with deformities because they were exposed to DU (as a soldier *or* civilian—on "our" side *or* "their" side . . . radiation poisoning has no political or religious preferences) or of parents who got cancer themselves and would leave their children without parents, the worker would quit his job immediately and do everything he could to stop the government-ordained

---

MAP OF CULTURAL RESPONSIBILITY
World Copyright © 2010 owner Clinton Callahan grants permission to use. www.nextculture.org

Where are you on this scale of taking responsibility for the culture you live in?

EVOLVE TOWARD HIGHER LEVELS OF RESPONSIBILITY

7. I invent new culture. I design and implement social pilot models in the world. I link up with other social pilot models and weave the system of influence for the emergence of next culture, archearchy.

6. I join an alternative social system with a culture having a different context (a different set of distinctions) than the context of mainstream culture. I can now shift from context to context, yet I prefer to live in my new culture.

5. What? There is something beyond the system?! It is possible to go beyond the system and still survive? There are others already out there?! My fears have become the gateway to adventure. I can explore and discover.

4. I have been fighting the system but I cannot beat the system. I can change myself but the system does not change. Like they say, "If you can't beat 'em, join 'em." Or?

3. Oh, my God! There is a system! Not only are there wolves (politicians), there are also pigs (businessmen)! They are collaborating to shear us sheeple. It is a conspiracy! I must fight the system!

2. Something is not fine here. I feel angry, scared, and sad – I feel betrayed, confused, distrustful. I want to create, but hey! There are wolves around! I must hide out and learn how to survive.

1. Everything is fine. I stand numbly in line with the rest of the sleeping sheeple. I give my responsibility away. I give my center away. I give my authority away. I am good at keeping myself in denial. After all, it could be worse ...

START AT LOWER LEVELS OF RESPONSIBILITY

---

but illegal proliferation of these materials, and would force the cleanup of contaminated sites.

If a modern consumer felt the stunning nightmare of losing the once exquisitely beautiful tropical reefs due to ocean acidification produced by automobiles, ships, airplanes and coal-fired electric power plants, she would cease driving her car, buying imported foods and clothing, vacationing in faraway lands, and would never turn on an electric light that was not powered by solar or wind.

If an adult man or woman felt quaking fear about the thousand gigaton planet-killer methane time bomb about to explode out of the Siberian tundra and shallow continental shelves due to global warming, and if that man or woman recognized there was a chance to defuse that bomb by abandoning almost every aspect of modern culture, they would not hesitate one moment to *just stop*. They would leave modern culture behind without regard for the uncertain consequences of leaving modern culture behind, because those consequences, *whatever they might be*, pale in comparison to letting modern society devour the future of humanity into oblivion.

I AM A BRIDGE TO NEXT CULTURE

What if you decided to use your daily life as an experimental laboratory for implementing elements of next culture? What if you decided to connect with people who are offering to be a bridge for you to get over into next culture?

There are all kinds of bridges. There are people who know how to grow and preserve beans, how to make passive solar living environments out of old tires (see <www.earthship.net>), how to deliver authentic ritual for consecrating rite of passage to adulthood. These people are bridges. What if you decided to learn from them and take steps across those bridges?

What if after awhile you decided to help other people to next culture by being a bridge yourself?

This is a time when courageous experimenting is required for humanity to make it through to the next century. Even more, this is a time for courageous experimenters to come together in community. For if the universe is holographic—as so many researchers confirm—then single individuals do not contain precise enough intelligence to create new opportunities out of today's complex circumstances. When people come together in bonded community, however, their intelligence can synergize. What if you started bringing pieces of the hologram together in a weekly meeting of next-culture experimenters?

The purpose for coming together in the radically responsible self-governing context of next culture is far from the familiar purposes of profit, competition, Gremlin-feeding power struggles, or mere distraction. The ship of civilization may be going down, but in your weekly meeting you are gathered together building bridges to next culture. Your purpose is to cointention a bright future through unfolding the full potential of every human being, to change the morphogenetic field of the human race. The meeting itself is a bridge. Each time you come together people take steps together and move further beyond modern culture's horizon.

Humanity has already crossed into uncharted territory. The future is unknown. Do not be too concerned about "the powers that be" getting upset about your experimenting. There are already too many heretics to keep track of. Your experiments actually serve modern culture by providing revolutionary spirits with something peaceful and productive to do: design and build bridges to sustainability.

Supporting a healthy and diverse ecology of sustainable microcultures could be the smartest insurance that any predominant culture could carry. As the ship of state goes down, the once proud protagonists may eventually come knocking at your door. When they come, you can smile kindly and say, "Hello. Welcome to the bridge. What are you feeling?"

Bridge builders who bring people together in autonomous next-culture enterprises, resilient organizations, and self-governing ecovillages are no different from yourself—spirited yet humble, courageous yet pragmatic, visionary yet relational. Finding your way to next culture is a natural consequence of liberating and applying the strength and intelligence of your conscious feelings . . . being no longer numb.

Welcome to the bridge. What are you feeling?

Feelings
are for
healing things
or for
handling things.

APPENDIX A:

LIST OF THOUGHTMAPS

APPENDIX B:

MAP OF TEN DISTINCTIONS FOR CONSCIOUSLY FEELING

What would happen to your belief system, your self-experience, your defensive strategies, your abilities to communicate and relate, if you consciously applied these ten adult, responsible distinctions to feelings?

TEN DISTINCTIONS FOR CONSCIOUSLY FEELING

1. There are only four feelings: anger, sadness, fear and joy. All feelings fit into one of these four categories, or are mixtures of these four.

2. There is a difference between thoughts and feelings. Thoughts come from your intellectual body's mind. Feelings come from your emotional body's heart.

3. There is a difference between feelings and emotions. Feelings come from yourself in the present moment. Emotions are incomplete feelings that come from the past, or inauthentic feelings that come from some other person or organization.

4. Feelings are absolutely neutral energy and information, neither good nor bad, neither positive nor negative. Feelings are feelings.

5. Feelings serve you powerfully in their pure form, not mixed with each other. Mixed feelings include depression, hysteria, jealousy, despair, melancholy, shame, guilt, schadenfreude, and so on. To shift out of these mixed feelings, simply un-mix them.

6. Feelings can be experienced from zero to one hundred percent intensity. In each moment you are feeling all four feelings, but one is always bigger. This is what you are feeling.

7. There are two *Phases* in *feelings work*. In *Phase 1* you learn to detect and avoid *low drama* through consciously feeling neutral, unmixed, one hundred percent intensity feelings. In *Phase 2* you learn to create *high drama* through consciously applying the vast information and energy resources of your feelings with adult responsibility.

8. As an adult you can consciously integrate feelings into responsible speaking and listening so that feelings serve you relationally and professionally.

9. *Feelings work* is part of a formal rite of passage that awakens (stellates) archetypal structures and talents that have been lying dormant within you, waiting to be turned on and used to fulfill your destiny.

10. Stellated masculine and feminine archetypes form the basis of a new and truly sustainable culture (archearchy), oriented more towards *being present* and *being with*, and less towards consuming, owning, having, going and *doing*.

APPENDIX C:

This is a map of what is possible right now.
What you are doing right now is creating conscious or unconscious stories about what is.
Without your storymaking, *what is* would have no meaning. This is not bad – it is how it is.
The world is rich in evidence, so you can make up any story about anything.
You do not make up stories for no reason. Every story has a purpose.
You are either aware of the purpose of your story or you are not.
If you are aware of the purpose of your story, then your actions serve conscious purposes.
If you are not aware of the purpose of your story, your actions serve unconscious purposes.
This map is not about good or bad. It is about conscious or unconscious creating.

CONSCIOUS PURPOSE

THE BRIGHT JEWEL OF RESPONSIBILITY
CREATES A RESPONSIBLE GAME :
"WINNING HAPPENING," "I WIN AS YOU WIN."
ABUNDANCE THROUGH TAKING RESPONS-
IBILITY FOR SOURCING THE RESOURCES.
SERVES YOUR TRUE PURPOSES (DESTINY).
YOUR BRIGHT PRINCIPLES.
USES THE ENERGY AND INFORMATION OF
FEELINGS TO CREATE HIGH DRAMA.

UNCONSCIOUS PURPOSE

THE SHADOW JEWEL OF IRRESPONSIBILITY
CREATES AN IRRESPONSIBLE GAME :
"I WIN, YOU LOSE," "HA - HA! I GOT YOU!"
SCARCITY THROUGH AVOIDING TAKING
RESPONSIBILITY FO R THE RESOURCES.
SERVES YOUR HIDDEN PURPOSES.
YOUR SHADOW PRINCIPLES.
USES THE ENERGY AND INFORMATION OF
FEELINGS TO CREATE LOW DRAMA.

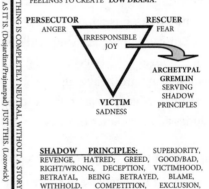

WHAT IS, IS, AS IT IS. (Desjardins/Prajnanpad) JUST THIS. (Lozowick)

EVERYTHING IS COMPLETELY NEUTRAL, WITHOUT A STORY.

BRIGHT PRINCIPLES: KINDNESS, DIGNITY, GENEROSITY, LOVE, CLARITY, RESPECT, ACCEPTANCE, POSSIBILITY, INTEGRITY, COMMUNICATION, TEAMWORK, DISCOVERY, FRIENDSH IP, COMMUNITY, EMPOWERMENT, TRANSFORMATION, GROWTH, RADIANCE, TRUSTWORTHINESS, HIGH LEVEL FUN, ETC.

SHADOW PRINCIPLES: SUPERIORITY, REVENGE, HATRED; GREED, GOOD/BAD, RIGHT/WRONG, DECEPTION, VICTIMHOOD, BETRAYAL, BEING BETRAYED, BLAME, WITHHOLD, COMPETITION, EXCLUSION, RESENTMENT, DENIAL, EXPECTATION, DISRESPECT, ETC.

This map is inside of you. Each of us has a bright world and a shadow world. This map is not about good or bad, only about the kinds of results you want to create. The king or queen of your underworld is your Gremlin, which feels glad when someone else feels pain and serves Shadow (*hidden purpose)* Principles. The king or queen of your upperworld is archetypal man or woman, who feels glad when someone heals, learns, changes or succeeds, when the game is about winning happening and serves Bright (*true destiny)* Principles. When you have gained clarity about both your hidden purpose and your true destiny, what you get is the possibility of making a conscious choice about what you are creating right now. This can be a most useful choice.

APPENDIX D:

BAMBI VS. THE COLLAPSE OF CIVILIZATION

This is a blog posted by Tim Bennett, a film maker living in northeast USA. Tim writes about making use of fear with rare and profound clarity. The original blog is available online at: http://carolynbaker.net/site/content/view/230.

Tim wrote, directed and edited the film *What a Way to Go – Life at the End of Empire* <www.whatawaytogomovie.com> produced by Sally Erickson.

Tim's writing is conversational *Americanese*, flamboyantly laced with 21st Century American slang and cultural referents. If you want further clarity about any of his terms, just google them. (For example, I just googled *hoodies*. They are heavy, upper-body garments with a hood, a hooded sweatshirt.) A good reason for reading Tim's original blog online is that it includes an abundance of valuable links not included the text below.

ORIGINAL BLOG POST – MONDAY, 26 NOVEMBER 2007

The people I see engaged in effective response have all faced into, sat with, chewed on, and stared down their fear. This does not mean they are no longer afraid. It means that they have confronted their fears and found themselves more than a match for them. It means they have found their power to respond even when afraid, which is the definition of courage. They are still standing in the headlights, for there is no real place to hide, but they are not frozen. They are readying themselves for the blow, however and whenever it comes, responding, moment by moment, intuitively, rationally, non-rationally, and with heightened awareness

    Don't be afraid to be afraid . . .

—Yoko Ono, *Beautiful Boys*

I have heard many astounding things in the four years since I began to make the documentary film *What a Way to Go*. The most astounding is this, which I have heard more than once, from real, living, seemingly intelligent and thoughtful people: "I refuse to be scared."

Imagine... refusing to feel one's feelings. As if such a thing is ever really possible. As if such a thing is even a good idea. As if such a disconnection from one's own body and one's essential humanity, as if this core-directed attempt at control and domination, isn't just more of the same. It's a bit like "I refuse to feel pain" or "I refuse to feel hunger." I mean, right on... pain and hunger can be a real downer, dude, so like, yeah, cool, groovy, far out, but like . . . um . . . shouldn't you take your emaciated hand out of that fire? It's starting to smoke.

Many great thinkers have wondered, Kurt Vonnegut amongst them, whether the hypertrophied human cerebral cortex will ultimately prove to have been a bad idea, and whether it will be soon selected against in the grand Walkabout that is evolution. My guess is that, if that should be the case, if we do go the way of the Yangtze River Dolphin or the Miss Waldron's Red Colobus Monkey (two species which have recently gone belly up in the shallow and quickly-warming end of the gene pool), it will be because this great, gray, wrinkled jelly-mold of an organ confers upon us the dubious ability to convince ourselves that we do not feel what we feel, and that we do not think what we think. To my mind, that's about as good a working definition of insanity as we're ever going to get.

"I refuse to feel scared." Could we ask for a more marvelous statement of willful denial than that?

It's understandable, of course. We live in a culture, and a system of governance and economy and production, that uses fear to control us. Just as it uses violence. Just as it uses power. And so, in the realms of power and violence and fear, we are left to stumble about at our most crazed and confused. Chafing under the dominating jackboot of the mortgage payment, the television commercial, the IRS form and our next employee review (what, did you think all dominating jackboots came hobnailed?), we seek to distance ourselves from any and all participation in such basic human animal responses as fear in the face of danger, or protection and defense in the face of attack: "Those bastards use fear and power to control us, goddamnit! No way am I going to let them make me be afraid!" In an attempt to "not become the enemy", we wrap ourselves in cloaks of noble courage and righteous pacifism and hope that these thin fabrics will protect us.

And why not? They HAVE protected us. If we're rich, that is, or at least middle class. If we're white. If we're male. If we're educated. If we're first world. If we're well-employed. Here in the Insulated States of America, much of our violence and power and fear, at least of the hob-nailed sort, has been outsourced, offshored and externalized so as not to upset us while we eat (bad for the digestion, you know). We on the top have been spared the most brutal and overt consequences of our actions for so long now that we have forgotten that there are any. We close our eyes and click our heels and zip up our *NO FEAR* hoodies and we're good to go, confident that all that wishin' and hopin' will work today just like it worked yesterday.

Which is, of course, why Peak Oil whacks us so devastatingly up-side the head. Because when we begin to look closely at the situation, it becomes very clear, very quickly, that wishin' and hopin' are about to go the way of the Yangtze River Dolphin and the Miss Waldron's Red Colobus Monkey in terms of effective life strategies.

It burns, doesn't it? It galls and vexes and maddens. I mean, isn't this what we spent ten thousand years trying to control? Haven't we worked long hours for low pay killing off everything we could that might chase us or bite us or poison us or eat us or claw us or irritate us or scare us or make us feel all creepy and oogly inside? Didn't we arrange things so that we could know where our next meal is coming from, and where our warm bed will be at the end of the day? Aren't we, by virtue of our millennia of effort, and by virtue of our exalted position at the very tip-top of the Great Chain of Being, actually and in no uncertain terms *ENTITLED* to not feel fear?

Well, sorry, no, we're not. We can't have that. First, because that Great Chain is a load of horseshit (my apologies to horseshit, which, composted, can be really great for your garden), and second because our delusional attempts to control something as huge and complex and chaotic and self-directing and autonomous and sacred as THE WHOLE WORLD have succeeded only in pissing her off, and, as that great mall-rat-t-shirt says, "When Momma ain't happy, ain't nobody happy". Knock knock. Who's there? Climate change. Oh fuck.

Some people, cognizant of how silly it sounds to actually deny their own feelings, will tweak things a bit, saying, instead of "I refuse to be scared", something like "I refuse to live in fear," meaning, I think, pretty much the same thing (though now avowed as an actual policy), but sounding much better. That this is said with high nobility of purpose and the best of intentions does not surprise me, for we are nothing if not well-intentioned. That it's said with a straight face astounds me. Like . . . um . . . wouldn't the only reason to actually "live in fear" be if there were something in our lives that was ongoingly frightening and threatening? And . . . I'm embarrassed to have to write this . . . if there's something ongoingly frightening and threatening in our lives, don't we actually want to know about it, and maybe, the gods forbid, respond? Isn't that what fear is for?

Maybe that's not totally fair. Maybe it is. At some point, we have to do the work of teasing apart a healthy and useful feeling of fear from an unhealthy and useless feeling of worry, of fear mired in molasses and J-B Weld, which can be both debilitating and paralyzing. Perhaps it's the difference between a creative response and a reaction. Fear has an in-the-moment quality to it, as a response to an immediate stimulus, and the possibility of openness and creativity exists therein. Worry has a long-term gnawing quality to it, as if fear has taken up a dwelling-place in our hearts, with plans to stay and eat all our potato chips, and there's nothing we can do to get rid of it.

We point to that ol' deer-in-the-headlights as an example of the paralyzing effect of fear. Well, let's think about deer for a second. I've met up with many of these "venisons of the deep" in my day, walking through the woods. When they hear me coming, they respond by running away. I've yet to have one stand there and let me walk up and pet it. Given the traditional choices afforded us animals, and knowing that fighting is probably riskier and may take more energy, and seeing an obvious escape route, the deer flees. Of course. Easy as pie. Deer ain't dumb.

But when I approach a deer encased in two tons of metal and glass and fine Corinthian leather, sometimes the deer takes the third option, the option that remains when fighting won't work and there isn't time to flee, or a place to flee to: it freezes. Not a bad strategy as a last resort, given the physiology of vision and the instincts of predators, but fairly useless against a Ford F-350 Super Duty diesel, or even a Toyota Prius. What works in the evolved world of lions and tigers and deers fails in the invented world of traffic and tramways and trucks. An oncoming pickup falls so far outside the traditional purview of a white-tailed deer that her first and most effective fear responses break down. Fight and flight appear to be out of the question and, unfortunately in this case, freeze doesn't stand much of a chance. Traffic and tramways and trucks. Oh my.

This, I think, is what some people are pointing to when they say they "refuse to live in fear." They look at oil and climate and environmental meltdown and mass extinction and overshoot and economic and political insanity and they sense that, if things are really this dire, there's no real way to effectively fight it (as in solving it . . . as in keeping this system going . . . as in SOL, dude . . .), no clear place to which they might flee for safety (where could we go where they don't hate us? . . . hmmm . . .), and they rightly surmise that freezing, in the face of something this huge, will probably not work either. What to do, what to do? There IS an ongoingly frightening and threatening presence in our lives. The coming storms lie so far outside of our purview that our traditional fear responses break down. We already know what usually happens to the deer. And being frozen in fear, apart from not working, really, really sucks. What to do?

I know! Let's refuse the situation. Let's *just say no* to our own reality! In fact, let's re-write reality. Let's do like Captain Kirk did with the Kobayashi Maru training exercise and reprogram the simulator. After all, he didn't believe in the no-win situation, so why should we? I mean, c'mon, people! We're Americans, aren't we? Damn straight! Lock and load! Let's roll!

Ahem . . . where were we?

When we douse out the fear, when we tamp down the embers of worry, we unwittingly, and unfortunately, choose ingrained reaction over creative response. We fail to let the fear and worry do their work, the work of alerting us, not only to the fact that we are in danger, but also that this danger is huge and new and so dire that our normal responses will not serve us.

Our culture in general (and those in power and control in particular) has used and abused fear and power and violence in order to manage our behavior and our beliefs, to sell us shit we don't need, and to siphon off the material wealth of an entire planet. In reaction to that, rather than in creative response, we end up forced through tighter checkpoints and down narrower chutes, further and further into the pen. Reacting rather than responding IS a life lived in fear. Reaction is always constrained. It is always less free. The irony, for those who say, "I refuse to live in fear", is that they already *do*, and that they probably always have. Refusing fear is a fear reaction to fear itself. (You came close, FDR, but no cigarette holder.)

There's a way in which the fundamental heart and spirit of my film *What a Way to Go* can be encapsulated in one short piece of voice over: "If what we want is to stop the destruction of the life of this planet, then what we have been doing has not been working. We will have to do something else." Something else, as in something *really* else, as in *"now for something completely different"* else. Not the same old tricks in a new shade of muddy green.

So what might that be, fellow deers? We've tried the Happy Chapter (TM), but that hasn't seemed to "work" (I'm defining "work" as "somehow avoiding our headlong plunge into global mass extinction"). We've done the studies and written the books and convened the conferences and made the movies and, standing there in the glare of headlights, we've looked up at that big ol' scary truck a'comin', yes we have, yes we have. But then, because it's so darned scary, and because everybody knows you can't leave people afraid and upset, and because everybody knows that you've got to give people hope, man, you've just got to!, we've tacked on conclusions and chapters and benedictions and epilogues and dénouements that say, "Hey, things aren't so bad. All we have to do is this-and-this-and-this and everything will be fine." And the effect on us has been to put us back to sleep. I mean, if somebody has figured out the this-and-this-and-this, then surely they're on it, right? So, I can get back to my shows, right? Cool. The truck? Oh, that. Yeah, don't worry. There's some guys in Colorado who have found the brake pedal.

(If only we had stopped to wonder why it is this culture never actually DOES this-and-this-and-this. *Here lies Humanity: They could have saved themselves, but they really sucked at follow-up!*)

We keep inching up to the edge of terror and hopelessness and despair, only to pull back and find solace in the arms of denial and false hope and slightly-less-unsustainable "green living." Doing so hasn't actually "worked." So . . . now what? What comes next?

Remember, the truck is still coming . . .

I am reminded of an old children's game we used to play in the one-room schoolhouse I attended in rural Michigan. One of us would lead and the rest would follow and we'd sit together and smack our hands on our knees and mimic the various motions and sounds as we went along. It was a hoot. Here, I'll lead:

Coming to some fear. *Coming to some fear.*

Can't go over it. *Can't go over it.*

Can't run away from it. *Can't run away from it.*

Can't go around it. *Can't go around it.*

Gotta go through it. *Gotta go through it.*

Alright. *Alright.*

OK. *OK.*

Let's go. *Let's go.*

Smack your hands on your knees, folks. Shout out and shake these bones. We've got some feeling to go through! (WARNING: DO NOT TRY THIS ALONE!)

Here's the thing: I think we all KNOW that we have to do this. We know it's the fact that Brother Al's movie [Al Gore's film *An Inconvenient Truth* <www.climatecrisis.net>] *was* so damned scary that it put Climate Change near the top of our national Honey-Do list (whether what the national Honeys are doing will actually "work" is another essay). We know that it's the *feeling* that has made the difference. And we know that it's the *feeling* that makes us come alive, which is why we spend $9 (plus $7.50 for popcorn and a drink) to go to a movie that will wrench our hearts and drain our tears and rouse our righteous indignation and scare the bejesus out of us.

What we don't know is how to do this whole "feel the terror" thing without it totally undoing us, without it leaving us debilitated and paralyzed. I mean, shit, pretty much every last thing the analysts and scientists I've been reading for the past four years have been saying is now coming true, with this exception: IT'S UNFOLDING WAY FASTER THAN EXPECTED. Foreign investors are fleeing, petrodollars are petrified and petrodenial is running dry, bubbles are bursting and dollars are dropping and the price for a barrel of light sweet is getting downright crude. The delusional belief system (aka "the economy", aka "the market") is staring on in dis-belief. Oh, and climate change? Well, let's just say that you might want to buy those new waders you've been looking at in the Cabelas catalogue. Today.

You know things are moving quickly when you get to be a prophet and an historian all in one lifetime…

Atomized and ruggedly individualized, riven from our tribal roots, deprived of our healing arts, numbed, dumbed [read *Dumbing Us Down* by John Taylor Gatto] and bummed by an insane culture, alone and without community, how for fuck's sake are we supposed to go through our terror? And why should we? If we can't fight, and we can't flee, what are we to do? If our terror is keeping us frozen, how do we know that feeling it and moving through it and unfreezing it (rather than denying it) will actually give us the power to jump before the truck turns us into road-pizza?

Well, here we are at the heart of it, folks, where the rubber meets the doe, so to speak. There IS no jumping out of the way. The truck is too big. And too close. And moving too quickly for us to even have time to get a good crouch in. So . . . perhaps it's time to remember that sometimes . . . sometimes . . . when deer and truck meet . . . the truck gets totaled. And sometimes . . . sometimes . . . the deer survives.

We're going to have to question some deeper assumptions here. Who says we can't take the blow? And who says deer can't protect themselves from attack? Who says we can't find effective responses that will give us a better chance of surviving the impact? And who says we can't align with the forces already in motion to help the death machine die with more dignity, and less destruction, than it otherwise will? Who says?

Ah, we poor Average Americans (TM). We've been bought off just like the Canarsies were before us (supposedly). But instead of the legendary "$24 worth of beads and trinkets", we got iPhones and plasma TVs and hot and cold running water and *The Sopranos* and Denny's Grand Slam Breakfast. We're so much smarter than those silly Indians, aren't we? Look what we got! And all it cost us was . . . well . . . our very souls, not to mention the health of an entire planet, which is, technically speaking, bigger than Manhattan.

We seem to have so much to lose (as long as we can continue to externalize those darn costs) that talk of taking the blow, of acting to protect ourselves and the life of this planet, scares the rest of the bejesus (that residual bejesus which has not been frightened away by horror movies) right out of us. Take the blow? I can't take the blow; I just got these new blue jeans! Fight back? Why, they'll put me in jail! I can't get a signal in there! Preparing for collapse looks, to those at the top, like hard physical labor and learning to cook possum and really greasy hair and no more trips to Caribou's. Fighting back looks like embarrassing headlines and a date with Bubba in the showers. With possum stew and jail food on the menu, the Extinction Basket with *pommes frites* and a Coke (TM) begins to look like an attractive option.

Pampered and purchased, it's pretty much agreed all around that the last thing Americans are going to do is rise up and take their lives back into their own hands. On the whole, that's probably true, at least until we've already lost our toys. But while masses do not seem to change minds on any sort of a time scale that will help us at this point, individual minds can and do change. People can step out of denial and get into real and effective response. You can. Yeah, I mean you. That's why I'm sitting on my ass right now writing. Because there are people out there who are ready to look where I'm pointing. Maybe you're one of those people.

We can take the blow. (We don't really have much choice.) Perhaps we can even survive it. We can begin by finding our place and our people. We can start an edible forest garden and clean out some old barrels for water catchments and walk down the road and meet all of our neighbors and get together for a potluck and a meeting and talk about what's coming. We can find a facilitator and do the feelings work we need to do, moving through the grief and the hopelessness, the fear, the anger, moving through them and beyond them, moving together, arm in arm, hand to hand, heart to heart, discovering that we are strong enough to bear such things, that we are still whole enough to not be undone by them, finding that together, we can stand and face the headlights, we can stand and hold each other as the truck hits, and finding, maybe, just maybe, that some of us are still alive after it has passed. Some of us need to do this work, because most will not. Refusing to feel their fear now, they will be forced to feel it upon impact, when the trauma is greatest, the losses so hard to bear. They will need our help.

And we can act to protect ourselves (the larger "ourselves", which includes everybody else). We have no real idea what small groups of us can do to that truck if we stand up to it when it hits, but we can acknowledge the possibility that the truck will end up overturned in the ditch, damaged beyond repair, never to "let's roll" again, while we manage to limp away and lick our wounds. It could happen. And since it's possible that finding some way to deflect the truck into a ditch will "work" (and remember I'm defining "work" as "somehow avoiding our headlong plunge into global mass extinction"), then it's worth the responding, the trying, the being, the doing. Things are going to get a bit crazy. The rules are all going to change. Stay awake. Stay aware. Stay poised. All will become clear.

The people I see engaged in effective response have all faced into, sat with, chewed on, and stared down their fear. This does not mean they are no longer afraid. It means that they have confronted their fears and found themselves more than a match for them. It means they have found their power to respond even when afraid, which is the definition of courage. They are still standing in the headlights, for there is no real place to hide, but they are not frozen. They are readying themselves for the blow, however and whenever it comes, responding, moment by moment, intuitively, rationally, non-rationally, and with heightened awareness. And they are getting prepared to play their parts in tossing that damned truck into the ditch.

It seems fair, in a way, that someone takes the blow. Not necessarily at the individual level, of course. There are many, many victims in this story. We were all born into this situation. I will not argue that any one of us in particular has a debt to pay. That's for each of our own hearts to know.

But at the collective level, at the level of our nation, and our culture, there is a fairness here that feels deep and clear. This particular troop of clever monkeys has acted abominably. As dysfunctional (if not self-acknowledged) members of the Community of Life, as supposedly informed and qualified delegates to the great Council of All Beings, we have amends to make. Perhaps feeling the fear we've engendered, the pain we've caused, the grief we've created, the anger we've provoked, the guilt we've earned and the clear and soaring joy we can step into at any moment, perhaps feeling deeply is one way to begin making those amends. Feeling. Then moving into defensive and protective responses that might actually "work". It's sort of a cosmic you-break-it-you-buy-it situation we find ourselves in. We created this, we "civilized" ones. We broke the Laws of Life. The results belong to us. So how much do we have in our wallets? Who are we going to be?

I know my path: I'm going to finish growing up. I'm going to do whatever it takes to rejoin the community of living souls as a fully initiated adult human being. Refusing to feel one's fear is just a dressed-up form of adolescent indestructibility, just another facet of Civilization's millennia-long PCP frenzy. Fuck that. It's time to grow up. I'm ready.

I'll feel my fair share of fear and grief and anger and shame and joy, and savor the sweet delight of being alive in this amazing time. I'll find those few people who see the truck coming, and sit with them in circle and share my heart, and my tears, and we'll stand together and watch the truck as it nears. I'll read the headlines, at the very least, in Carolyn Baker's Daily News Stories, and let the fear and anger wash over me and through me, and I'll use that fear to keep me aligned, and in response mode, with reality.

I'll use the fear, rather than refuse it. I'll use it to keep me awake and alive and in action. I'll use it as an antidote to the culture that seeks always to lull me back to sleep. I'll use it to help bring an end to that culture.

Damn, that feels good.

Bring on the truck.

FURTHER UNLEARNING

Your Box defends its sovereignty by claiming to know. Learning anything new challenges your Box's dominion. Since Boxes defend their territory with a vengeance, your first step in learning is to unlearn, to dismantle the certainty with which your Box paints its interpretations over your direct experience of the world. Adopting unlearning as part of your daily practice keeps you liquid enough that your Bright Principles can move you during the course of your daily life. The following are useful resources for further unlearning.

RECOMMENDED BOOKS

Baker, Carolyn. *Sacred Demise: Walking the Spiritual Path of Industrial Civilization's Collapse*. Bloomington, Indiana: iUniverse, 2009. <www.carolynbaker.net>

Baldwin, Christina. *Calling The Circle – The First and Future Culture*. New York: Bantam Books, 1998. <www.peerspirit.com>

Berne, Eric. *Games People Play – The Psychology of Human Relationships*. New York: Grove Press, 1964. Note: Eric Berne died in 1970, but there is an informative website about his work at: <www.ericberne.com>

Blanton, Brad. *Radical Honesty – How to Transform Your Life by Telling the Truth*. Stanley, Virginia: Sparrowhawk Publications, 2005. <www.radicalhonesty.com>

Callahan, Clinton. *Radiant Joy Brilliant Love – Secrets for Creating an Extraordinary Life and Profound Intimacy with Your Partner*. Prescott, Arizona: Hohm Press, 2007. (Also available in German under the title *Wahre Liebe im Alltag – Das Erschaffen authentischer Beziehungen*. Bremen, Germany: Genius Verlag, 2007.) <www.clintoncallahan.com>

Callahan, Clinton. *Wild Thinking – 52 Adventurous Thought Experiments – Radical Knowledge for Liberating Your Effectiveness and Delivering Your Destiny,* available as a PDF file on CD by request: info@callahan-academy.com. (Also available in German under the title *Abenteuer Denken – 52 Abenteuereisen zu größeren Möglichkeiten.* Bremen, Germany: Genius Verlag, 2004.) <www.clintoncallahan.com>

Carse, James P. *Finite and Infinite Games – A Vision of Life as Play and Possibility.* New York: Ballantine Books, 1986. <www.jamescarse.com>

Castaneda, Carlos. *Journey to Ixtlan – The Lessons of Don Juan.* New York: Simon & Schuster, 1972. Note: Carlos died in 1998, but there are various websites about him. A useful starting point is <www.wikipedia.org/wiki/Carlos_Castaneda>.

Dawson, Jonathan. *Ecovillages – New Frontiers for Sustainability.* Foxhole, Dartington, Totnes, Devon, UK: Green Books Ltd, 2006. <www.chelseagreen.com/bookstore/item/ecovillages>

Diamond, Jared. *Collapse – How Societies Choose to Fail Or Succeed.* New York: Penguin Group, 2005. <www.edge.org/3rd_culture/bios/diamond.html>

Dunhan, Bandhu. *Creative Life – Spirit, Power, and Relationship in the Practice of Art.* Prescott, Arizona: Hohm Press, 2005. <www.salusaglassworks.com>

Fritz, Robert. *Creating – A Guide to the Creative Process.* New York: Ballantine Books, 1991. <www.robertfritz.com>

Fuller, R. Buckminster. *Critical Path.* New York: St Martin's Press, 1981. <www.bfi.org>

Fuller, R. Buckminster. *Grunch* of Giants (*Gross Universe Cash Heist).* New York: St. Martin's Press, 1983. <www.bfi.org>

Garfield, Charles, et. al. *Wisdom Circles – A Guide to Self Discovery and Community Building in Small Groups.* New York: Hyperion, 1998. <www.wisdomcircle.org>

Gatto, John Taylor. *Dumbing Us Down – The Hidden Curriculum of Compulsory Schooling*. Gabriola Island, BC, Canada: New Society Publishers, 2005. <www.johntaylorgatto.com>

Glasser, William. *Choice Theory – A New Psychology of Personal Freedom*. New York: HarperCollins, 1998. <www.wglasser.com>

Goettner-Abendroth, Heide. *The Way into an Egalitarian Society – Principles and Practices of a Matriarchal Politics*. Winzer, Germany: Hagia International Academy, 2007. <www.goettner-abendroth.de> <www.hagia.de>

Gordon, Thomas. *P.E.T. Parent Effectiveness Training*. New York: Penguin Group, 1975. Note: Thomas Gordon died in 2002, but his wife and partner Linda Adams carries on the good work of Gordon Trainings along with her daughter Michelle Adams. <www.gordontraining.com>

Hansen, James. *Storms of My Grandchildren – The Truth About the Coming Climate Catastrophe and Our Last Chance to Save Humanity*. New York: Bloomsbury USA, 2009. <www.columbia.edu/~jeh1>

Hartmann, Thom. *The Last Hours of Ancient Sunlight – Waking Up to Personal and Global Transformation*. New York: Three Rivers Press, 1999. <www.thomhartmann.com>

Hawk, Red. *Self Observation – The Awakening of Conscience, an Owner's Manual*. Prescott, Arizona: Hohm Press, 2009. <www.hohmpress.com>

Hawken, Paul. *Blessed Unrest – How the Largest Social Movement in History Is Restoring Grace, Justice, and Beauty to the World*. New York: Penguin Group, 2007. <www.blessedunrest.com> <www.paulhawken.com>

Heinberg, Richard. *The Party's Over – Oil, War and the Fate of Industrial Societies*, second edition. Gabriola Island, BC, Canada: New Society Publishers, 2005. <www.richardheinberg.com> <www.postcarbon.org>

Hendricks, Gay and Kathlyn. *Conscious Loving – The Journey to Co-Commitment – A Way to Be Fully Together Without Giving Up Yourself.* New York: Bantam Books, 1990. <www.hendricks.com>

Hillesum, Etty. *An Interrupted Life – The Diaries, 1941-1943 and Letters from Westerbork.* New York: Henry Holt & Company, 1996. Note: Etty died in Auschwitz in 1943, but there are many links to information about her listed in Wikipedia: <www.wikipedia.org/wiki/Etty_Hillesum>

Jensen, Derrick. *Endgame, Volume I – The Problem of Civilization,* and *Volume II - Resistance.* New York: Seven Stories Press, 2006. <www.derrickjensen.org>

Korten, David C. *The Great Turning – From Empire to Earth Community.* Bloomfield, Connecticut: Kumarian Press, 2006. (The one thing I disagree with in David's thinking is when he several times equates Christianity with spirituality – fish of a different feather, in my opinion. The rest of the book is super.) <www.thegreatturning.net> <www.davidkorten.org> <www.greatturningtimes.org>

Kübler-Ross, Elisabeth. *On Death and Dying – What the Dying Have to Teach Doctors, Nurses, Clergy, and Their Own Families.* New York: Macmillan Publishing Company, 1969. Note: Elisabeth died in 2004, but the Elisabeth Kübler-Ross Foundation carries on with her work <www.ekrfoundation.org>. The Hospice movement was promoted by Elisabeth Kübler-Ross, more info at <www.hospicefoundation.org>.

Kunstler, James Howard. *The Long Emergency – Surviving the Converging Catastrophes of the 21ˢᵗ Century.* London: Atlantic Books, 2005. <www.kunstler.com>

Lankford, Valerie. *Four Feelings and What to Do With Them – Questions and Answers for Problem Solving.* Baltimore, Maryland: privately published pamphlet. Request through email: valerielankford@yahoo.com Telephone: +1-410-771-1234. <www.valcanhelp.com>

Lerner, Harriet. *The Dance of Anger – A Woman's Guide to Changing the Patterns of Intimate Relationships.* New York: Harper, 1985, 2005. <www.harrietlerner.com>

Lobaczewski, Andrew M. *Political Ponerology – A Science on the Nature of Evil Adjusted for Political Purposes.* Grande Prairie, Alberta, Canada: Red Pill Press, 2008. <www.ponerology.com>

Lozowick, Lee. *Getting Real.* Prescott, Arizona: Hohm Press, 2007. <www.leelozowick.com>

Lozowick, Lee. *The Alchemy of Transformation.* Prescott, Arizona: Hohm Press, 1996. <www.hohmpress.com>

Macy, Joanna. *Coming Back to Life – Practices to Reconnect Our Lives, Our World.* Gabriola Island, BC, Canada: New Society Publishers, 1998. <www.joannamacy.net>

McKibben, Bill. *The End of Nature – Humanity, Climate Change, and the Natural World.* New York: Random House, 1989. <www.350.org>

Meadows, Donella H., et. al. *Limits to Growth – The 30-Year Update.* White River Junction, Vermont: Chelsea Green Publishing Company, 2004. Note: Donella Meadows died in 2001, but there is an informative website about her work at: <www.sustainer.org/meadows>

Moore, Robert, and Douglas Gillette. *King Warrior Magician Lover – Rediscovering the Archetypes of the Mature Masculine.* New York: Harper Collins, 1990. Note: The *Conclusion* chapter was my original source for distinguishing the four archetypes of king, warrior, magician and lover. Associating the archetypes with the four feelings and the procedure for stellating (initializing) the archetypes were empirically developed during Possibility Management trainings and laboratories by Clinton Callahan. <www.mkpchicago.org> <www.robertmoore-phd.com>

Morris, Desmond. *The Naked Ape – A Zoologist's Study of the Human Animal.* New York: McGraw-Hill, 1967. <www.desmond-morris.com>

Peck, M. Scott. *The Road Less Traveled – A New Psychology of Love, Traditional Values, and Spiritual Growth*. New York: Touchstone, 1978. Note: M. Scott Peck died in 2005, but there is an informative website about his work at: <www.mscottpeck.com>.

Quinn, Daniel. *Beyond Civilization – Humanity's Next Great Adventure*. New York: Three Rivers Press, 1999. <www.ishmael.org>

Ray, Paul, and Sherry Ruth Anderson. *The Cultural Creatives – How 50 Million People Are Changing the World*. New York: Harmony Books, 2000. <www.culturalcreatives.org>

Rischard, J. F. *High Noon – 20 Global Problems and 20 Years to Solve Them*. New York: Basic Books, 2002. <www.rischard.net>

Somé, Malidoma Patrice. *Of Water and Spirit – Ritual,Magic, and Initiation in the Life of an African Shaman*. New York: Penguin Group, 1994. <www.malidoma.com>

Torbert, Bill. *Action Inquiry – the Secret of Timely and Transforming Leadership*. San Francisco: Berrett-Koehler Publishers, 2004. <www.harthill.co.uk/action-inquiry1/what-is-action-inquiry.html>

Welwood, John. *Perfect Love Imperfect Relationships – Healing the Wound of the Heart*. (Or *any* book by John Welwood!) Boston: Trumpeter Books, 2006. <www.johnwelwood.com>

Wheatley, Margaret J. *Turning to One Another – Simple Conversations to Restore Hope to the Future*. San Francisco: Berrett-Koehler Publishers, 2009. <www.margaretwheatley.com>

Wolff, Robert. *Original Wisdom – Stories of an Ancient Way of Knowing*. Rochester, Vermont: Inner Traditions International, 2001. <www.wildwolff.com>

RECOMMENDED DVDS

11ʰ Hour with Leonardo diCaprio <www.11thhouraction.com>

A Crude Awakening – the oil crash <www.oilcrashmovie.com>

The Age of Stupid with Pete Postlethwaite <www.ageofstupid.net>

An Inconvenient Truth with Al Gore <www.climatecrisis.net>

Ancient Futures – Learning from Ladakh <www.isec.org.uk>

The Corporation by Mark Achbar, Jennifer Abbott and Joel Bakan
    <www.thecorporation.com>

Deadly Dust by Frieder F. Wagner <www.telepool.de> (then search on
    Deadly Dust)

The Great Warming with Keanu Reeves and Alanis Morissette
    <www.thegreatwarming.com>

Home by Yann Arthus-Bertrand <www.home-2009.com)

In Debt We Trust by Danny Schechter <www.indebtwetrust.org>

Message from the Gyre with Chris Jordon <www.midwayjourney.com>

The Power of Community – how Cuba survived peak oil
    <www.powerofcommunity.org>
    <www.communitysolution.org/cuba>

The Story of Stuff with Annie Leonard <www.storyofstuff.com>

Wake Up, Freak Out – then Get a Grip by Leo Murray
    <www.wakeupfreakout.org>

What a Way to Go – Life at the End of Empire by Tim Bennett and
    Sally Erickson. <www.whatawaytogomovie.com>

The World According to Monsanto by Marie-Monique Robin.
    <www.seedsofdeception.com>

Zeitgeist Addendum by Peter Joseph. <www.zeitgeistmovie.com>
    shows the *Zeitgeist Movement Orientation Presentation*

RECOMMENDED EXPERIENCES

Nothing beats the instant and inarguable feedback of raw experience for learning to trust your own deep clarity and for building the matrix needed to bring you through a rite of passage into adulthood. I feel glad to tell you that my list of individuals and groups providing authentic elements of next culture rite of passage is growing too fast these days to list in a book. Instead we collect them on several websites.

<www.iamabridgetonextculture.org>

<www.nextculture.org>

<www.quitschool.org>

<www.possibilica.org>

You are a piece of the puzzle. To connect with others and serve as a bridge facilitating the shift to next culture, please go to <www.fouryearsgo.org>

If you recommend additional sources, please contact us through one of these websites and let us know.

Thank you.

INDEX

FURTHER EXPERIMENTS

I appreciate that you are reading this page. Each further experiment you try has the possibility of cutting new forms of consciousness that others can then more easily follow. This makes you a bridge to next culture. Someone must go first. In this case that someone is you. Please keep making personal efforts and being a bridge for others to do the same. Here are some suggestions:

1. Commit to lowering your numbness bar as part of your rite of passage to adulthood. Then, for the rest of your life, responsibly use whatever feelings come up for you to heal things or handle things.

2. Start a weekly *I Am A Bridge* meeting to develop your conscious feelings together with others, arm in arm, heart to heart. It can be too painful to do it alone.

    More info at <www.iamabridgetonextculture.org>.

3. Get copies of this book into the hands of your friends *and* your enemies. Keep talking it through with them. Share your personal stories and listen to theirs, all the while remembering they are merely stories. Invite them to continue these conversations with you at your *I Am A Bridge* meetings.

4. Use the authentic alchemical elixir *Tonic Gold*™ to build your energetic matrix. Building matrix helps you hold what you learned in this book and supports further conscious feelings experiments. I *highly* recommend *Tonic Gold*.

    More info USA <www.tonicgold.com>, Europe and Asia <www.tonicgold.de>.

5. Read my other books: *Wild Thinking,* and *Radiant Joy Brilliant Love.* Register to get our SPARKs newsletter every two weeks with further experiments to try. (SPARK stands for Specific Practical Applications of Radical Knowledge.)

   More info at <www.clintoncallahan.com> (click on the English flag at the top of the page)

6. Get yourself into an Expand The Box training or Next Culture Lab, or bring these trainings into your organization. Powered by the ingenious tools and thoughtmaps of Possibility Management, these trainings transform your life or workplace into a rapid learning environment.

   More info at <www.nextculture.org>.

7. Have fun!

Your mind is yours to play with and make into whatever you want.

Thank you for thinking wildly!

Clinton Callahan